# THE WIND AND THE CARIBOU

*Nobody knows*
*the way*
*of the wind*
*and*
*the caribou*

CHIPEWYAN
INDIAN PROVERB

ERIK MUNSTERHJELM

# The Wind
# and
# the Caribou

HUNTING AND TRAPPING
IN NORTHERN CANADA

TORONTO
THE MACMILLAN COMPANY OF CANADA LIMITED

*The names of some of the places mentioned in this book have been changed on official maps—a few of them twice—since the events here recounted occurred. I have, however, preferred to retain the old and familiar names by which these places still are known locally—names not subject to sudden governmental caprice.*

# CONTENTS

# CHAPTER I

## *Going North—Karl and I decide to go trapping —Preparations and canoe-building*

I<small>T</small> was January and ninety-eight degrees in the shade. For longer than I cared to remember I and thirty other unfortunates had been burrowing in a dry riverbed in the desert. Bossed by a foul-mouthed foreman, we had been digging holes for the foundation of a concrete bridge which was to replace an old structure of wood.

We had been shovelling since early morning, while the flaming sun rose higher and higher and parched our sweat-drenched bodies until they were covered with a sticky coating of salt that made dirty white streaks on our browned backs. This was just one in a monotonous row of similar, cloudless, stifling days.

There came a lull in the work. In the hope of finding a cooling breeze I climbed slowly out of my hole and up on the bridge and sat down. I wiped the sweat from my face and gazed dully out over the plain. Grey and dusty, spotted by an occasional cactus and sage bush, it spread out before me. Only to the north, beyond the shimmering haze, towered a blue-black mountain range crowned by violet peaks.

While I looked a downy cloud approached a peak, was split, and passed on, leaving the pinnacle covered by a shining white mantle. I stared.

Snow! Good God, snow!

It was as if an electric shock had gone through me. Something snapped. And, without thinking of the consequences, I walked over to the foreman.

'I'm quitting.'

'What? What's the matter, boy?' he asked, surprised.

'It's this heat, this infernal heat. It drives me nuts,' I yelled. Turning, I left him staring, and started for the bunkhouse. There

7

I stuffed my belongings in a packsack, got my wages, and jumped on the next train north.

I had had enough of sunny California. I had stood its perpetually clear sky, its burning sun and its everlastingly dry, hot and even climate for two long years. A northerner, I wanted to see snow again, feel the frosty wind in my face; even to hear a blizzard whistle past the corner of my shack would be a blessing. The shining mountain top was a beckoning signal. I was going north; back again to God's country.

It was the end of January when I arrived in Edmonton, the capital of Alberta. It was cold there, and there was plenty of snow, too, so I decided to stay and get myself a job.

That was not easy, though. The depression had started, and now it was winter, when even ordinary jobs were hard to get. For a week I haunted employment offices, factories, construction companies and other outfits that might need a man, but did not catch even the faint smell of a job. It did not look so good.

It was on one of these rounds of the employment agencies that I met Karl. He was looking for work, too, and we started making the rounds together. We hit it off well right from the start, and spent much of our time in each other's company.

Karl was a slim, wiry Swede of thirty-odd years and had been in Canada just two years. Like most recent immigrants, he had made his living the best way he could: by working on farms, in lumber camps and construction gangs. But he was like a fish out of water in these jobs. Since boyhood hunting had been his passion; it was in his blood. His father had been forester and gamekeeper on several estates in Sweden, and ever since he could walk Karl had carried a gun and roamed the woods. No wonder, then, that he longed to try his hand at the same things in Canada.

True, he had already tried. The previous winter he and two other lads had trapped north-west of Prince Albert, but with poor results. The country was poorly stocked with game and there were many hunters. That did not discourage Karl, though. His desire to trap remained, but now he wanted to try it in some really virgin territory, far from civilization and cities.

Wistfully he talked about his plans, and so one day—I do not remember who first proposed it—we decided to pool our resources and try our luck in the real unspoiled wilderness. The way it looked we would go broke before catching a job, anyway.

The next few days we studied all the literature and maps of the north that we could find in the public library, and selected the area north-east of Lake Athabaska as the most suitable. When we had made our decision I started to laugh.

'What's so funny?' said Karl.

'Well, I was going north all right, but I sure didn't intend to go that far. But I might as well go the whole hog. I've read too much Jack London and Curwood, and maybe it's the best way to get them out of my system.'

The next step was to buy an outfit. Edmonton is the proper place for that. This metropolis is the gateway to the great northland and the logical outfitting place for all who intend to go 'down north'. In the days before air travel the best method of reaching the great rivers that flow northward all the way to the Arctic Ocean was the railway, which began there.

In those days Indians in caribou parkas and pearl-stitched moccasins, trappers, prospectors, fur-traders and other weather-beaten denizens of the wilderness were as common a sight on Jasper Avenue as the bawdy ladies and gamblers who were trying to relieve them of their money. This is still true today, although less so, and in spite of oil and farming the north still sets its mark on the city. Below its surface veneer of respectability it is a rip-roaring paradise for all northerners; a place, the delights of which are discussed by the camp-fires or dreamed of during lonely winter nights in far-away cabins.

In Edmonton there are many stores that specialize in trapper's and fisherman's equipment. In one of these we bought as complete an outfit as our finances permitted, and then boarded the 'Muskeg Flier'.

The 'Muskeg Flier' is famous all over the north. It makes one trip a week over its three or four hundred miles of track between Edmonton and the town of Waterways on the banks of the

Clearwater River, a tributary of the Athabaska. Waterways is the southernmost port of that great system of rivers and lakes which comprises the Mackenzie basin.

The train consisted of about ten antiquated freight cars, with a wooden passenger coach from the last century attached to the rear. This cavalcade of relics was pulled by a locomotive which panted and trembled, not from eagerness, but from age.

When the train had started and we had made ourselves at home—comfortable is hardly the proper word for it—I studied the surroundings with interest.

Half a century before, the coach might have been the pride of some transcontinental crack train. Decorated bronze lamps hung from its ceiling, its walls were of mahogany panels framed by carved mouldings, and the upper parts of the windows were stained-glass mosaic set in lead. One could picture how, fifty years before, frock-coated gentlemen had attended bustled ladies with smiles and flattery.

Now the car resembled a bedraggled down-at-heel aristocrat. The panels and windows were cracked, the lamps spotted with verdigris, and everything was covered with a film of grime, except those parts of the benches where the seats and backs of passengers had rubbed it off. In one end of the car a set of benches had been removed to make room for a pot-bellied cast-iron stove and a rough fuel-box.

There were about a dozen other passengers in the coach: homesteaders, trappers and lumberjacks, and a couple of women. While I looked them over I noticed a thin-faced, bearded man who stared at me intently. I looked away, but when I glanced at him again he was still staring at me. Finally, when I gave him an annoyed glance, he came over and sat down beside me.

'You are from the outside,' he said accusingly.

It was not so much a question as a statement. I nodded, annoyed at being so easily recognized as a greenhorn. He continued hastily:

'Don't be sore. I knew you must be one. Nobody but a tough old-timer or an unsuspecting newcomer would dare make this trip. There are terrible experiences in store for you.'

He looked with satisfaction at my startled expression before he said:

'You see, a trip on this train is something of an initiation to the north, a test of courage and stamina. The mere thought of it keeps the chicken-hearted away from those rigours of the north that really test the fitness of a man. Anybody that survives a trip on the "Muskeg Flier" will have little trouble later.

'The average speed of this train is about four miles an hour, and that is about all a normal person can stand, anyway, without being shaken to death. In the summertime you can jump off the first car and pick a lard-pail full of blueberries in the bush alongside the track and still have lots of time to catch the last car as it passes by. In the winter the train crew run a trapline along the right of way and stop when they please to tend their sets. That is all right with most passengers, because it gives them some relief from the terrible shaking and jumping they have to endure when the train is moving.

'If it wasn't for that, only a person with the patience of an Indian fakir to watch a certain spot for several minutes would be able to tell if it is moving at all.'

The stranger interrupted himself for a moment to give me a searching glance. A look through the window assured me that we were moving all right.

'Nobody cares much if the train is only a day late. But once, when it had not showed up in Edmonton a week after it was supposed to, some impatient, prospective passenger phoned the railroad people and asked if he would be able to go north that year. The officials, alarmed at the possibility of losing a passenger to the aeroplane company, started hustling. They were very relieved when a farmer, who had driven into town in his buggy, told them that the train was coming all right because he had seen it pass his place on its way south a couple of days before. And, sure enough, it arrived the next day.'

The man stopped only to spit at the red-hot stove. I had by now decided that I was listening to a descendant of Paul Bunyan. He went on:

'The "Muskeg Flier" has a peculiarity which is perhaps a

world's record. It is the only train in the world that always, and
in both directions, is travelling uphill. You see, the track is laid
mostly on endless swamps and muskegs that sink when the train
passes; so that the locomotive is forever desperately climbing
out of the mire like a drunk trying to crawl out of the gutter.
So as not to lose their train altogether the railroad people have
welded the rails together and tied a red-painted gas drum to the
engine with a long rope, in the hope that the drum will float if
the train sinks out of sight. It's lucky for us passengers that they
haven't found out yet if the device works.'

My narrator stopped to spit once more and put another lid
full of snuff in his mouth. He had now warmed up to his
story.

'Yes,' he said, 'the line has never been completed. Maybe the
builders figured that they would never be able to reach the
Arctic Ocean, anyway, so what was the use of trying? So they
stopped construction, and the track ends abruptly miles from
nowhere. After all, it had to stop somewhere. Who cared where?'

The fellow got really going now. With hardly a breath he
rattled on:

'And the climate in this car is the most varied in the whole
world. When it is real cold, women and children freeze to death
in one end of it while their men-folks are roasted to death in the
other. They can't go to their rescue, anyway, because the car is
jumping around like mad so that nobody can stand, walk or
crawl. I lost my old woman and kid that way.'

He stopped and dried a tear out of his eye. I yawned loudly,
and, with a disappointed expression, he went back to his seat.
After this I tried to sleep, but I only froze my toes and singed my
hair. I could not sleep, anyway, because that fellow set up an
infernal wailing and moaning and claimed the railroad had broken
his leg. Karl said we shouldn't judge him too harshly, as he had
probably had his wits shaken out of him on some earlier trip.

After that the journey proceeded uneventfully, and soon we
arrived in Waterways.

There we heard of an empty cabin about twelve miles up the
Clearwater River. As break-up was still a good month and a half

away and we did not want to stay in the town, we decided to move to the cabin. We hired a man with a team of horses to take us there.

The next morning we started. Our teamster walked ahead, testing the ice with a steel-shod stick, and behind him came the horses in tandem, each pulling an oversize toboggan loaded with our equipment. After winding back and forth over the treacherous ice, which showed many open spots after a recent thaw, we arrived at the cabin in the afternoon.

It was built high on the river bank overlooking the wide, bush-covered flats of the other shore. This was a nice place in which to live, especially as the cabin itself was in fair shape and would, after some minor repairs, be habitable again. We unloaded our stuff, and our teamster left. The rest of the afternoon we spent patching the roof, installing a new window, building bunks and benches and putting up our stove. By nightfall we were snug and comfortable in our temporary home. It was small but cosy.

While living there it was our intention to trap and hunt a little; but our chief job was to build a canoe with which to continue our journey northward after break-up. That neither of us had ever built a canoe or hardly even seen one did not trouble us much. We had been used to boats from childhood, and Karl was a fair carpenter. Besides, we had a handbook in which the procedure of building one was described in detail. And in Edmonton we had bought tools, canvas, paint and other materials for the job.

Guided by the manual, we started to work with great enthusiasm. We split straight spruce wood for ribs, fashioned bow and stern pieces from a bent tree, hewed a keel and nailed the frame together. After a few days our craft began to take shape, and we eyed it with pride as it grew under our hands. Even though I thought the shape a bit odd I said nothing. One day, however, Karl laid down his hammer and scratched his head.

'I dunno, but I think the boat is too wide and too low in the ends. . . . And the bottom is too round, too,' he added.

'Looks a little that way,' I agreed.

'It looks more like a dough trough than a boat,' Karl said truthfully.

'But we've followed all the instructions,' I protested half-heartedly, although I had to admit Karl was right.

We studied the handbook again, and found that we had done everything just the way it advised. But our craft still did not look like a canoe. After some discussion we agreed that the handbook was no darn good and threw it away. We would have to start all over again.

This was our first acquaintance with manuals on woodcraft and other aspects of life in the wide open spaces. We had bought a stack of others, too, that dealt with camping, trapping, hunting and firearms, and studied them diligently in our spare time. All of them were, as we much later realized, worse than useless, because the information was completely misleading and caused us not only a lot of unnecessary backbreaking work but also did our trapping great harm. Had we but known it then, we could have saved ourselves many disappointments and hundreds of dollars by throwing all the books in the fire. These same handbooks are still being sold and widely advertised.

When we had torn our first abortive effort in canoe-building apart again and started to work according to our own ideas the craft began to take shape. It looked like a canoe this time. Thinking of the great northern lakes that we would have to cross, we made it large and sturdy: twenty feet long and with a four-foot beam. What to use for boarding gave us some worry at first. Then we discovered an old sternwheeler which had been pulled ashore and abandoned a few miles from our camp. Somebody had already 'borrowed' most of the lumber from it, but there still remained some cedar boards that we could use, when they had been planed down to the right thickness.

Besides the big one, we also built a small twelve-foot hunting canoe, which we lined with birch bark and covered with canvas. It was light and handy to portage, and would be just right for muskrat hunting in the spring in the Athabaska delta.

These days I also came to know my partner better. Karl was a broad-shouldered, sinewy six-footer, with black, curly hair and dark-brown eyes. He was a hard worker, and one would not have believed that such strength as he gave proof of could be hidden in his spare frame. Although big, he was quick in his movements and light on his feet. He was a born hunter, an exceptional shot and almost recklessly fearless. His greatest faults were a quick temper and occasional fits of truculence. Then he could be very unpleasant, but these fits went as fast as they came, and he would soon be his usual self again. We were partners for two years and got along fine together. We remained fast friends all the years we camped in the north, even after we had parted.

Karl was, however, very class-conscious; and because I did not spring from the proletariat or embrace the faith of Marx and Engels, he at times ticked me off. Once when we quarrelled he branded me a 'damn proselyte'. The meaning of this terrible epithet was at first lost on me. But since he, as I said, was very class-conscious, it finally dawned on me that he meant 'parasite'.

But Karl was a real man and a good partner. He was an excellent marksman and sometimes performed feats that made me stare. Sometimes he simply could not miss.

While we were building our canoes we also trapped a little. Mostly it was weasel and muskrat; other fur-bearers, except foxes, had been practically exterminated in these parts, and the foxes at this time of the year were so badly 'rubbed' that their pelts were worthless. We caught some fifty ermine and eighty muskrats, the latter mostly in a little slough near our cabin.

Once a week I made a trip to McMurray for mail and provisions. The town boasts two hotels, two churches and a main street. There are also a few automobiles which run up and down the three miles of good road which connects the town with the station at Waterways. The population consists mostly of Indians and half-breeds.

In spite of its seeming insignificance, McMurray is an important town. It is the jumping-off place for all the traffic that moves down the Athabaska, Slave and Mackenzie Rivers all the way to Aklavik on the Arctic Ocean, more than a thousand miles away. From here the boats are directed to all parts of that area of over a million square miles that comprises the basin of the mighty Mackenzie and its tributaries, the Peace, the Athabaska, the Liard and many others, and which encloses the Great Bear Lake,

Great Slave Lake and Lake Athabaska. This great river system is navigable all the way north except for a sixteen-mile stretch between Fitzgerald and Fort Smith on the Slave River, where everything, including boats and barges, has to be hauled over land. In the summer time this waterway is plied by picturesque boats, with the wheel behind, which push barges before them; it being easier to navigate among the sand-bars that way than if the barges were towed behind.

In McMurray the Hudson's Bay and other trading companies have warehouses, air-transport companies have their shops and a landing strip, and fish companies their depots.

In McMurray I met many men who had lived long in the north and knew it well. From them I got much useful information and good advice. And there on my last trip I also met Tex.

While walking from the station towards town I was overtaken by a slight, dark and very talkative fellow, who, with a rucksack on his back, was going the same way. He said that he had just arrived in Waterways by side-door pullman—that is, by freight car.

Then he told me that he was going 'down north', where he had been trapping several years, that he had made lots of money there, that he had gone outside via Alaska and spent all his money in a year, and that he now was on his way back to his old haunts on the Arctic Red River. In the same breath he asserted that he was from Texas, had originally been a cowboy and a ranger, was good with a lariat and an outstanding shot. He also wondered how he would get north, as he was dead broke.

I suggested that he work on a riverboat and pay for his fare that way; but he explained that he wanted to hunt rats in the delta to get some quick money and then buy an outfit here in the south where things were cheap.

I parted with him in town, finished my business and was on my way home, when Tex appeared again. In the short while I had left him he had found out that Karl and I intended to go to the delta on the first open water. Now he asked if he could come along with us. I evaded the question by replying that I had to ask my partner first and managed to shake him off without any promises.

But not for long. Perhaps an hour after I had got home that night somebody knocked on the door and in walked Tex with a loaded packsack. He had managed to get some food 'on credit' from the Hudson's Bay store and then borrowed a blanket from somebody else, found out the location of our cabin and left town shortly after. Then he had followed my tracks to our cabin. Tex was obviously a man of action. We invited him for supper and to stay for the night, since it was late.

Now Tex made us a proposition. Being an old hand, he could teach us greenhorns a lot about rat-trapping and many other things; he knew the river, the shoals and the channels, and could help us in many other ways, if we only would let him come with us to the delta. Besides, it would not cost us a cent; he had enough grub for himself, he said, and patted his well-filled packsack.

And somehow, I do not know how it happened, we agreed to take him along.

Tex was a man of small stature but of big words. During the next few days he filled us with stories of his feats as a cowboy, a Texas Ranger and a trapper. He was, by his own admission, an outstanding lariat artist, an extraordinary pistol shot—not quite as good with rifle, he said modestly—a hunter, a woodsman, a real river-rat, and so on. Some of his yarns had a flavour reminiscent of Wild West magazines, but that might have been just a coincidence.

Unfortunately he showed scant interest in doing his share of the daily chores or in helping us with the canoe-building. But instead he was ever ready to give advice, to direct or to criticize freely and willingly. We soon tired of him and his bragging, but, since we had given our promise to let him go with us, we had to abide by it. Besides, he might really be useful later, when we started down the river.

The signs of spring became more numerous daily; the snow melted, aspen and birch became tinged with green and the first mosquitoes appeared. We now expected the river to cast off its bands of ice any day.

So one day we heard a rumble and the ice in the river cracked. Suddenly it heaved, was rent from shore to shore, and surged forward with a muffled roar. Great sheets and blocks were up-ended and thrown aside, and a flood of muddy brown water rushed over them and up on the banks. Break-up was here. The stream swept logs and branches before it, and half a mile below our cabin the ice jammed into a barrier, which increased steadily in height and thickness as more ice floes were swept to it with the current. In a couple of hours the water had risen over the low-lying south bank and flowed into the forest. That night our cabin lay by the shore of a large lake, the surface of which was covered with ice-floes, tree-trunks, branches and all sorts of other debris. The opposite shore was flooded with ten feet of turbid water over which only the tall trees lifted their branches. But our shore was high and our cabin out of danger. We could wait calmly for the river to recede inside of its banks again.

The following morning the barrier was gone and the water was level with the banks. Driftwood and ice-floes had also decreased in quantity, and we decided it was safe to try out our hunting canoe. Karl and I lowered it into the water and paddled gingerly among the ice down the river. Because of its small size the canoe was a bit tippy, but it handled easily and held water well. But we had to be on the alert continually as we manœuvred among tree-trunks and ice in the fast water. It was easy enough to drift down with the current, but we had to dig in with all our strength to make any headway against it. We were exhausted when we arrived back in camp and we had shot only three muskrats.

Tex met us at the landing. 'I knew that you guys wouldn't get any rats. There aren't any when the water is high. You just let yourself in for some useless work.'

The next few days we hunted with varying success, but as the river fell our luck improved. Finally even Tex condescended to go along.

While we hunted we waited impatiently for the time when we could depart for the better hunting grounds of the Athabaska delta. We had heard that it usually took the break-up about two weeks to reach the delta after McMurray was open; then, one day, we met a couple of Indians, who told us that the ice still covered the Athabaska River but that the Clearwater had flooded McMurray and caused a lot of damage. So, although we were impatient, we knew it was too early to start. Meanwhile we hunted the surrounding waters.

One day, while I stayed in camp to bake bread for a week ahead, Karl and Tex went out in the little canoe. While I was busy around the oven I heard a faint yell. It was repeated and I went down to the river to see what was up. Then I saw Karl and Tex on the opposite shore. They waved excitedly, and Tex yelled at the top of his voice: 'Come over with the big canoe.'

We had not had the big canoe in the water yet and it was still up by the cabin, so I had to pack it down to the shore. And then I had to make paddles. Quickly I nailed some rat stretchers to sticks, threw them into the craft, and paddled as fast as I could through the current to the other side. There stood a pair of sheepish and very wet fellows. Karl had no hat and only one boot. Tex was coatless and bareheaded also.

Through chattering teeth they said that they had capsized and lost the canoe in the strong current. While they changed their clothes in camp I heard how it had happened. Tex, for once, said very little, and it was Karl who told the story with many bitter looks his way. Karl was so angry that his always halting English became worse than ever, and I could hardly understand him. Finally, when Tex, who obviously felt uncomfortable, went outside, Karl switched into Swedish and the story came out in a rush.

They had gone a few miles downstream, shot a few rats and turned homeward. Paddling upstream, they hugged the shore where the current was weak and an occasional eddy gave them a boost. When they came to a point past which the current swept with great force and where they should have edged into the stream with the bow pointing upstream as much as possible, Tex, who sat in the bow, made a wrong move and the canoe shot out into the current broadside. Before Karl had time to do anything they capsized and the boys were plunged into the icy water. Karl's foot had become wedged under a cross-bar, so that he was almost submerged; only his head was above water. He kicked and struggled to free himself and fought for air at the same time. Meanwhile Tex crawled up on the overturned craft, and howled for help at the top of his voice. He never gave Karl a thought and when the canoe passed under a tree which overhung the river, he grabbed it and let go of the canoe, leaving Karl to shift for himself. Karl finally managed to pull his foot free of the boot and tried to tow the canoe ashore. But the current was too strong and he was too far out. So he abandoned the craft and swam ashore. He then ran downstream, with one bare foot, on the chance that the canoe might drift close to shore where he could reach it. But he could not keep up with it and it just drifted farther out, so he gave up. Tex never made an attempt to help him.

'And when I found him the goddamned ass was sitting there on a tree-trunk, shivering and white in the face. And I get sore when I think of how I lay there in the water, like a frog, trying to kick loose, while that so-and-so clung to the top and yodelled. . . . And the last I saw of the canoe, it was going around a point hell-bent for Aklavik.'

After that the two compadres trudged homeward several miles until they reached the shore opposite the cabin, Karl with one bare foot.

They had been lucky to get out of the strong, icy current, but, even so, we had suffered a great loss. The canoe we had hoped to hunt rats in was probably crushed to matchwood in some ice jam. But, besides that, we had lost some traps, our parkas which the boys had used to sit on, and—the most important—our .22 rifle. Now we had nothing with which to shoot rats.

For once Tex was fairly quiet a whole day, and that was just as well, because now we were pretty angry and fed up with him.

But we needed a new rifle, and so we decided to go to McMurray and buy one and await break-up there. The next morning we loaded all our belongings in our canoe. It held us and our whole outfit easily, with plenty of room left over for the supplies we were to buy in the fort. We pushed off and paddled briskly down the river.

When we came to McMurray we found that the Athabaska also had broken its bonds, but we could not get ashore there because the whole shore and a channel between the mainland and an island was blocked by packed ice.

We landed on the island and considered the situation. The only way to the fort lay over the ice jam. It looked solid enough, and after some speculation I started across the jumble of heaped-up blocks and sheets, sliding and scrambling up and down and jumping from one block to another. When I got to the shore I saw that the flood really had done a lot of damage. A house close to the river had one wall stove in, another had been pushed off its foundation and a very necessary outhouse lay on its nose in the mud. After viewing the havoc, I spoke to three men who sat on a bench in the sun and had been watching my progress across the ice jam: 'It sure looks awful around here.'

The men looked me over, and then one answered slowly: 'Yes, but not half as bad as you would have looked if that ice had started moving while you were out there. It shifted about an hour ago.'

There was not much to answer to that, so, after chatting with the men for a while, I left them and went in to the fort. McMurray had been bathed in mud. Walls, doors, stairs, even the window-panes were covered by grey slime. Here and there somebody had tried to wash off some of it, but that only made the rest look worse by contrast. I did not stay there long. When I had found a trader, sold him some furs, and bought a rifle, some shells and other odds and ends, I returned to the river.

One of the men was still sunning himself on the bank.

'Are you going across that again?'

'Sure. I can't stay here; my partners are on the island,' I said.

'Go right ahead, I can't stop you,' he said, but when I left him I heard him mumble something about children and fools. I did not ask him what he meant, but clambered over the ice barrier to the island. I had some good news for the boys. When I told them that the ice had gone out two days before and that the

Athabaska was open they cheered. We decided to leave immediately. We could follow the break-up down the river to the delta and start hunting muskrats in one of the best districts in Canada, just when it was at its best, and every day counted.

The next morning we left civilization behind us. We were on our way to the real northland, the completely unspoiled wilderness.

Years were to pass before I returned. But, of course, I did not know that then.

# CHAPTER II

## Down the river—Muskrat hunting in the delta—Fort Chipewyan

THE Athabaska River has its origin in the Rockies and its upper reaches are rapid, with clear, cold water. But as soon as it gets to the prairies it becomes slow and turgid. By McMurray it is already a typical old river, with a channel that meanders through its bottom-lands in great bends from bank to bank. The bottom-lands, like the valley slopes, are covered mostly by poplar and birch, with only a sprinkling of conifers among them. The Athabaska and its northern extensions, the Slave and the Mackenzie, flow through an ever-narrowing wedge of bush-covered prairie-land that lies between the Cordilleran mountain complex and the Canadian shield, the tip reaching the Arctic Ocean.

Although this land is covered by bush it has the same fertile soil as the open prairies in the south, and wheat and other grains have been grown with success as far north as the Arctic circle, far beyond the present limits of cultivation. The subsoil is also rich; coal, bitumen and natural gas have been discovered in several localities, and oil near Fort Norman in the North-West Territories.

To become prosperous this great land needs only good communications and more inhabitants. Its climate is not nearly as rigorous as is generally believed. In our day it still remains in its natural untouched state, the habitation of bear, moose, wolf and Indian. Its scattered white inhabitants live mostly along the waterways and exist by trapping and fishing.

At the south-west end of Lake Athabaska, the river, together with the adjoining Peace, forms a large delta, which consists of a maze of sloughs, shallow lakes, blind channels and ox-bows, teaming with wild life.

In the summer time the river is plied by picturesque, flat-bottomed steamboats with high smoke-stack and towering superstructure. They navigate among islands, sandbars and driftwood in the best traditions of the Mississippi. These boats have the wheel in the stern and are fired with wood; for the winter they are pulled up on the banks to dream away the seven months between sailing seasons.

We were the first to start northward that spring. The river was littered with ice-floes and driftwood, and we had to navigate slowly and carefully among all the debris. A sharp root or block of ice could easily pierce the canvas and cause a leak which would damage our supplies.

There was evidence of the recent floods everywhere. Great trees had been broken or torn loose from the banks and were floating in the current or hanging down from the shores by a few undamaged roots. One cabin had been completely destroyed, so that only a heap of logs remained, another had been moved, and one was covered by a glittering mountain of ice, one of the many that the floods had left behind on the banks. No people could be seen; they had all fled to higher ground. We passed two riverboats resting on logs on the shore; *The Northland Echo* had been badly battered and the *Athabaska River* had part of its super-structure bashed in.

We advanced slowly, keeping well behind the flood crest and paddling in and out of bays and channels, shooting rats as we went. At night we camped on some island, where we sat through the long evenings talking and fighting swarms of blood-thirsty mosquitoes. To keep them at bay we lit smudges, which often managed to drive us away, too. Long after retiring we lay in our beds and listened to the night birds and the hum of thousands of frustrated insects outside the net of cheese-cloth which protected us.

After a few days' journey we came to McKay, a little settlement situated so high on some bluffs that it had escaped the flood and therefore had not been evacuated by the inhabitants. As soon as we landed we were surrounded by people who wanted to hear the latest news from the 'outside' and—the price paid for muskrat pelts in McMurray. And, lastly, they asked if we had any .22 shells to spare.

We soon found that all the people we met along the river asked us the same things. We were the first arrivals after break-up, and they had been isolated for several weeks. The people were all anxious, because there had been a slump in the fur market just before communication with McMurray ceased, and muskrats were their chief source of income. Also supplies were running low.

North of McKay the river became wider and the shores lower. The high banks receded farther in the distance as we proceeded, and islands and sandbanks increased in number, and so also waterfowl and muskrats.

A village near Poplar Point had been completely flooded. Here the river had really gone on the rampage; the buildings had been thrown around, tilted and even razed. Household goods, tools and clothing littered the ground, a boat had been smashed, and among the trash glittering blocks of ice lay melting in the sun as a mute evidence of who was to blame for it all. Not a human was in sight, but it was evident that the people had been taken by surprise and been forced to flee without a chance to salvage their belongings.

Here we became acquainted with another facet of our friend Tex's character. He searched eagerly among the buildings to 'find' things that he could take along. Had we only let him he soon would have filled the canoe with tools, clothing and dishes. Only with harsh words did we convince him that the things were to be left where he had found them. He evidently considered us not only a pair of great fools for not taking what we could, but mean, to boot, for preventing him from doing it. He sulked for several days.

By now we were completely fed up with him. After the episode with the canoe he had soon become his old bragging self again. He found fault with everything we did and talked con-temptuously of greenhorns, although he himself made many blunders hardly excusable in a self-admitted old-timer. He was also lazy and often gave us reason to ask if he was afraid of breaking his paddle, because he put so little weight on it. His knowledge of water was a myth, and twice more he showed his yellow streak.

Once we paddled across a wide part of the river where the waves ran quite high and we shipped a little spray. Tex, terrified, almost dropped his paddle and asked if we wanted to drown him. I told him that the temptation was great, but that we did not think we would take the trouble. He also frequently talked of our ignorance of currents. Finally Karl asked him where in hell he had learned about such things on the dry prairie, adding that we two had been used to water practically from birth and had handled boats almost since we were able to walk. Tex had no answer to that and went into another sulk.

One morning, when we were paddling slowly downstream, I suddenly saw a deer standing among the trees on the shore. I pointed and cried: 'A buck.' And I reached for my rifle. But Karl was faster. He sat in the stern, with his rifle handy. He grabbed it, got up, aimed and shot, all in one smooth, sweeping move. The shot went off just as the animal disappeared in the bush. From where I sat I could not even see if he had hit it or not.

'You missed,' exclaimed Tex almost triumphantly.

'I don't think so,' replied Karl, unruffled. 'Let's go ashore and see.'

We clambered ashore and ran up the bank. There was the buck, dead, in the edge of the bush, shot through the heart. That was real shooting. If anybody thinks it is easy to hit a running deer from a moving and rocking canoe when the animal is visible for only a few moments, let him try. But Tex would not give Karl even a grudging compliment. 'If you hadn't hit it, I'd say you were a poor shot,' was the best he could do. He had shown himself to be only a mediocre shot, but that did not seem to bother him.

Now we had fresh meat for several days ahead. We were also getting near the delta, and were very glad of that, because that was as far as we had promised to take Tex. As soon as we were there we would get rid of him at the first opportunity.

The day we shot the deer we heard a voice hail us from shore. A man was standing by a log cabin in a clearing waving to us. When we landed he invited us for a cup of tea in exchange for news.

We entered the cabin. While our host, a lively dark-haired fellow, busied himself by the stove, he told us that he had just returned from the woods farther inland, where he had evacuated his family to a platform in a big tree. He had come to view the damage done by the flood and to see if he could bring back his family.

This spring the flood had been worse than for many years, he said, and everything in the house except the ceiling had been soaked. While he talked he opened cupboards and chests and looked at their contents. In one chest there were clothes. He laughed loudly and lifted up some cotton dresses. The bright colours had all run together and produced an indescribably garish result. 'The old woman has always liked bright clothes and now she'll sure get her fill,' said our friend and laughed again.

He seemed to take his loss so lightly that I was surprised. When I remarked on it he just grinned and said casually: 'Well, the hunt has been good; I guess I can afford to buy her some new ones.'

He told us that we now were at the beginning of the delta, but that we were not allowed to hunt on the west side of the river. That belonged to the Wood Buffalo Park, a great, recently established sanctuary for the last remaining herd of wood buffalo. Only those trappers who had been on the ground before the park was established were granted permission to hunt in it. But our host gave us a good description of a spot farther down the main channel, where nobody had hunted that spring, and told us how to find it.

He also told us of a trader who lived close by. Tex immediately became interested. Here was a chance to get some more food on credit. The stuff he had brought when he joined us had long been gone, and lately he had lived on ours. Karl winked at me. I understood; here was our chance to get rid of his nibs.

Soon after, when we had given our friendly host a piece of deer meat and some .22 shells in exchange for rat pelts, we departed, leaving him waving on the shore.

Now we went to visit the trader. Here Tex used all his powers of persuasion and talked the man into giving him some food, a .22 rifle and some shells. When the transaction was finished, Karl told Tex that he no doubt could shift for himself now and that we were leaving him here. He looked disappointed, but did not protest; he probably realized that we were in earnest. So we parted, and neither Karl nor I shed many tears.

Continuing our journey, we paddled briskly on towards the place where we had been advised to start our spring hunt. Just before that spot the main channel was supposed to split into two parts, swerving off in opposite directions forming a 'T'. We were to continue a couple of miles down the right-hand channel and stop there, on the left bank.

The advice sounded simple, but proved harder to follow, because here the river became a confusion of arms, blind channels, ox-bows, small, connected sloughs, islands and sandbanks. It became increasingly difficult to keep track of the main channel in the almost still, muddy water. Finally we found the place, though; the 'T' was easy to recognize once we came upon it.

About two miles below it, on a knoll covered by poplars in their first sheer foliage, safe above the surrounding swamps, we pitched our camp. We rigged up our tent, built a stage for drying muskrat hides and a fire-place in the shadow of the trees. Then we prepared lunch and went out to look at the land.

It was absolutely level. There was no tall timber; poplar and birch grew in the drier spots, but mostly there were only alder and willows. The islands resembled plates with high rims built up by the river. Their interiors consisted of swamps, damp grassland and shallow, muddy sloughs and lakes interspaced with thickets of low bush. The flats teemed with waterfowl. There were ducks, from mallard and canvas-back to small, brightly-coloured butter-balls no bigger than a squab; several species of geese, among them wavies and Canada geese. There were loons, seagulls, cranes, teal and snipe, and countless species unknown to us.

When we wandered over the grass plains nesting ducks flew up all around us, and out on the sloughs flocks of wary geese watched us with their long necks erect. These usually wily and shy fowl were easy to shoot here as they let us approach within a hundred feet before lifting. Most of the waterfowl use the delta only as a resting-place on the trek farther north, and some of them go all the way to the arctic islands to nest. In spring and fall the wild life here is at its peak.

One fall a wealthy sportsman, who had heard of this hunters' paradise, came here with a party of friends to shoot geese. After a few days they left disgusted. 'This isn't sport, it's just plain slaughter', one of them summed up the opinion of the party. Without trouble they had shot their bag limit for the whole season the first day.

Muskrats were also plentiful; there were many houses on the shores of the sloughs, and some of the lakes seemed to have been ignored by hunters this spring. At least we found no signs of traps or other human activity, and decided to stay until the end of the season. We set our traps on the rat-houses and on the little platforms at the water's edge where rats came to eat, and in their runways between the ponds. We even waded out in the lakes to place traps on mudbanks and floating logs. One month later we would have sunk out of sight in the bottomless mud, but now the frost was still in the ground and we were able to walk around on the frozen mud which lay a few inches below the bottom of the lakes.

In the morning and evening twilight we paddled on the small channels and sloughs and hunted with our guns, calling the rats to us and shooting them when they came near. An Indian had taught me the trick of calling them. One presses one's lips hard together and forces the air inward through the corner of the mouth. This produces a peeping sound that resembles the mating call of the rats; at least it was enough to fool most of those that were honeymooning all over the place. When they heard these counterfeit sounds of burning passion they came towards us eagerly, like small steamboats with a swell around the bow, and swam right into perdition. Karl, who sat in the bow with the rifle handy, let them come quite close before he dispatched them with a bullet through the head. The rats were not even afraid of the crack of the rifle. At times we got several, one right after another, as fast as we could shoot. One night we shot about forty in one hour. Let that be a warning to anybody blinded by passion.

These days we had little time for sleep; the season was too short. At daybreak we were hunting; then we went out to see to our traps, and came home for lunch wet and dirty. When we had changed and eaten we skinned and stretched our catch, scraped the hides free of fat and hung them up to dry on the stage in the shade. When that was done it was time to go over the traps once more. It was supper-time when we came back. Sometimes we gathered a hatful of mallard eggs for the meal. This took only a few minutes; as the ducks flew up before us we picked a few eggs out of each nest and soon had enough for a good meal.

After supper, which usually consisted of eggs, a goose or muskrat hams (which are very good to eat when one has conquered one's natural aversion to them), we rested for a while. Then out to shoot muskrats again, until it was too dark to see the rifle sights. We did not get many hours of sleep.

Besides the muskrat pelts we also saved the castors. These are a pair of auxiliary sex glands that are located just below the tail and are found in both sexes. They secrete a substance with a sour, musky smell and are used in perfume and medicines. The beaver, the muskrat's closest relative, also has them. I have often recognized the smell when passing some well-dressed and well-scented lady on the streets of our cities. Trappers dry and sell them for a good price, or use them in lures to catch other fur-bearers. Mink, marten, lynx especially, and, of course, the rats themselves, go for it in a big way.

In catching rats one sets the trap about one inch below the surface of the water in front of places where the rats go ashore, and puts a peeled willow stick, with castor smeared on it, behind the trap.

Besides muskrats and waterfowl, beasts that prey on them also live in the delta. Great owls flitted silently and shadowlike through the night; falks, hawks and ospreys circled the sky in daytime and in the mud we saw fresh tracks of otter, fox and mink.

The axiom that the wilderness is quiet did not apply here. Day and night the air was filled with sounds of all kinds. Waterfowl quacked, seagulls screamed, owls hooted and hawks whistled. The syncopation in this cacophony was supplied by large bullfrogs that produced a sound bewilderingly like the water-pump on a steamboat: *oomph-cluck, oomph-cluck*. And like the long sustained tone of a cello, rising and sinking, was the buzz of millions of mosquitoes.

We did not see many neighbours. Occasionally we heard a rifle shot or the sound of an outboard motor in the distance. One evening a lone Indian paddled by. Otherwise we saw nobody. . . . Oh yes, I almost forgot Tex.

One night I saw a camp-fire a little way down the shore from our tent. When I went to see who it was, there Tex sat munching sardines and oranges. Now he also owned a tent and a little skiff. The tent he had bought, he claimed, and the boat he had found in the willows, where the flood had left it. He had also got a lot of rats and sold them at a good price, he said.

What business he had there he did not tell me, though, but perhaps he had come just to show us how well he was getting along or maybe to see if he could 'find' some pelts. However, the next morning he was gone again. And that was the last time we saw him, although our paths were to cross once more and we were to hear some more about him.

He seemed to be a more unsavoury character than we had even suspected. During the years he had trapped near the Arctic Red River he had run up a big debt at a local trading post. Then one spring, when the debt had grown to two thousand dollars, and Tex had made a good enough hunt to pay it, he sneaked across the mountains to Alaska instead, sold his fur there and went to the States, leaving his debt unpaid.

A year or two after we left him he came to the fort near his trapping grounds with much more fur than anybody had expected, because he was known as a poor trapper. But that year one of his neighbours disappeared and was never found. Furthermore, no fur was found in his cabin, although he was known to have made a good hunt. Tex was suspected of foul play, but nothing could be proved.

On the sixteenth of May the season ended. In a little over two weeks we had caught some four hundred muskrats. It was a very modest catch compared with that of some other hunters, who averaged between fifteen hundred and two thousand. But the older trappers had their carefully chosen and protected areas, and usually a squaw as well, who skinned and stretched the catch, leaving the men free to devote themselves solely to hunting. But even at that, two thousand rats represent a lot of hard work.

At all events we were satisfied with the result, and on a nice sunny spring morning we broke camp, loaded our canoe and turned its bow downstream again on the next lap of our journey.

The delta became flatter yet, if possible. The islands became mudbanks, the channels wider and shallower, and the vegetation consisted of grass and reeds, with an odd willow thicket here and there. And then beyond some grassy green flats we spied the wide blue expanse of Lake Athabaska.

Even out on the lake we had to stay in the channel, which was marked here by logs driven into the bottom. Outside it the lake was choked by silt, and we ran aground on mudbanks a couple of times when we tried to take a short cut. It is about sixteen miles from the mouth of the river to Fort Chipewyan on the north shore.

We arrived there without incident and pitched our tent on a sandy beach on the eastern outskirts of the settlement. Then we went sight-seeing. It did not take long to become familiar with the place.

Fort Chipewyan was then the largest settlement on Lake Athabaska. It is also the centre of the muskrat district, where in good years some quarter of a million pelts are sold. There is a Hudson's Bay post situated on a knoll overlooking the lake, a Catholic church and Indian mission, a few free traders, and a hotel with an adjoining restaurant run by a Chinese, who is probably the most isolated member of his race on the continent. (It is significant that a Chinaman prospers where another *entrepreneur* would starve.) There is also a detachment of R.C.M.P., led by a sergeant. The inhabitants are mostly Indians and breeds plus a few whites. They live, directly or indirectly, by trapping.

When we visited a trader to sell our fur and buy supplies, he told us that he was short of many things until a fresh supply arrived by boat. As the first one was due in a few days we decided to wait.

One afternoon a Mountie, resplendent in scarlet tunic, blue breeches with yellow stripes, and a wide hat and brass buttons, came visiting. He was friendly but inquisitive. He wanted to know who we were, where we came from, where we were going and what for, what kind of an outfit we had, and so on. Finally he said that the North-West Territories had been closed for trapping to anybody who had not trapped there before. At this a thought struck me.

'You must have met a man who calls himself Tex,' I said. Yes, the Mountie admitted he had. He also said that Tex had told the police that we intended to go to the Territories and they naturally had to investigate whether he had spoken the truth. Besides, they had to keep track of everybody in the north, anyway, especially newcomers, who might get lost or drown or get into other sorts of trouble, and see if they were properly equipped. 'So don't feel bad about it. As long as you behave you can do as you like and go where you like—except the Territories, of course,' he added, smiling.

We told him that we knew of the new law, and that our intention was to go to Stony Rapids in the east end of the lake.

'Well, you look like a couple of good fellows, the kind we like here. Furthermore, don't worry about Tex. We know of him—he is in our books.'

Now that the official part of the visit was over, the constable sat down for a cup of tea and a long chat. He was a likeable man, who, despite his youth, had already been many years in the north.

This was our first meeting with the Mounties, that fine body of men that represents the law in the north. We were to meet many more, and become fast friends with some. Most of them are not only fine fellows, but also real men.

A few days later the first boat of the season arrived. It was freshly painted and gay with bunting, and in the stern it flew a big red flag with a golden HBC in the corner.

There was noise and merriment on the wharf. The whole population, it seemed, had met up to greet the boat, because the arrival of the first boat is a tangible sign of the arrival of summer and also means that the long isolation of the winter months is broken. The boat brings letters, newspapers, fresh fruits and vegetables. More than the honking of the geese overhead, it says: 'The summer is here. Enjoy it.'

It is an occasion for celebration—especially as there are parcels containing joy in liquid form in the cargo. And since there has always been heavy betting about when the first boat will arrive and which one it will be, the sorrow over losing or the triumph of winning can be drowned in 'real stuff'.

That night was a happy one in Chipewyan. Noisy parties were in progress everywhere and a dance started in an empty warehouse. Karl and I drifted there and watched the proceedings. The dancing was executed with more enthusiasm than skill; in some instances the performance was very wobbly. But the more or less bronzed maidens did not seem to mind the condition of their partners at all. They executed the intricacies of the square dance with evident enjoyment, although their faces remained stolid. The music was produced by an accordion and two fiddles.

But suddenly there was trouble. Two Indian lads, who had been competing for the favour of a doe-eyed maiden, and had given each other black looks, abruptly decided to have it out right then and there. And the battle that followed was something absolutely new to me both as to technique and execution. One boy kicked his adversary in the pants and was grabbed by his long, black curls in return. With a scream of rage the curly one turned, scratched his opponent's face and grabbed hold of his throat. The other retaliated by biting his thumb, with a screech of his own. Then there was a flurry of scratching, biting, kicking, slapping, hair-pulling and pounding. The two opponents rolled on the floor, hitting each other's heads on the planks, tearing brand-new white shirts into shreds, and they grunted, yelled and swore. It looked awful and sounded worse; in fact the noise was like that from a pack of wild-cats let loose. I thought there was going to be a repetition of what happened to the Kilkenny cats. Others probably thought so, too, because they rushed in and separated the two braves.

But the effects of all the ferocity were distinctly disappointing. The shirts of both fighters were torn, they had a few scratches in the face, and one bled from a bite. Karl thought that the material results of that terrific expenditure of energy were very small.

When the fighters had been led away, the dance continued. The doe-eyed maiden, stolidly chewing gum, was put through her paces by a new partner, and the men made more frequent trips behind the corner for refreshments. Karl and I left.

The following day we got the remainder of our supplies from our trader, loaded our canoe and left. The Mountie we knew stood on the dock when we pushed out.

'Well, good luck, boys. Give my regards to Corporal Nicholson when you arrive in Stony Rapids.'

We waved back, turned our bow to the east and started rowing.

# CHAPTER III

## *Lake Athabaska—Stony Rapids—A lesson in history—Trappers*

We rowed across the calm lake towards the south shore. To begin with, while we still were near the mouth of the river the water was turbid and sluggish with grey mud, and driftwood logs monotonously poked their grey roots and branches over the water. Even the alders and willows seemed grey. The only contrast was provided by white splotches of seagulls droppings on trunks and stones.

But after a day's journey the picture changed. The water became clear and blue; the mudbanks and grassy reed-covered flats turned into sandbeaches; driftwood became scarce.

We now rowed past a smooth white sandbeach that extended ahead of us for miles in even, shallow curves. Inland the beach ended abruptly in a steeply rising bank that was capped by a thick mat of mountain cranberry, moss and juniper. Spaced evenly on the edge stood great, gnarled jackpine, their orange-coloured branches, covered with bright-green needles, reaching out towards the lake.

Beyond the banks, which sheltered the land like a wall, lay mile-wide sandflats, where tall pines grew far apart as though in a park, and where the ground was covered by a thick carpet of needles and brittle grey lichen that crunched underfoot. In moist places dark-green spruce grew close together in moss and Labrador tea a foot deep.

In one day we had left the prairie landscape behind and come into new surroundings. It was as if a great unseen hand had washed everything clean in one night, thrown away the muddy water and poured fresh and clear water into the lake instead. We had entered the Canadian shield.

These surroundings resembled my homeland so much that it was as if I had suddenly been transplanted there. I saw and recognized more and more familiar plants and trees. For years I had not seen juniper; here it grew in profusion. Blueberry and wild strawberry were blooming, and in the muskegs I picked arctic cranberries from the fall before. The sight of prairie crocus or anemone, or a marsh violet, were constantly fresh reminders.

I had never before experienced much homesickness, but to be moved suddenly into a land with the same natural surroundings as I knew from childhood brought on a violent attack. For a few days it tormented me like a physical pain; everything that reminded me of my home was like a fresh stab.

Karl, who saw how down in the mouth I was, was very—or as I thought—overtly scornful, and made remarks about sentimental sissies, but he was a bit serious himself at times. Soon, however, the mood passed and was forgotten. But we felt more at home here than anywhere we had been since crossing the Atlantic.

The south shore of Lake Athabaska was a two-hundred-mile sandbeach. In shallow, wide bays it stretched from the mouth of the river almost to Fond du Lac. In some places the water was so shallow that we had to travel a mile or more from shore to stay clear of the sandbanks. This held true especially around the mouths of the small rivers that fell into the lake.

It was the beginning of June. We were in no hurry, because we had been told that the ice usually did not leave the northeastern parts of the lake until the middle of the month. Consequently we travelled slowly. To begin with, we rowed in the daytime, but as we had an almost continuous head wind we started to travel at night instead, when it was usually calm.

We did this also because of an incident that taught us caution. One day, when we for once had a favourable wind, we hoisted our square sail and steered eastwards at a good clip. But the wind turned gradually north and increased, until we started shipping water. Then, because flour, sugar, salt and other supplies could easily be spoiled, we turned towards shore. The beach seemed to be only half a mile away, but when we got there we found that the distance was at least two miles. By then we had taken in a lot of water and had bailed out many gallons, and the greater part of our provisions had been soaked. Beans, peas, sugar sacks, dried fruits and salt had to be spread out on tent and tarps in the sun to dry, and clothes hung on branches. We lost a couple of days and a lot of food. After that we were careful of windy weather.

This was so far north that it never became quite dark. Even at midnight we could see points away ahead above the mirror-calm water. And across the lake the mountainous north shore was silhouetted like a dark, indigo-coloured saw-blade against the orange sky. To the east and west the horizon was an unbroken line. Straight above us the sky was dark blue, and often the phosphorescent draperies and flowers of the northern lights waved back and forth. Northern lights at midsummer time! It was an eerie but common sight here, less than a thousand miles from the magnetic north pole.

Except for the splash of the oars, the stillness of the warm nights was broken only by countless loons that had gathered far out on the lake. What they did away out there, and why loons, which usually were unsociable, gathered in flocks, was a riddle to me, but it gave one a creepy feeling to hear first one cry, then several, and finally hear a chorus of—as one thought—insane laughter echo over the lake. One felt as though sailing through an asylum.

In the daytime we mostly rested, bathed and sunned ourselves as much as was possible with the insects, and wandered over the lonely sandflats. We, of course, also slept, although it sometimes was almost impossible for the mosquitoes and another yet worse tormentor, the blackfly. These nasty little creatures fly right into eyes, ears and the mouth, and crawl in under the clothes. They do not sting; they bite off a chunk and the bite burns like fire and leaves an itchy swelling. They pester both man and beast, especially those that are dark in colour. They can chew a dog bloody between the legs, in the eyes and ears, and in any other spot where the fur is too thin to protect the skin. One becomes immune to mosquito poison in time, but to blackfly bites— never. The last bite burns and swells as fiercely as the first.

This summer I became acquainted with them, but later I was to have many battles with the accursed pests. In some regions they are a real menace and are known to have literally driven men mad. Their only redeeming trait is that they rest at night— probably to give the mosquitoes a chance.

We had many new experiences on the lake. It was our habit to keep well away from the shore and hold a straight course from point to point. One night we steered towards one that seemed to be about five miles away. But when we had rowed for one hour it still seemed to be as far as when we started. One hour after that it had come no nearer. Finally, several hours later, it loomed somewhat higher, but it was seven o'clock in the morning when we reached it. The seemingly low sandy point was, in reality, a high esker that protruded far into the lake. Distances are difficult to estimate when one has only the sky and water for comparison. Later, when we looked at a map, we found that we had travelled thirty miles that night, and at one time had been ten miles from shore.

The lake was, as previously mentioned, very shallow. One morning we came to the mouth of a river, where there were sandbars so far out that we had to stay two miles from shore to keep clear of them. Just then a squall sprang up, and in a short while the waves started to splash over the gunwale.

We were in a ticklish situation. Between the shoals the breakers ran high, and frequently we ran aground on bars. However, we had to get ashore. After trying in several places, we finally found a channel, where, by winding in and out among the sandbars, we managed to bring the canoe to within three hundred yards of land. There we ran aground and could get no closer. The waves were bouncing the craft against the bottom. After taking off shoes and socks and rolling up our pants, we jumped into the water and dragged the canoe a little farther. Then we started unloading.

Each took a hundred-pound bag on his back and waded ashore through the shifting sand. And then back for another. After each trip we pulled the canoe a few yards closer to the shore, and finally it was resting empty on the bottom two hundred feet from land. There we had to leave it, but could not find a single rock that we could use for an anchor in the vicinity. Instead we drove a stake into the sand and snubbed the canoe to that. In the evening, when we wanted to leave, we had to go through the same procedure in reverse before we could continue our journey.

Once we were held up by a storm. On this occasion we had camped by a high point, where an esker came right to the shore and ended abruptly with a sheer drop into the water.

Indians had lived here years before. There were signs of their tents and camp-fires, a few cast-off utensils and, farther out on the point under the pines, overlooking the wide, blue lake, a simple white cross surrounded by a white picket fence.

One could hardly be buried in a more beautiful spot. The pines formed an awning of green overhead, the crowberry vines a soft carpet around. Here I sat for hours and watched the spectacle of the white combers breaking on the rocks, looking out over the blue water which changed colour towards the shore. First it changed into dark indigo, then lilac with greenish shades, then orange, and finally bright yellow, where it was shallow. The sky, the water and the land looked as if they had been freshly painted or washed, so clear were the colours.

So we travelled day after day, mile after mile. Lean forward pull back, lean forward pull back, one two, one two. Every so often we changed places and took turns rowing and steering. We never saw a soul during the whole trip, though we saw a couple of empty cabins. And one calm night we heard the far-away drone of an outboard motor, so far out that we could not see the boat.

The whole journey lingers in my memory as a long holiday. I remember its long, sunny days filled with light, sand and clear water, its calm light nights and the complete absence of other humans, which gave me a feeling of peaceful contentment: One was glad just to be alive.

After three weeks we came to Poplar Point, where the lake becomes narrow; at this point it is on the average only four miles wide. Here also the sand ended and the shore became rocky. We were now seventy miles from Stony Rapids, and now we could travel in the daytime even when it was windy.

. And here our luck changed. The first morning there was a fresh westerly breeze. Up went our sail and soon we coasted along at a good clip. At noon we passed the settlement at Fond du Lac, but did not stop. We wanted to go as far as we could while the wind held; and, anyway, we had no business there.

That night we had come a long way before the wind dropped, and it was getting dusk when we went ashore on an island and started unloading. I was just handing a bundle to Karl, when I saw an animal that resembled a muskrat swim along the shore. While I watched, it suddenly splashed so that the spray flew and dived. Wham. It sounded as if somebody had hit the water with the flat side of a paddle.

'A beaver. It must be a beaver,' I thought, as I grabbed my rifle and yelled in excitement to Karl, who had walked away and was piling up sacks. Then I ran down the shore. Karl rushed to the canoe and grabbed his gun and followed. The beaver came up and dived again with another loud splash. Now I could see it lift its tail high and slam it on the surface before it went under. I stopped, and waited. Soon it showed itself again and I shot. The animal turned slowly over and lay still, with its legs in the air.

We had killed our first beaver. There was no mistaking it. We examined its flat, hairless tail, its webbed feet and its long, curved front teeth. Then we dug out our handbooks and skinned the animal according to all the rules; we made a stretcher of willows in the form of a big hoop and began stretching the skin. But it would not take on the nice, rounded egg shape it was supposed to get according to the pictures in the book. No matter how we pulled, it still looked like a calf-hide with tongues projecting in all directions. We looked in the book again and found that we had done everything right. We scratched our heads, but stretched the hide, anyway, hoping that we had not spoiled it. Later we sold it for the full price in Stony Rapids, and found out how to skin a beaver properly. It was not at all the way the manual had it.

Then we were going to have a real feed of beaver meat. We placed our biggest pot on the fire and, licking our chops, we put the best parts of the beaver in it. But we were due for an awful disappointment. The meat was fat and tender, but tasted awful. It was like fat pork boiled with poplarbark. Which is only natural, since the beaver lives mostly on poplar and birch. But after a few bites we had to throw away the whole mess, and we made our supper of bannock and tea.

Beaver-tail soup—the famous delicacy of Uncas and Leather Stocking—also proved a disappointment. Although we cooked it with care, it tasted like dishwater, and when I tried to eat the tail itself I almost retched. One more illusion destroyed.

Later I found that the myth about the tastiness of beaver-tail soup is a product of somebody's imagination that is repeated by every ignorant tourist expert, who, after a fortnight's trip to the wilderness, absolutely must write about his wonderful experiences. This is usually done after reading works written by other equally competent experts, who probably never have seen a beaver except in the form of a hat on somebody's head. In this manner the fiction about the goodness of beaver-tail soup is kept alive, together with other equally absurd conceptions about the north. Not one of my many friends among the trappers has said that he likes beaver meat or beaver-tail soup. All of them have eaten it in a pinch, but none profess any love for it.

Indians like beaver. But they like any meat as long as it is fat—even mink. The taste is of no importance to them, or else their taste is different from ours. And beavers are usually fat.

We did not have to eat beaver meat, however, because fish were plentiful. In these waters we only needed to throw a spoon hook in the lake and row a few hundred feet to get a bite. When we caught a lake trout we filleted it, rubbed salt into the pink meat, and roasted it by the fire. It was a wonderful change from all the beans and bannock we had eaten while travelling along the south shore, where the fishing was poor.

The lake became gradually narrower, and one day we arrived at the mouth of a river. Here the lake also ended. We were close to our goal; Stony Rapids was supposed to be about three miles up the river. We dug in with a will and started upstream.

Soon we spied a cabin on the shore and heard a motor. A canoe with two men in it came shooting by. 'How far is it to Stony?' I shouted. 'About a mile,' came the answer.

Then the river widened to a little lake beyond which, partly obscured by an island, a foaming rapid rushed down. On the shores of the lake, the island and the rapid lay groups of buildings. We stopped to look the place over and then steered towards a cluster of houses standing among some tall poplars on a grassy shore.

When we landed, a couple of men came to meet us. 'Hello,' said one, a flaxen-haired broad-shouldered fellow, and added, after a sharp, scrutinizing glance, in Swedish: 'Hur star det till?' 'Very well, thank you,' we answered, and were invited to the cabin, where the other man, after putting a pot on the stove, said grinning: 'Well, well, a couple more Scandihovians, so help me God if this country isn't going to the dogs, and fast. . . . Sit down. I suppose you drink coffee any time, day or night, like Bill here.'

After this friendly welcome we soon became acquainted with the two companions: Bill, the blue-eyed, blond Swede, and Joe, his stocky, dark American partner, both about forty years old, trappers and fine fellows. While we talked, a couple of other men—Charlie, who was another Swede, and Ed, a Norwegian— entered. Joe's verdict that the place was full of 'Scandihovians' seemed true.

When the introductions had been taken care of and the coffee drunk they all helped us unload and showed us a good spot to pitch our tent. When we had our camp in order Ed came over and said with a friendly smile: 'You are hereby invited for supper with the beachcombers' association.'

After the meal we sat by the camp-fire and talked. Karl and I were the first to arrive from the outside that year, and now the boys wanted to hear about everything that had happened in the world since Christmas. They had all come out of the bush after the close of the trapping season, only a few days before, and had heard no other news than local gossip and what they got out of newspapers several months old. The mail service was a bit sketchy. Letters and papers arrived for Christmas and Easter and a couple of times during the summer. The reception on the primitive radio sets of those days was very poor.

But in spite of that they were surprisingly well informed on what had happened in the world. Now they badgered us for more detail. We talked and answered for hours, until our tongues felt like sandpaper and our throats were dry, in spite of the many cups of tea that came out of the pots permanently suspended over the fire. And as a camp-fire draws people like the proverbial candle draws moths, our company soon had increased to a dozen men, who all sat around smoking and talking. Finally, when our store of news was exhausted, a general discussion started. As I so often later noticed, the people of the north are well versed in what is happening in the outside world, in spite of their months-long isolation.

The worsening depression and the coming presidential elections in the U.S.A. were discussed thoroughly; and if the viewpoints offered at times were startling and the conclusions reached were amazing, they nevertheless gave proof of some original and pretty logical thinking.

After six hours of it Karl and I retired, leaving the rest of the gang still in full discussion. While we prepared for bed we decided that we had to correct our ideas of some of the 'strong and silent men of the north'. They might still be strong, but they were certainly not silent. And while we lay in bed comparing and digesting our impressions, Karl suddenly sat up and said: 'You know, Erik, a couple of those fellows are plumb crazy and some of the others I am not sure of. But, oh boy, can they ever chew the fat.'

Stony Rapids was to be my home for many years. If only for that reason I shall here describe the place and some of its inhabitants.

The settlement was never planned—it just grew. It got started when some men, who had been working on the railway to Mc-Murray, came north to trap after its completion and built their cabins at the foot of the rapids that mark the end of navigation for bigger boats. Stony Rapids is a natural terminal; from there on east, north and south-east the rivers abound in rapids, and travel is possible only by canoe.

Oscar Johnson, an old trapper and prospector, built the first cabin there and was consequently considered the grand old man of the place. Others soon arrived and settled. Then Hudson's Bay opened an outpost and the R.C.M.P. stationed two men there. More trappers and traders followed.

The little community was beautifully situated on the shores of the little lake below the rapids and consisted then of about fifty dwellings, the majority unusually well built for those parts. But then, Stony was the aristocrat among the little forts up there. The population was almost wholly white. All lived by trapping, most of them were good workers and their hunting-grounds were also good. Many were quite wealthy, at least compared with the rest of the people in the north. Many nationalities were represented, although Scandinavians were in the majority. Some of the men were married, and a couple of white women had followed their husbands there.

To most of the men Stony was only their headquarters, where they lived during the summer and the few days in winter, when they came to sell their furs and buy supplies. The rest of the year they spent on their trapping-grounds. But here they spent their vacations, which meant that during the scant two months between arrival and departure they had nothing to do but fish for their dogs, cook their food, fix fish nets, paint canoes, inspect and repair and complete their outfits and make home-brew and drink it. They usually arrived in Stony after the spring hunt in the beginning of June, and in the beginning of August they departed for their traplines again. Some of them had two months of portaging and travelling before reaching them.

But during the summer there was life and activity. At all times, day and night, motors hummed or somebody was paddling home from a party or a tryst with some willing maid from the Indian settlement on the Stony Lake, a few miles away. Some of the trappers made a quick trip to Edmonton for a taste of civilization or to get married. Then courtship, proposal and wedding had to be conducted at top speed, as the time was limited.

A couple of times during the summer the steamboats arrived with supplies. Then everybody pitched in to help unload the cargo.

There were three stores. The H.B.C. post was run by a young Scot, another was owned by a Pole and a couple of Syrians were trading in the third.

The Indians, who disliked the Pole, called him 'You-Chile', the rag-dealer. But when the merchant started calling himself 'You-Chile' the Indians retaliated by calling him 'You-Chile-Asee', or the ragged rag-dealer.

That the two Syrians had landed there was a source of surprise to me until I learned that there were many others, all traders, in the north. This pair of levantines were real businessmen; they managed to pay less for fur and sell more below standard merchandise than any four other men. Ali something or other was one, the other was Andy. He had had another name before—Allah only knows what—but had taken a new handle, easier to pronounce, upon arrival in Canada.

The law was represented by two Mounties, a likeable young Canadian Les, who was the corporal, and his red-haired Welsh assistant. They were police, judges, game wardens, forest rangers and, on certain occasions, parsons, when they had the right to marry, baptize and bury in emergencies. They were also tax collectors. Their district was bigger than many provinces, but its population was small and scattered, consisting of less than a thousand souls. A half-breed Indian was their interpreter, guide and general handyman.

As mentioned, Bill was a Swede. He had come to Canada as a seventeen-year-old and almost at once had gone north. He possessed considerable physical strength and was very proud of that. As often he got the chance he showed off by wanting to compete in 'breaking arm', lifting big stones, etc. Usually the boys let him win, because if he lost he would sulk the rest of the day.

Bill was a bit conceited also in other ways. He thought himself an exceptional ladies' man, and, although his methods of conquest were so elementary that even the Indian girls laughed, he sometimes managed in spite of blushing and stammering to win the favour of one. After that there was no prouder man in Stony; he strutted around like a turkey gobbler.

But Bill's great passion was education. He had probably never acquired more than grammar school, but he wanted more. One fall he bought a big stack of very popularly written booklets at five cents apiece, each one of them dealing with some branch of science in about fifty pages. All winter Bill and Joe drank devoutly from these wells of knowledge, and when they returned to the fort in the spring they were educated to the gills. They held forth with authority on the most varying subjects for their ignorant friends, and if somebody dared question their veracity they immediately referred to their mentor: 'But McCabe maintains.' Bill literally spouted science until all his friends were sick and tired of him. And just then Karl and I arrived. Bill was overjoyed at getting two new victims. Several nights in a row he paced the floor of his cabin and lectured. Biology, astronomy, chemistry or history—he knew them all.

I remember especially one night when he discoursed on what he called 'antique history', an endless story about emperors, kings and fair maidens. I recognized faintly certain characters and incidents in the yarn, but time and place never bothered Bill. Without compunction he took a Roman emperor from the first century A.D., placed him as a king in Babylon two thousand years earlier, and made him compete with Paris for the hand of Helen of Troy. He made Alexander the Great a contemporary of Kublai Khan and had them fight for the hegemony of the world. It was a whale of a story, but hardly history. However, Bill went to bed very satisfied that night; my face must have shown that I was impressed. . . .

Some years before, Bill and Joe had trapped along the edge of the barren lands and made a very good hunt on marten and white fox. So they decided to leave the north to go outside and live like gentlemen. They went to Vancouver and there they bought a tugboat, of which Bill was captain and Joe engineer. Joe met a widow a foot taller than himself, fell violently in love and got married. But business was poor and they had to sell the boat at a loss. Next they bought a poolroom, but lost money on that also. When summer came they had to sell again. They gave the money to Joe's wife and returned to Stony Rapids and trapping. But Joe had more grief coming: his wife sued him for non-support and later divorced him. So ended Bill's and Joe's adventure, and neither thereafter talked of going outside to live like gentlemen again.

But they were both fine men and helped me a lot. I learned much from them about the surrounding country, which they knew like the palms of their calloused hands, and received a lot of good advice on trapping.

Charlie had hunted farther north a few years, and one winter he had even ventured out on the barrens. He was so proud of this that he always talked of it and consequently acquired the name of 'Barren Land' Charlie.

Ed, the Norwegian, was another character. Sometime in his earlier life he had been a circus acrobat and was still very agile and quick. He was rumoured to have quite a lot of money, but kept it cached under tree-roots, corners of buildings and so on. He had once lost his savings in a bank failure and did not trust banks any more. A couple of years after our arrival he married a two-hundred-pound Indian virgin, with three illegitimate children, and lived happily ever after as a fur trader way down north.

Old Bert, the father of the community, was a splendid man of sixty. Broad-shouldered and provided with long muscular arms, he was the best canoeman in the land. He also liked to impress people. He loved big words and was very proud of his atrocious English. When he started talking about prospecting—his favourite subject—he loaded his speech with long intricate terms. He added a few extra syllables to the words, pronounced them wrongly and with a strong Swedish accent, but he made an impression on the listener all right. When he spoke I used to sit with my head on one side wondering what it was all about.

Prospecting was Bert's passion, and every summer he searched for his mine. He never found one, but he never became discouraged. He was always sure of finding one—next year.

One summer Bert found a glacial boulder, rich in silver, on the shore of Lake Athabaska. A mining concern became interested and came to Stony with men, equipment and aeroplanes, and started prospecting. They found no silver, but discovered a low-grade copper deposit some miles west of Stony Rapids. They built a warehouse, an aeroplane base and a radio station. But then the price of copper dropped, and the company abandoned the prospect after spending a lot of money on it. Only the radio masts and the warehouse remained in Stony as a witness of a great past. But the trappers lived as before. There was still fur in the bush and fish in the lake.

These people were very generous. Frequently, when some friend had met with misfortune and returned broke, everybody chipped in and gave what they could afford to help him on his feet again. And often a new, poorly equipped arrival was given dogs and harnesses and other gear to help him get started. For that reason most of the trappers who have had hard luck outside return to the north. But also because it has become their home. Those on whom the north has once cast its spell are not happy elsewhere—they are lost to the outside world.

# CHAPTER IV

## *The land and the inhabitants—Eastwards*

STONY RAPIDS is, as I said, the end of navigation, and he who wants to travel farther must from here on use a canoe. He is now in the Canadian Shield, that vast area, underlain by granite, that surrounds Hudson's Bay in a great arc; a land of thousands and thousands of lakes, rivers and other waterways, from inland seas like the Great Bear Lake to little, marshy sloughs. The streams are mostly only a succession of lakes connected by short spillways, full of rapids and falls. It was almost as if the land were submerged, with only the highest parts rising out of the water, just emerging from a deluge. A journey here is frequently interrupted by rapids and falls, past which all equipment must be portaged before one can continue to the next obstruction. Here the canoe is the only practical craft. In some areas the traveller is not dependent on rivers but can travel over lakes almost in any direction and portage over the narrow necks of land that separate them. Age-old portages, although seldom used, are found everywhere. The approaches are usually marked by trees stripped of their lower branches and blazed square.

It is typical glaciated country, where the ice-sheet has scraped away all soil, leaving the rock bare and polished, and deposited the sand and gravel in other areas in the form of sandplains, eskers and moraines, filling the old riverbeds through which the land was formerly drained. The relief is low; hills, eskers, lakes, muskegs, rivers and sandplains alternate all through the area.

Fauna and flora are poor in number of species. Black spruce is the most common tree; jack pine, black and yellow birch next. Black and aspen poplar, tamarack, alder and willow just about complete the list.

The northern parts of the land are barren. The border between the wooded country and the tundra, although indistinct, runs in a roughly straight line, from near Aklavik on the Arctic Ocean, south-east. It touches the north-east corner of the Great Bear Lake, passes just north-east of the Great Slave Lake and continues to the south tip of James Bay. From there it angles north-eastwards across Labrador.

The fauna of the tundra differs greatly from that of the woodlands. Caribou, like its faithful consort the wolf, live in both, but white fox, musk-ox, arctic hare, lemming and some other species never venture far south of the timber line, and few species of the woodland fauna wander far out on the barrens.

Except for the influx of the white man the population has remained unchanged for centuries. Around Lake Athabaska and north as far as the Great Slave Lake live the formerly numerous Chipewyans, who, like their northerly neighbours the Slaves, Dogribs, Yellowknives and Louchoux, belong to the Athapascan language group. Formerly the Chipewyans lived much farther south, but were decimated and crowded northward by the Crees, who were pressing in. Of the once great tribe only some fifteen hundred or two thousand souls remain, scattered over a wide area. Their features are Mongolian and their bodies squat.

The Crees, who belong to the Algonquin language group, are more like the cigar-store Indians, tall and slim, with hooked noses and narrow faces.

The Chipewyans hunt mostly in the woodlands, but in the winter some of them venture out on the tundra in search of caribou. That part of the tribe, sometimes called Caribou Eaters, are as dependent on caribou for food, clothing, light and, formerly, shelter as the Arab on the date palm.

Along the coast and inland on the barrens live the Eskimos. Their nearest village lies only about a hundred and fifty miles north-east of Stony Rapids on the shore of the Ennadai Lake. There is a sharp line between the domains of the 'Huskies' and the Chipewyan, as neither trusts the other or encroaches on his hunting-grounds.

Formerly Eskimos used to come to Fond du Lac to trade, but now none has been there for several decades, possibly because of the following incident.

One winter a Husky came to the fort with his komatic (a long sleigh with runners) to buy ammunition and other supplies. On his way out he happened to camp with some Chipewyans. There was little conversation; they did not understand each other's tongue. But, instead, one grinned at the other in a friendly way over the camp-fire and used sign language, smoked and drank tea, and exchanged small gifts. Both parties were anxious to be friendly and to show that the old enmity was forgotten. All went well until the Husky, in exchange for some other gift, gave one brave a hunting-knife with a nicely carved handle of walrus tusk. The grateful Indian, who was also something of a prankster, grinned, pointed at the Husky, pulled the back of the knife across his own throat and lay down and closed his eyes, all in an expressive pantomime and as an attempt to joke about the old feud.

He should not have done that. The Husky just looked at him without a smile. Eskimos do not understand jokes; to them everything is deadly reality. A little later he walked over to his sleigh to which his dogs were still hitched, pulled out his rifle and started shooting at the surprised Indians, wounding several before they had time to escape out of the fire-light. Then yelling at his dogs, he raced away, leaving the howling braves to their fate. Since then no Eskimo has visited Fond du Lac.

The primitive Eskimo, who lives isolated from the white man and the blessings of his civilization, is honest and helpful. He will gladly give you any assistance you need, and lend you his belongings, including his wife, without asking for anything in return. But you have to ask him first. To make off with his wife or daughter without his permission is to him like stealing his dog or gun. All are his property—chattels and equipment necessary for his livelihood. Retribution comes swiftly to any man who tries it.

Their morals, customs and standards are entirely their own and quite logical. They have been developed through ages of struggle against a hard climate. But to a white man they are often confusing, and the actions of the Husky himself unpredictable.

Some years ago a missionary in the far north encountered a

band of Eskimos living in their natural state, completely isolated from the outside world and the white man. They still hunted with bow and arrow and worshipped their heathen idols. The missionary talked to them about his God and persuaded them that He was more powerful than their own, and that prayers to Him would bring much better results than worship of their own gods. He baptized the whole band and remained with them as their shepherd. But that fall the caribou herds failed to come as usual and stayed away in spite of the most burning prayers. The Huskies then concluded that their old gods had turned away the caribou in revenge for being scorned. The Huskies accused the missionary of falsehood and became so hostile that he was lucky to escape with his life.

Those that have come in contact with civilization acquire many of the white man's faults and often become untrustworthy. One spring two trappers, one Gene Olson and his partner, were found, one with his throat cut and the other shot through the head, in their tent out on the tundra. Although the murderer was not found, it was generally believed that Eskimos had done it, because all the men's belongings, except one rifle, were intact. An Indian or a white man would have taken their furs and supplies also. . . .

The trappers from Stony Rapids scattered over a great area for the winter, several as far as the Dubawnt Lake, about two hundred miles north of the timberline. At this time at most a score of white men had ever seen this great lake one hundred miles long and sixty wide, where break-up comes in July and where some ice remains all through the summer, until it starts freezing again in September. Here they caught hundreds of white foxes some winters and were almost wealthy in the spring. But then came some poor years when they hardly made their expenses. But every third year on the average was good, and that more than made up for the poor ones.

The life on the barren lands is hard. All winter the trapper lives in a tent, and the only way of heating it is with a small kerosene stove on which he also cooks his food. Often he cannot remove even his parka for months at a time. There is no wood for fuel, or for shelter against the roaring blizzards that sweep over the plains and last several days. Sometimes these start so suddenly that a man can save his life only by digging himself down into the snow and crawling into his sleeping bag for the duration of the storm.

Some of them have been lucky enough to find one of those scattered bluffs of timber that sometimes occur in sheltered valleys way north of the timber line proper. Many trappers prefer to stay at the edge of the bush, where there are trees for fuel and to build a cabin.

Many of the Stony Rapids trappers also go south-east up the Fond du Lac River—locally called the Black River—as far as the Wollaston Lake, or south up the Cree River.

In those days there were no registered or restricted trap-lines. If somebody was dissatisfied with his hunting-grounds and wanted to move elsewhere he was free to do so. But courtesy demanded that he discuss his intentions with his prospective neighbours and find out where they trapped and what grounds were open. Together they decided on the limits of their respective territories; and the newcomer was told where there were empty cabins which could be used, about lakes where the fishing was good, about country where the caribou usually were plentiful, and a number of other things that would be helpful. These things were discussed amiably; everybody gained by having his grounds to himself, and there was plenty of room for all. As a general rule, before going out, neighbours also agreed where and when to meet during the winter.

Karl and I inquired early about suitable grounds for us and were given much information and good advice. Finally we decided on the Porcupine River, a tributary to the Black River, flowing into the latter from the north-east. Bill, who proposed it, said that no white man had trapped in that district for years. Porcupine was so full of rapids and falls—on the average one per mile according to the Indians—that nobody travelled along it. For this reason the men in Stony Rapids knew very little about the Porcupine River country, and the Indians were supposed to go there only in the winter-time.

We tried to get more information about the district. Henry, the police interpreter, gave us a description. About forty miles up there existed a plateau of sorts where two other rivers, the Nest and Grease-lip Rivers, joined the Porcupine within a mile of each other, and around this place, called The Forks, lay a delta where muskrats were plentiful. Below that the river broke through several mountain ranges and was very rough all the way down. The Grease-lip had come by its name from the herds of fat caribou that used to range there during the winter. Both the Grease-lip and Nest Rivers drained several large lakes. The Indians never travelled on the river, but used a roundabout way.

Formerly the Chipewyans had hunted there almost every year. But one year a fever—probably the Spanish flu—came along, ravaged the tribe all winter and killed many. Death hit those who lived in the Porcupine area the hardest, and about one-third of them died. The Chipewyans, who are very superstitious, buried their dead there and left the area, believing that it was under a curse. Since then few had dared go back. Now, since it had been left alone for many years, the land should be good for fox, muskrat and especially mink, who like running water. Furthermore, the mink cycle was expected to hit its peak the coming winter; all the trappers expected to catch many of them.

The more we heard about the Porcupine the more we liked it, and we decided to go there in spite of the discouraging stories we heard about rapids and falls on the way.

We caught travel fever and immediately started to prepare for the trip. We were going to leave right then and there. The other boys tried to dissuade us: it was too hot now, the first of August was plenty early, and so on. But we did not listen.

First our canoe had to be cut down in size and weight. We made it several inches lower and removed several crossbars, the seats, and anything else that was too heavy. Then we packed our equipment in bundles of about one hundred pounds, each suitable for portaging, and made packboards to make the carrying of big loads easier. Finally we completed our outfit and bought more provisions. It was July and we had to take along enough food to last us until Christmas.

Our provisions were bought according to one simple idea: the most possible nourishment in the least possible weight and bulk. That meant dried beans, peas and vegetables, rice, oatmeal, powdered milk, bacon, lard and dried fruit. Tea, coffee, tobacco, butter and such were packed in airtight containers, and salt, sugar and other foods, liable to become spoiled by dampness, in canvas bags treated with paraffin. Heavy and bulky and perishable foods like potatoes, jam and eggs were taboo. When everything must be packed on one's back over many portages not one pound of superfluous weight is allowed. Despite that, we could not take along enough supplies to last us through, and intended to live mostly on fish and game.

Naturally we also took along fish-nets, spoon-hooks and rifles. They are indispensable to a trapper. Karl's rifle was a cal. 270 Winchester, and I had a 6.5 mm. Mannlicher carbine. Both were good rifles, but had one drawback: ammunition was difficult to obtain in these parts, where the .30–30, .25–35 and .32 special were the most common guns. Although they were not so good for caribou, they were still widely used, because they had become firmly established and ammunition could be had at any post. Karl managed to buy two boxes of shells for his rifle, but I got none for mine. In all we had only about one hundred shells for our large-calibre guns but plenty for our twenty-twos.

Now we were ready and on the seventeenth of July we started.

Just before we left, Old Jack came and offered us a dog. He said he had too many; and even if we did not intend to use a dog team, we needed a watch-dog, anyway, to keep bears and scavenging Indian dogs away. We listened a bit dubiously; from what we had seen of his outfit we did not believe he wanted to bestow any prize on us. However, as we did not want to insult the old man, we accepted with thanks.

Old Jack was a peculiar chap and the dirtiest I have ever met. He never washed; he maintained that water was bad for him. He had the so-called seven-year itch, which those who knew him claimed had been his at least fourteen. Moreover, he never changed his underwear; he just pulled on a new one when the undermost rotted off. And when he scratched himself, which was incessantly, it sounded like somebody scraping a board with a rake.

Because of his high-pitched voice the Indians called him the Black River Loon, which name was not exactly complimentary, as they considered the loon a crazy bird. But occasionally Jack showed signs of an education above the average. He knew music and literature and used phrases that suggested a cultured background. But all that had long ago been buried under a thick layer of filth. However, he brought us the dog, an old white-haired pooch, and we walked down to our canoe with it in tow.

We had no maps showing our route or destination. Only the outlines of the largest lakes and rivers were drawn on the maps that then existed: the hinterland was blank. The Black Lake and the Black River were shown, but the Porcupine was marked only by a broken line that joined the Black River. Later we found even that to be incorrectly drawn. But Henry and the other boys had made us a pencil sketch which proved very useful, although it did look mostly like a row of sausages with lots of string between.

To begin with, we were to follow the old portage route to the Black Lake, used hundreds of years ago, although surrounded by a land still as virgin as it was then. We were glad of that, and, feeling like Peter Pond, Samuel Hearne and Livingstone rolled into one, we pushed off and rowed out on the Stony Lake, followed by the good wishes of our friends.

# CHAPTER V

## *Over the portages—Indian villages on the Black Lake*

AFTER rowing ten miles we came to the first portage, which leads past Woodcock Rapids, where the river drops eighty-one feet in two miles. In the last quarter of a mile it breaks through a sandstone ridge and tumbles down fifty feet, in a narrow gorge, in three successive falls.

We went ashore below the falls from where a well-cut and blazed portage leads to the Middle Lake, two and a half miles away. At once we noticed that the portage was used a lot, because by the landing there was a wharf of sorts and a stage on which to pile one's outfit out of reach of dogs and other hungry marauders.

The portage started with a veritable Jacob's ladder up the slope of the sandstone ridge. Here some travellers had placed big, flat blocks of stone in a row to form a rough stairway.

Here we made our first acquaintance with portaging. First the trail took us straight up and, when we were well there, straight down again to the edge of a swamp. Then it led on across a row of slippery logs and sticks over the mud to the other side. On these one was supposed to balance over the swamp with a big load on one's back. Generations of travellers had cut down trees and thrown them into the mud, where they soon sank out of sight, so that the vicinity was clear of bush. Over a creek that flowed through the middle a rough bridge had been built. That, we found out later, had been constructed by the Indians that same summer so that their priest could pass through unsullied.

Right at the beginning we had a mishap. Walking single file, each with a flour bag on our backs, we navigated along the soap-slick shaky path. Karl, who walked ahead, suddenly slipped off a log and sank to the hips in the mire. I thought it looked so funny that I started to laugh. I should not have done that. The next instant I myself lay on my belly in the goo. And to get out was not easy. We could not put our flour sacks down in the swamp and there was no other place to put them. With hundred-pound packs on our backs, and trying to keep it dry, we had to crawl back on the logs and stand up. When we finally succeeded, after slipping back a few times, we were wet to the skin and covered with slimy mud from head to foot. Then we continued the rest of the way across the portage.

But when we had made two more trips, and got wet every time we crossed the swamp, we concluded that this was not the best way, so we packed everything first to the edge of the swamp, then across it, and finally the rest of the way to the Middle Lake. By doing it in this way in easy stages, we escaped being wet all the time. With short intervals all along the portage there were stages, cut from trees, where one could place one's load and rest.

We had to shoot the dog. Although we were green, we soon saw that Spot wasn't fit even for 'hitting the devil on the fanny with', as Karl put it. He was not capable of walking more than a few hundred feet without a rest. By palming him off on us Old Jack had simply wanted to save himself the task of killing an old hunting partner. Oh yes, Spot was good for one thing. After one meal we had left our dishes unwashed. When we returned to the tent, Spot had carried every plate, spoon and pot into the shade of a tree and licked them clean as a whistle. There he lay, with dishes in a ring around him, looking proud and wagging his tail. That was a trick Jack had taught him, we thought; too lazy to wash dishes himself. But old Spot was put out of his misery.

We soon had a dog, anyway. When we, at the end of one trip, came to the Middle Lake we caught a glimpse of a yellow dog under the stage. I took a piece of bacon and, walking towards it, succeeded after much coaxing in calling it to me. The animal, a bitch, poor as a crow, growled and showed her teeth as she came closer. But hunger won, and finally she came so near that I could give her the bacon and a pat on the head. And now, when friendship had been made, she became wild with joy. She tore around in circles, ran back and forth between us, and then around and around again. Her happiness at finding new masters was boundless. That day she never let us out of her sight for a moment. We did not even have to tie her up, because after we had fed her and she regarded us as her masters she never touched our stuff. From then on she guarded it instead.

That was necessary, too, because on the portages there were other dogs the Indians had left behind them when they travelled. Left without food, these starving marauders would eat almost anything. Soap, shoes and greasy frying-pans were coveted titbits and would disappear without a trace. They would even tear open flour sacks when they could. We had been told about them and warned to keep all our stuff out of their reach. Besides the bitch, we glimpsed a couple more dogs, but they were so shy that we never got near them.

In three days we had packed everything over the first portage and proceeded to the next one, which started on the other side of the Middle Lake and led past the great Elizabeth Falls. Here the Black River drops one hundred and ten feet in less than four miles, and the water boils down over a series of steps in a thundering maelstrom, through which no man could go alive and which makes the solid rock tremble. The roar of the falls can be heard for miles, and when one walks over the portage their deep rumble is constantly heard. One thinks involuntarily of all the water power that goes to waste here.

This portage, which leads for nearly four miles over a evenly rising sandplain, is as level and wide as a highway. Here most of the trappers used a primitive wagon, constructed from a couple of logs hollowed out in the middle to the shape of a spool of thread. It had a shaky rack on top and pieces of bacon rind for bearings. They hitched their dogs to the wagon and transported their canoes and equipment over to the Black Lake in a few trips. But the wagons had to be kept well hidden, because if the Indians found them they would break them up for firewood. And that they were well hidden I can testify. Although we had been given descriptions of a few hidingplaces, we did not find a single wagon and had to carry every pound of our equipment on our backs.

We had packed our first load over and returned to our tent, when we received visitors—a couple of Indians from the Black Lake out duck-hunting. They both spoke English and introduced themselves as Joseph Beau and Ed Johns. Then they hastened to explain that they did not belong to 'these Chipewyans'. They were from the south, had gone to 'white man's school' and were civilized persons. They had come to these parts only the year before.

Most of the other Indians had gone to Fond du Lac for their 'treaty money', but these two did not receive theirs here and had stayed behind to look after the friends' dogs and other property. They were both about thirty years old, muscular and taller than the average Chipewyan, probably of mixed Cree and Chipewyan ancestry. Since they lingered and eyed our grub pile hungrily, we soon grasped the idea and invited them for tea and bannock.

While we ate we asked them about the Porcupine River. Joseph could tell us quite a bit about it; he had been there with another man the winter before. He warned us earnestly: nobody ever travelled on the lower part—that was called the Dead Man's River by the Indians and was considered unnavigable. They always used a roundabout way along a string of lakes. When I asked Joseph how many of them had been in the area, he told us that only he and a hunchback, with their families, had lived there. These Chipewyans, he said contemptuously, were still afraid of the place.

Before Joseph and Ed left they asked us for food. We promised them some if they helped us pack our outfit over the portage.

The following days they helped us, too. And at packing they proved themselves real humdingers. With hundred pounds on their backs they ran all the way across, using a short, shuffling gait. They did not use packboards but tumplines, wide leather straps that pass over the head just above the hairline and are attached to a couple of thongs tied to the load. Most of the weight rests on the head and the pack hangs low on the back. I tried this method also, and found that at first it puts a great strain on the neck. One's neck and shoulders are sore and stiff at first, but once one gets accustomed to it it is the best way to carry big loads.

We made three trips a day over the trail. That meant twenty-four miles, twelve of them with a hundred pounds on the back and something else in each hand, in burning sunshine, with vicious mosquitoes and blackflies forever biting where one could not reach them. The canoe was taken over by all four of us together. Were we ever glad when we finally had packed everything across!

If our helpers were good packers, they were also matchless at the table, and the amounts of bannock and fish, tea and sugar that disappeared down their gullets would have sufficed for a platoon of hungry recruits. Luckily the fishing was good, but the inroads they made in our stores were still amazing.

The wind was increasing and the lake was becoming quite choppy when we laid out from shore. So when Joseph invited us to visit the Indian encampment we accepted. That was a real experience.

The camp was situated on a high, bald point, where the wind blew free and kept away mosquitoes and flies from the tents. There were only five families on this point, but about thirty more lived scattered along the lake shore. We camped on the sandy beach a little way from the tents, and we walked over and got acquainted.

The camp was one great jumble. It swarmed with dogs and children of all sizes among the tents. Squaws with gay, voluminous skirts and shrill voices seemed to be continuously chastising a dog or scolding a child. Motley clothing and ragged fish-nets were hanging on tree-stumps four feet high, which had been left when cutting tent poles. The air was full of diverse noises and remarkable smells, none pleasant. One had to be careful where one stepped, too, to avoid treading on a pup—or something worse.

The women cooked over open fires in front of the tents, washed clothes, cut wood or changed diapers on their papooses. Here I got an explanation for all the yellow muskeg moss that hung in festoons all around the tents. The women packed the moss around the lower parts of the babies to absorb that which came out of them. Moss was plentiful and did not have to be washed.

The men who remained in camp reclined in the tents, unconcerned about it all. An old, wrinkled and grey-haired man sat alone by a smudge and beat a tom-tom—*ta-tam*, *ta-tam* he went—and sang a monotonous dirge, in which the A-sound seemed to dominate.

The oldster, Ed John's father, was still sitting and singing in the same spot when evening came. Around him gradually gathered a flock of listening youngsters, and later even the grown-ups joined them. Joseph explained that the songs were old tales—about heroes in the wars with the Crees, stories about fairies, hunting and witchcraft—and that the old man had a limitless supply of them. Apparently he was the bard of the tribe. He sang for hours, occasionally interrupting himself for some explanation. The melodies were monotonous but haunting, and the beat of the drum never changed. But the audience listened with rapt attention, their stolid faces unmoving, except for the play of the firelight on them. I would have given much to be able to understand it and take it down in shorthand. Here was a store of folklore probably never recorded.

The hate of the Crees and the fear of their 'medicine' still live strongly among the Chipewyans. They have no medicine-men themselves, but believe implicitly in the power of the Cree conjurers. Evil spirits, curses, bewitched objects, the evil eye, conjured sickness and other bad medicine are real dangers to them. And in case of sickness medicine-men are still consulted in spite of all the interdicts of the Church.

These Indians are all Catholics, and the Church wields great power over them. But, although they have been Christians for generations, religion has not succeeded in uprooting all their heathen beliefs and superstitions. Many tabus still regulate their life. To shoot a dog, or feed it moose-head or bear intestines, brings ill luck. On certain days one is not supposed to set traps for marten, break camp or start on a hunting trip. Beaver castor smeared on the nose will keep evil spirits from entering—and probably some evil smells, too. Those are only a few random examples of the profusion of don'ts that regulate the life of the Indian.

In other respects the Church has great influence among them, and when a prelate makes a tour of their encampments he travels with all the pomp and ceremony inherent in his station. He rides in a sleigh behind the tribe's best dogs while the fastest snowshoers run ahead breaking trail. Or he sits in a canoe propelled by the best paddlers. Verily a triumphal march!

Those braves who had remained behind to take care of the belongings of the men who had gone to the treaty obviously believed that this applied particularly to the wives, which were given special attention at the expense of the famished dogs. Although the Black Lake teems with fish, the Don Juans hardly had time to look at the nets or patch them; and to move them to a better place when the catch was poor was out of the question. But the wives were attended to, and there was much visiting in the tee-pees, especially after dark.

Joseph seemed to be a special favourite with the ladies. He was a good-looking chap and had the added attraction of being a foreigner of sorts. And the Indian women resembled their sisters elsewhere in their admiration of all imported things. So Joseph was a successful ladies' man, and a very busy one; there were many grass widows on the lake.

The Indians' morals are loose. If the man is away his wife is always ready for a little fun with some other brave. Besides, a woman's prestige is in direct proportion to the number of her lovers. It also gives her something to brag about to her envious sisters. The discussion and appraisal of a man's physical attributes and prowess as a bedfellow is then frank and detailed. Many a man has acquired a formidable reputation via this moccasin telegraph.

The whole thing is a vicious circle. Sometimes a man beats his woman on suspicion only; if she has not been faithless she certainly will be soon. After that he goes and sleeps with his neighbour's wife. But the men remain good friends. If one's woman has seduced a pal it is not his fault. The flesh is weak, and woman the root of all evil. The sum total is that the number of children in each tee-pee is great, and if somebody contracts a venereal disease the whole band soon has it.

However, the Indian loves his children and tries to take good care of them. But child mortality is so high that the survival of the tribe is always in danger. Among the grown-ups the number of deformed and ailing is great. Tuberculosis and scrofulous diseases are widespread, as a result of the one-sided meat-and-fish diet, crowded living quarters and complete absence of hygiene.

Ed John had fallen desperately in love—with a pair of blue serge trousers of Karl's. If a brave has a pair of those and a white shirt he is as elegant as Beau Brummel. Ed just had to have them, and, after much persuasion, Karl traded them for a dog. He was a sturdy, white husky with long ears, but only a short stump of a tail and one eye. In spite of that he looked like a good dog, and Ed assured us he was just that. His name, Wapush, meaning rabbit, fitted him well. We made yet another good trade. I gave a pocket-knife for another unbelievably long-haired little husky, Bobby. His owner had named him Shliuahsee, but we did not think even a dog should have a name like that, and so we changed it.

The Indians were forever begging for something, and we were soon tired of their eternal 'give me' and the starving curs that everything had to be guarded against. But the wind was still strong and the waves high, forcing us to stay for two more days. Then one night the old man said: 'Tomorrow nice day, wind no', and pointed at the lake.

Believing him, we gave a farewell party that night. At dusk the men gathered around the camp-fire, and the women sat down a little way off, by a fire of their own, chit-chatting. If we spoke to them, they tittered and gazed at us shyly or laughed, with the whole of their brown faces, whether they understood us or not—probably more when they did not. They baked bannocks and boiled countless pots of tea, while a can of tobacco was passed around and around. The party was a great success, because all summer these people had lived almost exclusively on fish and smoked kani-kinik, a mixture of swine-berry leaves and willow bark, which burns like fire on the tongue, though the smell is fragrant enough.

E

The men sat and smoked and talked late into the night, and Karl and I heard much about the land, the caribou and hunting. Joseph, who spoke the best English, told stories about animals or translated, assisted by approving grunts from the others, while the twilight deepened and the camp-fire died.

The next morning was clear and calm. As soon as we started to load the canoe a terrible clamour broke out among our dogs. Wapush, Bobby, and Queenie—that was the name of the bitch— howled and barked and jumped in their chains as though possessed. They were used to moving and also to being left behind, and were anxious to leave this place. Wapush and Bobby, ever since we tied them up by our tent and gave them a fish apiece, had been aware that they now belonged to us, and they did not want to be left behind to starve with the Indians. When I went to lead Wapush to the loaded canoe he tore loose and made a bee-line to it, jumped in and lay down motionless on the bottom, only growling a little at the other dogs.

To lie absolutely still in a canoe is something that the dogs in the north have to learn well, and it is very important, too. When one travels in a canoe loaded so that it has only two or three inches of free board and has also several dogs balanced on that load, one of them can upset the whole thing if he moves. Therefore they have been taught to lie as still as statues. If one dares to move the least bit the others will growl ferociously. The flat of a paddle is also a good teacher.

We left the Indian encampment and rowed out on the lake. It was early and nobody stirred in the tents. Only the howl of the hungry dogs echoed over the water and followed us on our journey.

# CHAPTER VI

## *Ascending the rapids—The Porcupine true to its name—The Forks*

THE Black Lake is a smaller replica of Lake Athabaska. It is some fifty miles long and ten miles wide; the south shore is sandy and shallow, the north shore rocky and deep. It is famous for its fishing and is said to have the finest lake trout in the land. For that reason the lake has, ever since long-forgotten times, been the home of that branch of the Chipewyan tribe that is called the Black Lake band. Because of the rivers flowing into it, it has also been a sort of crossroads for the rudimentary traffic of the whole area.

Few whites had visited the area before the turn of the century, and the natives were, even later on, quite hostile; there were some clashes between the Indians and the first white trappers.

About 1925 a trapper by the name of Peterson lived by a large creek branching off the north-east corner of the lake. It was then typical of the conditions that when he died, sometime during the spring—nobody seemed to know just how and when—word of it reached the nearest police detachment in Fond du Lac in the summer. And it was late summer when the police arrived on the scene to conduct an investigation. A questioning was held and a record made on the spot; then the police conducted the burial service. The body was left where it lay on the bunk and the dirt-covered roof of the cabin was caved in over it. Officially the matter was disposed of, but the white population was not completely satisfied with the performance. For a long time it was whispered that something had been amiss with Peterson's death. Most of his belongings, furs, money and a gold watch, were missing when he was found, and a chest, which had belonged to him, was found empty in the willows on the shore of Middle

Lake in the summer of 1934. But nothing more was done about it—the case was closed.

After rowing briskly all day we arrived at the mouth of the Black River the same night. Right there we came up against the first rapids, Burr Falls, a ten-foot sheer drop—past which we had to portage. So we camped below the falls and set our net in an eddy. In the morning there was a good catch of white-fish, trout and pickerel—all that the dogs could eat and more. A big heap was still left over when they had had their fill. Queenie was getting fat already, and Bobby walked around and smelled just from a life of plenty.

Wapush had appointed himself guardian of the fish heap; he lay beside it all day and growled if the other dogs came near, but he did not touch the fish himself until we gave him one. Here we could observe the difference between the dogs. When we packed over the portage the others ran along with us, rushed back and forth, chased squirrels and barked. But Wapush remained calmly beside his fish heap and watched.

Only when we lifted the canoe, the last thing to be carried over, did he follow, and then without having to be called. He knew when it was time to leave; he had travelled before. But when we were halfway across he suddenly was gone again. We cursed the damn dog and whistled; now he had probably gone back to the fish, and we would have to go all the way back again just for him. But we had not walked many more steps when I heard Karl, who was behind me, laugh. 'Look at Wapush; he's back, and he's got a big fish with him!' I called, and, sure enough, there he came with a big trout in his mouth and wagging his stump of a tail proudly. He carried it all the way across, too, and did not let go of it until he was in the canoe. And there he kept it between his paws and growled. Wapush had starved so often that he just could not see so much good fish going to waste without making sure of at least one more meal. And then there are people who say that dogs cannot think!

Above the falls the land was level; there was a delta of sorts, with several channels, and very little current, so that it was easy to row against it. It continued seven miles to the mouth of the

Porcupine. There we camped on a nice sandbeach, where the signs showed that somebody else had been camping earlier that spring.

In the middle of the night I was awakened by a faint noise in the tent. When I sat up a dark shape disappeared through the door and our dogs broke into a frenzied barking. I ran out and stood there a minute scanning the surroundings, but I could see nothing and went back to bed. However, in the morning we saw a dark-brown dog slink around among the trees that surrounded the camp. We called and he came closer, timidly whining. The last yards he crawled towards us on his belly, looking at us beseechingly with his brown eyes. When we patted him on the head he just licked our hands gently and remained still. He was an old, long-haired, almost toothless dog, and grey around the nose. He had probably been left behind, the spring before, by some hunter. Oddly enough he was quite fat, although we could not understand what he had been living on.

We took him along with us, but he could not, or possibly did not want to, follow us along the shore with the other dogs, and he was left behind the next day. We turned back to look for him, but he was gone. He had probably returned to wait for his master who would never come; and he probably starved to death at the old camp-site.

Now we started up the Porcupine, but after only a few miles we reached the first rapids. When we had passed them there was just a short way to the next. After that came a fall, then another rapid, and still one more. We navigated past four rapids and two falls that first day. Fortunately we could lead our canoe, empty or partly loaded, through some of them, and, though we were awkward at it to begin with, we soon became used to it. When we came to a stretch of fast water, where we could not row but did not have to portage, we just jumped out, sometimes up to our waists in water, and started pulling. One of us went ahead along the shore with a rope and pulled, while the other held on to the bow and guided the canoe among the rocks. In rapids with deep water we used a bridle. A line was fastened to the waterline of the craft about four feet behind the bow. The current would then pull the canoe out into the middle of the stream until the line became taut. Walking along the shore we were thus able to pull the canoe through the rapid. By tightening or slackening the line we could steer it arourd rocks and shoals.

But it was very hard work, and when we were waist deep in water, with the current tugging at our clothes, we had to be careful not to slip on the slimy rocks and lose our footing. We had to lean forward all the time and sometimes unexpectedly sank down to our necks into a deep hole. Then one felt completely helpless and at the mercy of the current.

Once we had to get through a canyon where the water was fathoms deep right at the shore and the current too strong to row against. We were then just above a fall and a faulty manœuvre would have swept us over it. I tied a rope around my waist and pulled myself forward from branch to branch along the willows that leaned out over the water, until I had the rope taut. Meanwhile Karl held on to a willow with one hand and the canoe with the other. Then, straddling the bow, he pulled himself and the canoe over to me, when it was my turn to go ahead again. In that manner we proceeded until we were past the dangerous stretch.

That night was our first on the Porcupine. Our camp was just above a rapid and ahead of us we heard the rumble of others. There was a little widening of the river in front of our camp. It was a clear and calm evening.

We had just thrown our stuff ashore, when the stillness was abruptly shattered by a horrible racket. The dogs howled and growled as though beset by the devil; the clamour did not sound like a normal bark but like a good free-for-all.

We ran there with sticks in our hands to part the fighters. But when we got there the dogs stood in a ring, stiff-legged, around a big grey ball. A porcupine! It shook and rattled its bristling hair and slapped with its tail, so that the dust flew when one of the dogs came close. That the tail already had found its mark was quite evident. The dogs' noses looked like pin-cushions. We chased them off and made a thorough job of killing the porky. We were both glad and mad at the same time. Now we had some meat for supper, but also the additional chore of pulling quills out of the dogs' noses. Porcupine is good meat; so while Karl skinned the creature I hung a kettle on the fire. Into the pot with the intruder.

While the pot boiled we pulled quills. It was not easy. Sitting on the dog, I pressed it to the ground and held its head between my knees, as though in a vice, and Karl jerked out the quills with pliers while the dog howled like an air-raid siren and tried to wriggle out. Bobby and Queenie were small and easier to handle and were soon free of quills, but we had a job with Wapush. He stood for the pulling of about a dozen quills. Then he tore himself loose and nothing could hold him. Then he roved around like an accursed spirit for a while, after which he came back voluntarily, whining pitifully, and submitted to the extraction of about the same number again. Wapush must have been in this sort of predicament before, as it all seemed like an old story with him.

On the whole dogs are pretty sensible beasts, but some never seem to learn to let a porcupine alone. Wapush was the wisest dog I have known, but in that respect he was incorrigible or just stubborn. He tried again every time he met one; some day he was going to get the best of one of the pesky critters, he thought. Wapush was a character.

A porcupine does nobody harm; he just waddles along minding his own business, grunts and climbs into birches and pines and eats bark. He is very deliberate, never in haste. If somebody attacks, he just rolls up into a ball of needles and waits for the aggressor to realize his folly. But if that foolish one persists, he is not slow. Like lightning he bats the attacker on the nose with his thorny tail. The quills are sharp and barbed and fastened loosely to his tail, but they attach themselves that much more surely to the attacker's nose. The quills are hollow, though, and had we but known it then we could have pulled them out much more easily if we had snipped off their tips first. But they came out, anyway.

Then we sat down and ate their erstwhile owner, who now was cooked. It was a big specimen, weighing maybe twelve pounds.

The meat was tender. It tasted like pork flavoured with resin; but we had not had any meat for a long time and enjoyed it in spite of that. When we had eaten the best parts the dogs got the rest.

During the next few days we ate many porcupines and pulled a lot of needles out of the dogs' noses. We could testify that the river had been properly named.

So we continued up the river. Next we came to a series of canyons, where the river broke through several ranges. And here we saw rapids and falls. There was no end to them. Although we passed one after another, there was always a new one ahead. Sometimes there was a little lake, across which we could row, but forthwith we came to another gorge that spewed water like a drain-pipe after a downpour. We packed and pulled, lined and waded, and slithered and scrambled over rocks. Sometimes it was difficult even to pack, as the slopes were so steep that we had to hang on tooth and nail as we climbed.

We toiled and struggled for three days and were wet from morning till night. Only when we had finished for the day were we able to change into dry clothes. But although we were wet all day we did not get sick. The weather was warm, and flu virus does not thrive in the wilderness.

Then we came to a lake a little larger than the others and thought that the country looked flatter ahead. We hoped that the rapids would end. When it started to rain, we decided to rest a day and patch up our canoe and clothes. The canoe had stood a lot of abuse and had started to leak badly when we had pulled it over rocks in the shallow rapids. I stayed in camp while Karl went out to hunt and take a look at the river higher up.

When I had patched and painted the canoe I suddenly remembered the net. I had forgotten to set it and the canoe had to dry for several hours before it could be used. There was nothing else to do but build a raft of dry logs. When the makeshift raft was ready, I grabbed a paddle and started out to set the net. There was a bit of a current at the point where I tied the end of the net to a bush. It swept me along nicely as I paid out the meshes. Then one mesh caught on a snag and I leaned out to loosen it. The raft tilted and almost upset. I struggled feverishly with the paddle, just managing to right it. But the current had swung the raft around, and another branch had caught in the net. Now started a one-sided fight against the current, the tricky raft and the tangling net. When I loosened the net from one branch it caught on another; the raft swung around in circles and tried to upset and wound the net around itself. I sweated and worked and cursed and swore, but the only result was that the net just got wound up worse and worse, until it was just one unholy mess. Finally I just sat there and almost wept. Then I paddled ashore again and spent an hour loosening the net from the raft and untangling it. Then I tried again, and by being very careful I managed to set it this time. I was just back on shore when Karl returned, and I praised my luck that he had not seen me. That I would never have been able to live down.

Karl was empty-handed and looked downcast. I asked what he had seen.

'Rapids,' he said bitterly. 'Not many, just six or seven, and one is a helluva big fall.' He had been up on a high mountain, where he had had a good view of the river. The report that there was one rapid per mile seemed to be true; so far we had had ample proof of its veracity. And that the traffic was not overwhelming was equally plain. Such signs of human activity as cut tree-stumps, beds of camp-fires, blazes and trails just did not exist. The few axe-cuts we had seen farther down had been old, proving that nobody had been here for at least a decade.

And the fishing in the lake was poor. I had only a couple of small jackfish for all my trouble. But one could not afford to be discouraged. We just set our teeth and tackled the rapids again.

That was the beginning of another white-water journey longer than the former. For five days we were hardly in the canoe at all, except when we were under it packing it across a portage. Again we lined and pulled, waded and dragged. Sometimes we got off a little more easily by unloading the food and pulling the canoe up half empty.

Once we almost lost it. We had just pulled it past a point when the current threw it against a big rock and a wave surged in, filling it with water and almost turning it over. Before we had time to pull it back behind a sheltering rock, a sack was swept overboard and disappeared in the whirlpools. We saved the rest, but that sack contained most of my winter clothes. It was a great loss to me—a worse one than I realized at the time.

One evening we came to a high fall. The river plunged out of a sheer gorge over a twenty-foot shelf down into a little, almost round lake, with high shores covered by spruce and birch. A high rock on the brink split the cascade in two and several birches leaned over the water, their branches almost touching the surface. The spray glittered in the sun. It was very beautiful, and I was admiring the sight, when I was rudely interrupted by Karl: 'How in hell are we going to get up here?'

That called me back to hard reality. The cliff, over which the river plunged, continued uninterruptedly on both sides. It looked really bad; I did not see a break where we could get through. But time enough to worry about that tomorrow. We pitched our tent below the falls and started supper.

Below the falls the fishing was fine. By standing on a flat rock and whirling the spoon-hook over my head, pitching it out about fifty feet and pulling it in again, I caught half a dozen big jackfish in a few minutes, and the dogs got their first square meal in several days.

The next day we found that the only way we could get up was to build a rough stepladder to a ledge, from which we would be able to climb to the top of the cliff. It took half the day to drag and carry the canoe and outfit up there, because there were other lower ledges to negotiate before we reached the crest. From there it was easier, although we had to descend into a muskeg and climb up another hill and then go down again before we reached the shore above the fall.

And there we had another rapid right in front of our noses! Those days we were never farther from white water than the roar of it.

These days we were often short of dog food into the bargain and had to shoot squirrels to feed them. Luckily these were plentiful, but it took many to fill a dog. The dogs soon learned to catch them as they fell out of the trees.

Once poor Wapush got a very live squirrel in his mouth and it did not at all like the idea of disappearing into a hungry dog's stomach just like that. So the squirrel bit Wapush in the lip and Wapush yelped. But he did not let go; he just chewed and whined alternately and, whether it wanted to or not, down went the squirrel.

This second string of rapids ended in another big fall, beyond which there was a large lake. Here the country got much flatter, and we were able to row about ten miles without having to step out of the canoe. Now we began to see signs of people again. On the shores there were old stages for fish and caribou meat, and tent-poles, and tree-stumps cut three to four feet above ground. These were sure signs of Indians; they never cut down a tree close to the ground—too lazy to bend over.

Although we soon came to a new mountain range and another rapid, we were in good humour. Here were lots of signs of people; we were getting close to The Forks.

But we had to beat four really bad rapids yet, and in one we had an adventure that could have ended in disaster. This rapid was so shallow by the shore that we had to wade up along a shoal of boulders in the centre. From there we had to get across a channel over to the main shore again. I started out, with a rope around my waist. Out in the middle the water reached my chest. Just then I slipped and was swept away by the current, while Karl stood in the lee of a boulder and held on to the canoe for all he was worth, straining among the slippery rocks, with the current tugging at him. But just before the rope jerked taut and my weight was added to what he already held, I managed to scrabble to my feet and waded to the shore. How it would have gone if I had not I hate to think about. Then I walked up the shore until the rope was taut, and pulled the canoe across.

Karl's comment on the incident that night was typical. 'Sure it was nice for you to go bathing while another poor devil hung on to the canoe for dear life.'

Then we came to another lake about six miles long. According to our estimate we had now travelled about forty to forty-five miles from the mouth of the Porcupine. We had been on the river for almost two weeks; that meant only three miles a day. But we should be very close to The Forks by now, if the descriptions of the area were true. There was supposed to be a big lake just below The Forks. In high spirits we rowed across the lake and, when it ended, up the river. But a short way up we were faced with another rapid.

By now we were pretty tired and gaunt, and decided to rest a day before continuing. Also the canoe needed patching again, as there were several tears in the canvas and it leaked badly. And there were other chores: clothes needed mending, bannocks had to be baked, and so on. Besides, we did not really know how far we had to go yet; it could just as easily be eight miles as forty. The Indians have no exact measure of distance and a big lake could be five or fifty miles long. We found a nice spot for our camp, and the next day we rested.

Karl was patching the canoe and I made bannocks. I had just baked a couple and laid them on a log to cool, when I happened to turn and saw Bobby sneak up and snatch one of the fresh breads. With a yell I made for the dog, who dropped half of the bannock in his haste to escape. I could not catch him, of course, but I grabbed a stick and threw it at him. It hit him square on the behind and he howled to high heaven, but he didn't drop his loot.

Karl came up while I was cursing the cur and asked what all the infernal racket was about. I swore, and then told him what had happened, to which Karl, who also was tired and nervy, said in an irritated voice: 'The dog did not take any bannock—you ate it yourself.'

That settled it. I exploded. Then we stood there and barked at each other like a pair of angry dogs and glowered like bulls. We called each other all the names we could think of, but before it came to blows Karl grabbed his gun and disappeared into the bush, leaving me, muttering and swearing, to finish the baking.

He had been away only one hour when he returned. He was still quite a way from the camp, where I sat and sulked, when he shouted excitedly: 'Hey, Erik, I've found The Forks.'

And then he told me that another river joined the Porcupine from the east only a mile or so upstream. At once all our troubles and differences were forgotten and we grinned happily at each other, a little ashamed of the morning's quarrel.

A little later we went over the last portage with renewed spirits and arrived at The Forks half an hour later. There we found a suitable spot and camped. It was two very happy fellows who sat by the camp-fire that night and looked at the land of which we were to take possession.

It had taken us two weeks to make the forty miles up to The Forks. How many rapids we had passed we did not know; we had lost count of them long ago. But we were there. We had rowed and paddled almost three months and six hundred miles to get there; packed, waded and roughed it—but we had reached our goal. We were there.

# CHAPTER VII

## *We make ourselves at home in our domain—*
## *The caribou-run*

THE next few days we rested, or rowed around exploring at our leisure the three rivers that met near our camp, and at the same time looking for a suitable place on which to build our cabin for the coming winter. It was only the middle of August then, but quite soon, in the latter part of September, we could expect cold weather, and then it would be nice to live in a warm cosy cabin.

Two rivers of about the same size join at the lower Forks; the Porcupine from the north and the Nest River from the east. At their junction they are both wide and slow. The Porcupine runs between swampy, grassy and reed-covered shores. Connected with it by narrow gaps lie shallow sloughs, where ducks find nesting-places and muskrats are plentiful.

The Nest River flows between sandy, pine-covered shores, and, about a mile farther up, another tributary flows into it from the south. This is the Grease-lip River, which has been so named by the Indians because of the herds of fat caribou that live around it in the winter. These two rivers join just above a little rapid; and although small rapids still are numerous farther up, the country between is fairly flat. Here the rivers flow through lakes and wind their way between sand plains and eskers, where pines and reindeer moss cover the ground, the otherwise dark verdure broken only by an occasional birch or poplar.

These are wonderful pastures for caribou. The whole area seems clean and unspoiled, primeval. Eskers alternate with muskegs, granite hills, plains, lakes and creeks. Spruce and pine are the most important trees, whilst on the more fertile ground grow aspen and poplar, and on the shores of watercourses willow, alder and birch, the latter also covering the burned hills. In the muskegs grow stunted spruce, together with tamarack, some of these being over one foot in diameter. Their crowns of yellowish-green soft needles rise high over the surroundings. Some disease has ravaged them years before and many of them are dead, but their bone-dry trunks still stand erect, pointing their gnarled, skeleton fingers towards the sky.

Not far from where the river widened into a little lake there was a pine-crested knoll near the shore. In a glade on the southern slope, with a sandy shore and a view of the lake and the river, we built our cabin. The pines made good building timbers, and on a burned ridge nearby there was plenty of dry wood for fuel for the winter.

In one day we felled all the logs, about sixty in all, that we needed for the house; the next day we carried them to the glade and piled them up. Then we chose a level spot, drove four pegs into the ground to mark the corners of the cabin, and started building. Laying the thickest logs underneath, we cut slots in the ends of others and laid them on top, and hewed the side that faced inwards. From a nearby muskeg we fetched moss, which we stuffed between the logs for chinking. When the walls were high enough we cut openings for door and windows. The cabin was fourteen feet long by twelve wide, the window facing south-east and the door south-west.

For a ridgepole we cut the biggest pine we could find, and the roof was made of four-inch peeled poles. On these was laid a thick layer of moss, and on top of that we shovelled so much sand that the ridgepole sagged under the weight.

Dry trees were hewed into planks from which we fashioned window and door frames, table, benches, bunks and shelves. The windowpane was a sheet of thick celluloid. The floor was dug a foot down into the ground, and the sand we excavated was used to bank the walls, to make them warm and draught-free.

The cabin took two weeks to build, and when it was ready we eyed it with pride. Karl had built cabins before, but this was my first effort, and my pride in it was perhaps therefore permissible.

By the shore we constructed a dock, and near the cabin we piled up our wood for the winter.

Occasionally we took time off to go picking berries or hunting, or scouting for a better place for our fish-nets than the one we had. Spruce grouse and ducks made a welcome change in our diet of fish, beans and bannock. One day Karl had real luck. He came home with four geese that he had shot on a slough up the river. A great flock had been resting there on their migration south. He had crawled through the grass within range, shot three times with his rifle into the flock and got four geese before the rest lifted.

They were a tasty variety; but we got no more, although we often hunted for them and heard their calls high overhead as they winged their way towards warmer climes. A few bits of down floating on the surface of the sloughs bore mute witness of some flock having rested there recently.

The geese reminded us that winter was coming and that a lot of things had to be done before its arrival. The rivers had to be explored farther than we had ventured so far, small overnight cabins built for the winter and fish caught for bait and dog-feed.

We decided to take turns at exploring our grounds; so that one of us went out while the other stayed at home, looked after the dogs and fished. We flipped a coin, and I won.

One clear and sunny morning at the end of August I rowed up the Grease-lip. After three miles I came to the first rapid. Beyond that was a big lake with many narrow bays, and beyond that, separated only by a short rapid, another, yet larger, full of islands and points, between which I could see long vistas of water. I had scouted only a small part of it when I found a fresh beaver dam in the mouth of a creek. In a lake just beyond was the lodge.

I had never before had a chance to study and follow the activities of beavers, so I decided to stay there for the night. After supper I stole back to the little lake that the beavers had dammed up and sat down between the dam and the house to watch.

It was already almost dark. From where I sat on the eastern shore I could only dimly make out the outlines of the other side; only the line of the bush against the light evening sky and its reflection in the calm water were clear. The beaver-house was shrouded in darkness and its outlines could be more easily imagined than seen. A loon clamoured somewhere; the hum of the mosquitoes was the only other sound.

Then, on the water in front of the house, there appeared a silvery ring which soundlessly widened. From the ring a band crept slowly along the water in the shadow of the spruce; it came nearer, changed into a V, and then I could distinguish a dark spot that grew as it approached at its apex. There came a beaver, closer and closer. I held my breath and tried to be still quieter. On he came like a little boat with a swell around the bow; he swam along the shore, every so often pointing his nose upwards and sniffing the air. He passed so near that I could plainly hear the faint ripple of the bow-wave, but he did not discover me. Beavers have weak eyes, and, as the little breath of air that existed was towards me, he did not catch my scent. He continued his tour of the lake back to the house, where he dived. And so all was quiet again.

But not for long. The report must have been reassuring; the scout had found all in order, because soon a new ring, with a dark spot in its centre, appeared on the water, then another, and after that several. Soon the lake was crisscrossed by silvery streaks and waves.

One beaver swam to the dam, crawled over and disappeared behind it like a shadow. Another clambered ashore on a little platform, level with the water, only twenty feet from me. There he sat on his flat tail like a squirrel, twirling and gnawing a willow twig that he had brought with him. He was hungry, because the nibbling went on briskly, but he was also choosy; he stopped at times and turned the twig, looking for the most appetizing parts. He was not going to chew on just any junk that came his way. Only the juiciest parts for him.

From the mouth of the creek brisk gnawing now could be heard. It sounded loud and business-like; it continued almost uninterrupted. That meant that the logger, Old Man Beaver himself, was at work. After some minutes there was a loud crack, a large birch leaned, and fell with a splash into the water.

Almost instantly the gnawing resumed; the logger was already cutting the birch into pieces. Now my beaver also quit eating and swam over to help his pal.

Soon after, a member of the family came past, pushing a branch towards the house. He had trouble with his rafting, because every so often he changed position and started pushing in another direction. Slowly but surely he guided the branch towards the pile of brush and fresh branches that was the family storehouse. They expected an early winter, since they already were gathering their supplies.

It was getting too dark to see any more, and I rose to go back to my camp. I had hardly taken a step, when a loud splash sounded quite close to me and several other splashes repeated the danger signal in different parts of the lake. I had been discovered and, literally with a bang, the whole family disappeared. All was still again; only a few ripples travelled slowly over the lake. The beavers had dived, either to the house or to the small airholes, with their entrances under the water, that they had dug into the banks.

However, while I boiled a cup of tea before going to bed a loud splash echoed in the still air, and the last sound I heard when I lay in my feather robe about to fall asleep was the bang of a flat beaver tail against the water.

I could see in the morning that the beavers had worked all night in spite of my alarming presence. The brush pile before their house was much higher than the night before, and freshly peeled poles and mud still wet had been put on the house itself. The food supply had to be secured and the house repaired, even when danger threatened.

Continuing up the river through a narrow passage with swift water I came to another large lake. On the shore near the narrows I saw what looked like an old camping-ground and went ashore. Here were numerous signs of old habitation. The bush was cleared off far inland and countless yard-high stumps attested that Indians had lived here for a long time.

They must have camped here for ages, for several hundred yards along the shore the ground was covered with tee-pee poles.

Tee-pees were the old circular tents, covered by rolls of caribou hide, that the Indians used long ago, before they learned to use the lighter and more practical canvas tents of the white man. The tee-pees were heated by an open fire built on the ground in the centre.

The poles lay so close together that one could have walked on them for hundreds of feet without stepping on the ground. Most of them were decayed to mere outlines, and covered by fresher poles, as the campers had left them when they departed in the spring. Scattered around were discarded cooking utensils, rusty sardine tins—even up here King Oscar had found his way—and mouldy pieces of clothing. Broken caribou bones and bits of hide lay mixed with worn-out moccasins and empty rifle shells.

It was just here—as I found out later—that part of the Black Lake tribe had been living that winter when the 'flu came. They left in panic, never to return again.

That is why the camping ground still was littered with objects that they had lost and forgotten in the snow in their haste to depart. There I found axes, dog chains and traps, and old copper kettles, of the kind that the Hudson's Bay used to sell long ago, and even a rusty long-barrelled shotgun. And on the shore stood partly crumbled stages for fish and caribou meat. This was then evidently a good fish lake, which pleased me, because the fishing was poor around our camp, and we could come here for our fall fishing if we wanted.

That lake was quite large. I never rowed to the end of it, but glimpsed a wide expanse of water beyond some islands and saw several long bays. On a sandy point I spotted a good site for a cabin for the coming winter's trapping trips. Many creeks, which looked good for mink, fell into the lake, and the islands and points looked like good places to catch foxes.

I then set out on my return trip. I had stopped at a rapid to boil tea, when I heard a rustling in the bush. Noise in the bush meant game, game meant fresh meat, and that was something I had not seen for some time. Quickly I snatched up my rifle and ran as silently as I could in the direction of the noise. I heard the rustle again, and there, two hundred feet away, a pair of grey-brown animals fled between the trees. Caribou! I aimed quickly at the disappearing animals and pulled the trigger. Click. . . . Damnation! I had forgotten to push a shell into the breach. I loaded hastily, but by then the game was gone. Cursing heartily, I started slowly back, when I discovered one of the animals standing in a glade a hundred yards off calmly inspecting me. With trembling hands I raised the rifle, aimed and shot.

Hurray! A master shot! The animal dropped as if hit by a sledge-hammer. I rushed over. There it lay, stone dead, a fine caribou buck, shot right through the head. While I admired my prize, it suddenly struck me that I had aimed at the body when I shot, but that the bullet had hit the head. But I shied away from such thoughts and started to dress my game. My first caribou! I had shot a moose and a few deer before, but I had never seen a caribou except in a zoo.

When the animal had been dressed and loaded in the canoe, I continued homeward in high spirits and at a fast clip. I had just passed a point and turned my head to look ahead, when I saw a big herd of caribou swimming across the river, and on the shore a few hundred yards farther another herd.

Soon there were caribou everywhere. The country teemed with them. While I rowed I saw herd upon herd. They ran back and forth on the shore and plunged into the river without paying any attention to me. Those that came out of the river stood calmly and shook the water out of their coats before they trotted into the bush. Great bucks with velvet-covered horns led their harems of sleek does, and fleet, braying fawns followed. They came in a never-ending stream and their numbers must have given them a sense of security, because my presence bothered them not at all; they acted like tame cattle. I could have touched some of them with an oar as they swam past, and once I almost rammed one. The land that a few hours before had been so peaceful and quiet, and where one at the most had seen a lone loon or duck splash in a bay, was now bursting with life. In an unbroken stream the caribou welled through the woods and across the water, and the country reverberated with the cracking of branches, the braying of fawns and the lowing of bucks and does; and their pungent smell pricked my nostrils. How many I saw that day I cannot even guess, but for about fifteen miles I was forever seeing new herds. The summer migration to the north, towards their breeding grounds, had begun.

The most important thing now was to get home as quickly as possible, and I rowed on at my fastest clip. We needed meat, but to shoot caribou here and haul them home was unnecessary work. Better to get there and get our meat on the spot.

It was already getting dusk when I arrived. The joyful bark of the dogs greeted me as I landed, and Karl came down to the dock.

'Have you seen any caribou?' I asked anxiously, because during the last hour or so I had seen hardly any.

'Yes, I've seen a few and shot one,' Karl answered calmly.

But when I told him of the herds that I had seen he became excited, and right there we planned to go that way early in the morning, so as not to miss the migration and be left without meat.

There was no need to go anywhere, however, because the next day there were lots of them right around our cabin. The dogs had kept us awake since midnight with their barking, and every so often we heard the pounding of fleeing hoofs and the crash of breaking branches.

In the morning I walked over to a spot where a large muskeg ended in a narrow pass between two hills and where I had noticed some time before that the caribou trails were more numerous and deeper than elsewhere. There I sat down on a boulder and lit my pipe and waited.

I did not have long to wait before a herd approached. I shot a big buck out of that one, went over and dressed it, and returned to my post. The buck fever from the day before was gone. Now I sat calmly and chose the biggest and fattest caribou out of the herds that passed, almost ashamed as I picked or discarded. Talk about hunting! This was plain butchery. We needed meat and, because shells were scarce, we had to get the most with the least number of shells.

While I sat there I heard Karl's rifle boom over to the south and knew that he was getting his share of game. About noon, when I had shot and dressed about a dozen caribou, I went home for lunch. Karl and I then had about twenty-five of them together, and decided that that was enough for our needs and all we could take care of.

Now a busy time started. The meat had to be looked after and cured. We worked like beavers, skinning caribou and stretching their hides between trees to dry, hanging the meat high up in the tree-tops, where it was out of reach of blow-flies and where also the wind would partly dry it on the outside. In the evenings we cut hindquarters into thin slabs, that were hung above the stove to dry.

Dried meat is made in the following way: a whole muscle is loosened and its ends cut off; then it is held in one hand and rotated while one, with a sharp knife, cuts a slab starting from the outside as if one was unfolding a jelly roll. The resulting slabs are laid on poles over a fire or above the stove. The meat is turned every day, and after four to five days it is cured. . . . It is then hard and crisp, and will keep indefinitely if stored in a dry place. It can be eaten as it is and makes a very nourishing and tasty food. Crushed into powder and mixed with tallow and dried berries or raisins, it becomes pemmican, the staple diet of all arctic expeditions in former days. The Indians sometimes mix sugar with it instead of berries.

By the time we were through we had several sacks of dry meat hanging in the corner of our cabin.

From the back fat, which on some animals was three inches thick on the rump, we rendered tallow. And the tongues— oh, the tongues, for which an Indian will sell his soul and his woman her virtue—we boiled until they were tender, and ate with devotion, the fat running from the corners of our mouths.

These were days of plenty for the dogs also. They lay panting in the sun all day long, with great chunks of meat all around, and did not even bother to growl at each other. The caribou, at which they had barked themselves hoarse at first, still marched past, but the dogs paid no attention to them any more. It was only when one came too close that they, purely from a sense of duty, barked half-heartedly, and lay down again with grunts of relief when it had fled.

The caribou-run continued unabated for several days, then it gradually petered out; finally, about a week after its start, it was over. Only the deep black furrows, where their trails crossed the muskegs, and the bare and trampled patches in the lichen and reindeer moss, on the flats, reminded us of the run that had come and gone again.

With the caribou also came the fall. Up to then it had been summer, but with a week of rain and wind the water became cold and the leaves turned yellow. When it cleared again we had frost every night.

# CHAPTER VIII

## *Fall chores—An unsuccessful bear hunt— The two vagrants*

THE coming of autumn hurried our preparations for the winter. True, we still had a month until the rivers and lakes would freeze, but we also had many things to do before then.

Karl still had to make a trip over his trapping-grounds, and our overnight cabins had to be built. But our most important chore was to catch fish for dog-food and for bait for fox and mink. The large lake that I had visited was too far off, and we were thus forced to fish in another, closer by, where we could look at our nets every day.

The fish for the dogs was hung on a stage near the dock. Ten fish were pierced and hung side by side on a stick and suspended between two poles eight feet above ground. There the wind partly dried them. But the bait-fish had to be rotten. The worse they smelled the better the foxes would like them. So we hung them close to the ground in a damp place, where they soon decayed, so that the whole vicinity was enveloped in a disgusting odour. But the thought of how seductive the stinking fish would seem to game made us endure it.

That it already was seductive to somebody I discovered one day. At least ten of our bait-fish were gone. When I examined the place I came to the conclusion that a bear had been there. It had left a very plain 'calling card' close by.

We had to catch him in short order. Not only to protect our bait, but also because bear meat is good to eat. In the fall, after living mostly on berries, it is also tender and fat and we could render a lot of grease from it. Furthermore, the pelt would make a fine rug or bedspread. But we had to catch him first.

Karl and I spent a whole day making a dead-fall of big logs

and stones. First we built a pen, two feet by three and open in one end by means of poles driven into the ground. In front of the opening we laid a big log and braced up another above it. A piece of meat was skewered on a sharp stick that projected into the pen and was attached to a trigger arrangement on which the top log rested. If the bear touched the meat the trigger would spring and Bruin would get the log in the neck. To make this guillotine heavier we laid a couple more logs and some heavy rocks on top. And, to make the trap more alluring yet, we added a putrid fish to the bait. If that bear goes there he will be flat as a pancake in a second, we mused, as we left after the contraption had been set.

The next morning I was there bright and early. Yes, something had been there; the logs were down and the bait gone. But there was no bear; there was nothing at all. I cursed some and set the trap again, baiting it with a new piece of meat. The next day it was the same story, but now half a dozen of our precious bait-fish were gone also. Now we were really angry. 'Tonight we're going to get that so-and-so blankety-blank,' we said, and rigged up a really diabolical trap.

We trussed my rifle rigidly to a tree, tied a fish on a string and led the string over a branch to the trigger of the gun, so that the fish hung right in front of the muzzle. If Bruin so much as touched the fish he would get a bullet in the head. Then we moved all our bait-fish to the stage out of reach of all marauders and suffered from the smell the rest of the fall.

It was dark. We had just eaten supper and were sitting on our bunks smoking our pipes, when we heard a shot.

In a flurry we grabbed axe and knife and ran, stumbling in the dark, towards the trap, while the dogs, disturbed in their sleep, howled and barked. We got there panting, but there was no bear. The fish was on the ground, and in the tree behind it was a nice round hole where the bullet had gone in. We took down the gun and walked home again wondering how the bear could have escaped. Our self-confidence was badly shattered. We had done everything just as we had been told, and still the quarry had escaped. So we did not try to catch him any more. We had no more tricks up our sleeve. Although it tasted bitter, we had to accept defeat.

Some black hairs in the bushes near the trap showed us, the next day, that Bruin had been in an awful hurry to leave the spot and had jumped right through the brush.

A few days later the enigma was explained and my self-confidence partly restored.

Karl was away on a trip and I was alone at home, when the dogs, who had been let loose to stretch their legs, suddenly ran off into the bush barking and growling. Cursing porcupines and bears, I ran after them, and there, growling fiercely, with his back against a big rock, his hair on end and teeth bared, crouched a black dog. When he saw me he crouched lower yet and whined a little. He wanted to be friends, but he was scared, too, so he bared his teeth and snarled when I came near, watching the stick I carried, uncertainly. I threw it away, called to him and walked closer. It took a while before he let me get so close that I could let him smell my hand. After that he licked it timidly and I patted his head. The rest was easy. I just led him home, tied him up and fed him. Also I named him 'Bear', because he was without doubt the marauder who had been so hard to catch. He was small enough to be inside the pen when the dead-fall was sprung, and the shot had gone over his head.

Bear was very glad that he did not have to fend for himself any more. Whenever I came near he wagged his tail, looking at me with adoring eyes, and just wriggled from pure rapture when I patted him. The other dogs soon accepted him as one of the gang, and we had another sleigh-dog.

A few days later we started to build our overnight cabins, four of them: one downstream on the Porcupine and one upstream on each of the three rivers. In a sandy spot we dug a pit, about three feet deep and seven feet square. On two sides of the pit we drove a forked stick into the ground and placed a ridgepole between the forks. Then we leaned a layer of poles from the edge of the pit to the ridgepole, forming a V-shaped roof; we built the gables the same way. Then we covered the whole thing with a thick layer of moss and shovelled sand on top. In one end of the hut we built a fire-place and chimney of flat rocks, and from a caribou hide stretched over sticks we made the door—and the hut was ready. It took one day to build.

On these trips we had to take our dogs along and no one was left at home. One evening when we returned from one of our trips we saw a big grey husky sitting on our dock with his head askew and wagging his tail just like any other dog welcoming his master home. He only went twenty feet away when we landed, and sat down, still wagging his tail, not at all afraid. When we whistled he followed us eagerly to the cabin and did not even make any attempt to escape when we tied him up. He was a magnificent specimen: light grey, with sharp ears, sideburns, the tail curled over his back and slanting wolf's eyes, just as befits a true husky. We had another sleigh-dog. We called him Jack. For many years I drove him in my team.

Later I heard that Bear and Jack had been 'lost' the spring before by an Indian who hunted beaver some twenty miles from our cabin. All summer they had rambled around, living on what they could find; probably carrion, mice, berries and the like. They must have picked up our scent on their wanderings and followed it to our cabin.

A dog without a master is an unhappy being. Although most sleigh-dogs have quite a few drops of wolf blood in their veins, the instinct of the dog to serve man is strong. In addition, the dog has almost lost his ability to provide for himself. Generations of captivity have made him dependent on man; so he prefers to serve him in exchange for his keep. Even the most abused Indian dog that only gets bad treatment and often starves prefers pulling a sleigh to having his freedom, and if he is left behind he laments his loss in a way that would wring tears from a stone.

We now had five dogs, but since we had made no plans to use dog teams at the start we had no sleighs or harnesses for them. Good, factory-made, hickory toboggans and leather harness can be bought from any trader in the north, but we now had to make our own. Out of rope, pieces of caribou hide and strips of canvas, we fashioned harnesses that were not exactly elegant but were quite serviceable.

The toboggans gave us more work and trouble. Birch was the best available material, but birches big enough for the purpose were scarce. They had to be straight and without branches or rotten heart wood. Finally we located some by a creek several miles from home. But that was only the beginning. We cut and split quite a number before we found two that filled the bill. Then the work really started.

When we had brought the split logs home we hewed them into rough planks first, which we then trimmed with axe, knife and a six-inch plane—all the tools we had—until they were about three-quarters of an inch thick. The hardest work of all—to bend the front end of the sleigh without breaking it—remained. It cost us several broken boards, many new trips to the creek, much patience and a lot of bitter curses before we finally had our toboggans made.

The toboggan is the only practical sleigh in this land of deep snows, endless forests and no roads. It is usually about eight feet long, sixteen inches wide and turned up in front about eighteen inches. About two feet from the back end is placed a backboard, a contraption resembling the back of a chair. Between the top of the bend in front and the top of the backboard and down to the back end of the sleigh two ropes are stretched, one on each side, and on these is suspended a cariol made of heavy canvas, in which the load is placed. When the trail and the speed are good the driver rides either standing on the back of the sleigh or sits in the cariol. But mostly he runs behind or, if the snow is deep, breaks trail on snowshoes in front of the team. The dogs are hitched up tandem and the usual number used is five or six.

Among other preparations for the winter was the boiling of the traps to remove all human smell. This was done by lowering a bunch of traps into a vessel of boiling water, to which spruce boughs, alder twigs and bees-wax had been added—every trapper has his own recipe—for a few seconds. Then the traps were hung on trees far from camp until they were to be used.

In the evenings we also made stretchers for the fox and mink we hoped to catch, and sewed parkas from canvas to replace those we had lost in the spring. Most of my winter clothes had been lost in the rapid on our way up the river, and I now had only one pair of moose-hide moccasins and two pairs of woollen socks to do me until Christmas, when I could go to the fort again. I had to be very careful with them, and until late into October, when there was snow on the ground, I walked with my bare feet in a pair of rubbers; sometimes, when it was cold, wrapping pieces of burlap around my feet.

To have something to change into, I also made some make-shift moccasins from raw caribou hide with the hair still on. They were not beautiful, nor strong, and when they became wet and warm, a very unpleasant smell emanated from them. But I had to choose between freezing and stinking, and I preferred the latter.

Just about that time, a disaster, worse than any other, befell me. I lost my last pipe.

One calm, moonlight night we were rowing home and I was sitting in the stern, steering and paddling, with my pipe in my mouth. When I tried to light it, I found that only the stem remained clamped between my teeth. The head had fallen overboard.

When I left McMurray I had half a dozen pipes, but a couple had broken, one had fallen out of my pocket, one had been forgotten somewhere and one had gone with that ill-fated sack of clothes. And now even the last one was lost. Up until then I had always had a pipe in my mouth. Once I had even forgotten it was there when I jumped in the lake for a swim and had suffered Karl's jibes and scorn for a month afterwards. And now my last pipe was gone!

I tried to make a new one of birch; it tasted awful and soon broke. I carved one from an alder root; it was even worse. Then I fashioned one from clay, but it cracked the first time I used it. Then I gave up and started rolling cigarettes of pipe tobacco in pieces of newspaper. When I finally went to Stony Rapids I did not buy any more pipes, because I did not want to risk losing them again. From then on I rolled cigarettes.

The first snow came around the tenth of October. The little lakes froze and ice formed along the shores of the river. Then we also started seeing tracks and found that there was much game in our territory. Mink tracks were common along the river, near the mouths of creeks and around the rapids. The foxes ran along the shores, and out to points and islands, which they visited now that the lakes had frozen. On a lake we found tracks of a wolf pack, and on a hill a marten had run on the ground for a little way before climbing a spruce. Game was ranging far now that the lakes were frozen but the snow not yet too deep to hinder travelling.

On the ice of the sloughs and bays off the river muskrats had been building their 'push-ups', which are breathing-holes covered with balls of water-weed and grass that look for all the world like heaps of horse dung. These were quite numerous in some places, and we had hopes of a good muskrat catch in the spring.

One clear sunny morning about the middle of October I walked on the ice following a string of lakes. There was fresh snow on the ground and the sun shone brightly on the frost that powdered the trees. Some fresh tracks of ermine, mink and rabbit stood out like writing on a clean sheet of paper; here a porcupine had sauntered his stolid course in search of a den, and there a spruce partridge had lifted off the ground. Ptarmigan, which had recently arrived from the barrens, sat by the hundreds, like big snowballs, in the willows along the shore. Everything seemed clean, new and unspoiled. I sauntered slowly along, enjoying it all.

In the afternoon I was on my way homeward, when a herd of caribou came out on the ice and stopped to inspect me. They stood perfectly quiet for a while. Then a couple of fawns came running towards me with their legs swinging in a funny, wagging gait, and stopped spread-legged, a few hundred feet away, and looked again. Then suddenly, with a snort and a jump straight up, they were off again. It was very funny to see them slide and slip on the glassy, slick ice, galloping almost in one spot, before they got going. With the rest of the herd behind them they sped back into the bush.

Soon there were caribou everywhere again. They swam the river, wandered over the sandplains and lay chewing the cud on the ice. The fall run had started. Going homewards I saw more and more of them. The land was no longer white and unsullied. On all lakes a network of paths and tracks crisscrossed, and on the sandplains, where the reindeer moss grows, it was soon hard to find a square foot of untouched ground.

This time they did not seem to be in as big a hurry as in September. They wandered around sniffing curiously at rat push-ups, tufts of reeds and other interesting things; they browsed and ruminated and lay down for a rest. Often I saw bucks butting each other, or scraping the velvet from their horns on trees or stumps, until the horns shone bright red.

A herd of twenty to thirty caribou were crossing the river and I stopped to watch them. Unafraid, they walked out to the edge of the ice, jumped in and swam in a tight formation towards the other shore. While the others milled around out in the current, a big buck took the lead, swam up to the ice and started breaking his way through it. The caribou have their own method of breaking ice, and here I saw how they did it. As the buck swam forward he knocked the knees of his forelegs against the ice, shattering it from below, until it became too strong to break.

Then he turned and swam back a little way, turned again and came full speed back to the edge, reared up and, throwing himself half over on his side, slid up on it and a good distance towards the shore. There he stood up, shook the water out of his coat and trotted slowly away. The others followed one at a time in the same manner, each animal sliding a little farther on the lengthening, increasingly wet runway.

This time I did not try to kill any, but walked briskly homewards. When I was quite near the camp I came on two big bucks, who, oblivious of everything else, were engaged in a fierce combat, butting each other savagely. Their great horns flashed red, as though covered with blood, as they strained and pushed. I watched them for a while before I shot. When one dropped, hit by the bullet, the other shook his horns in triumph, butted his fallen adversary and snorted proudly, believing that he had won in a fair fight. But his triumph was short-lived; a minute later he lay beside his fellow, a victim of his pride.

When I started dressing them a most unpleasant musky smell hit my nostrils. Both bucks stank to high heaven. Then I remembered; somebody had told me that the caribou bucks smell during the mating season and for some time after. I had to admit that that was the truth. These two stank so much that they were unfit for human food, and I wondered if the dogs also would scorn them.

Karl had also shot a buck that smelled bad. Then we also noticed that the bucks were not nearly as shy as the other caribou. The bad odour was their protection; what self-respecting wolf would want to sink his teeth into such a stink-bag when there were lots of tender does about?

After that we killed only does ourselves and as many as we were able to get, because now it was so cold that the meat would keep fresh all winter. Also we did not know if they would stay in our district all winter, or were just passing through as in September. But now they were also much harder to hunt, as they did not use their passes much but roamed all over, especially on the lakes, where they could see us far away.

The meat was much leaner than earlier in the fall. The rutting season had been hard on the caribou. The few bucks we shot by mistake were practically skin and bone, and the does also had lost most of their fat. Only an odd one had a thin layer of back fat. It would take months of browsing before they would be in shape again.

This time the migration lasted only a few days, but even after the great herds had passed through on their way farther south many still remained in the neighbourhood all winter.

The migrations of the caribou are unpredictable. There is hardly a rule that always holds true. In theory the barren-ground caribou wander north, just before break-up in the spring, to fawn on the wind-swept tundra, where the flies do not torment them as badly as in the bush and where they can see an approaching enemy far off. Their summer is spent there wandering and browsing, but some of them, mostly bucks, go south and return to the barren grounds again for the rutting season. After that, and sometimes while the mating is still in progress, they follow the freeze-up south again, sometimes wandering a thousand miles before they stop for the winter.

But none of these rules is always followed. The caribou's migrations sometimes seem to follow no plan at all. One year thousands of caribou stayed in the sand country south of Lake Athabaska all summer and the following winter, and then went north the succeeding spring. Sometimes they migrate through the same district year after year, as regular as clockwork, and then, apparently without rhyme or reason, they abruptly change their route and go some other way the next year. Several years later they appear in their old place again, just as capriciously as they left. Occasionally they advance on a front several hundred miles wide, at other times on a narrow strip of twenty to thirty miles. And these themes are varied ad infinitum.

One circumstance which certainly influences their wanderings is that the forest fires every year destroy thousands of square miles of bush. That the caribou try to avoid these feedless areas is natural. But, apart from that, their migrations are guided by other factors unknown to us. The result is complete uncertainty. 'Nobody knows the way of the wind and the caribou,' says a proverb of the Chipewyans.

The inland Eskimos and some Indians, especially that part of the Chipewyan tribe called the Caribou Eaters, are almost completely dependent on caribou for their food and clothing. Thus the dearth or plenty of caribou means life or death to them, and in years when caribou are scarce they range far in search of them or starve. When they describe some part of the country an inevitable comment of theirs is: 'Lots of caribou there', or the opposite.

How many caribou are there? That is a question still awaiting an answer. There have been many attempts to take a rough census, and each time widely different results have been achieved. Their true number will remain a secret for years to come. The caribou wander over a vast region, sparsely populated or completely uninhabited, and the majority of the inhabitants are Eskimos or Indians. To get reliable information is therefore impossible. The best guess seems to be that there are two to three millions.

One winter caribou came south, arriving at Lake Athabaska and the Black Lake simultaneously. The migration over this three-hundred-mile front lasted, on the average, a week, and from all points along these lakes came reports of plenty of caribou. That winter they were plentiful all over that area, although the main body went south, some as much as three hundred miles farther. And that herd was only a part of the whole.

Yes, the caribou is a topic of unending discussion by the camp-fires. It is the 'to be or not to be' of the Indians, and an important factor in the life of all other inhabitants of the north. Most trappers depend on caribou for a big part of their food and dog-food, some for all of it.

During the late 'twenties Jack Hornby, an Englishman of good family, went out on the barren lands north-east of the Great Slave Lake to trap, together with two young men, reportedly his nephews. Hornby was old in the north, and a man whose passion for adventure had driven him to make longer and riskier trips than perhaps any other man had attempted, living mostly off the country and pitting his life and skill against the hunger and cold of the tundra. His two companions were completely green, fresh out of school. The three intended to live wholly on the country, depending mostly on caribou for their food. On the last portage, before parting with another trapper, they urged him to eat as much as he could of their provisions, so that they would have less to pack. When the trapper, noticing that their food consisted of a single bag of flour, refused, Hornby laughed, and, making a sweep with his hand, said: 'There is lots of grub walking all around us and fish in the lakes, too!'

But when they arrived at their destination there was no caribou, and none came all winter. Even fish were scarce. They ate their dogs, and finally pieces of hide and bones. Then they died. One of the younger men lived a few weeks longer than the others and kept a diary to the end. Finally the caribou came, but then the man was too weak to hunt, and he died also. Months later they were found. By depending on the caribou Hornby had stretched his luck too far.

But there is no word that puts more speed into a Chipewyan

than 'Caribou', shouted in his own tongue: 'Eh-thin! Eh-thin!' Even his dogs know that word; they have heard it before and it means food. One only needs to say it to them, and they break into a gallop and run as fast as they can looking all around for the promised steak.

Like most dog-lovers, I could write a whole book on dogs. When one has lived with them for years, and they sometimes have been one's only company for months at a time, one cannot avoid knowing them intimately and appreciating them. Among them there are both knaves and faithful workers, and each dog is as much individual as any human. Some of my best friends have been dogs, and I am sure that I never will be, nor have been, so liked by anybody as by some of them. A man feels he is some fellow when he has a faithful dog.

The husky is the original sleigh-dog in the north, developed by the Eskimos through generations of selective breeding. It is a powerful and chunky animal, with a thick woolly pelt, sturdy legs, large paws and a wolfish head with sharp ears, slanting eyes and sideburns. Its bushy tail is curved over its back, and the colour varies from white to black. Another typical marking is the spectacle-like ring many have around their eyes. Their weight varies from forty to seventy pounds. A better all-round sleigh-dog does not exist.

Unfortunately the strain has been mixed with all imaginable breeds, sometimes in an effort to increase speed or size, and probably no pure huskies can be found in our day anywhere except among some isolated Eskimos in the far north. Most sleigh-dogs are, however, some parts husky, and have retained some of the strain's good qualities.

An ideal sleigh-dog should be strong, fast, enduring and a good worker. Besides, it should be able to endure bitter cold and long periods of hunger. That is quite a bill to fill, and where can one find all these qualities combined in one individual? Still, a dog has a greater proportion of them than a man.

Contrary to common belief and to writers of adventure stories, sleigh-dogs are seldom vicious. Like other useful individuals, they are, on the whole, better mannered and more docile than their more civilized brothers, who are led in leash along our streets and cock their legs against fire-hydrants. They are often shy and afraid of strangers, which is only natural, since they seldom come in contact with people other than their masters. But with good handling, and a little spanking at times, sleigh-dogs are well behaved and obedient. When a dog loves his master he wants to please him.

There remains, however, a primeval wildness in them, which is often brought out by the smell of blood. When dogs get into a fight among themselves and one is wounded the others will gang up on him and kill him, sometimes even if he is one of their own litter. Also there are cases on record where women at certain times have been attacked and killed by their own teams. Dogs owned by Indians often fear a white man and vice versa. There is apparently a difference in smell—or perhaps in the degree of it.

In the bush country the usual number in a team is five. They are hitched up in Indian file and guided by commands, more or less standard. Most 'dog skinners' use signals and gestures of their own, besides.

How good a team is depends to a large extent on the lead-dog. It has to be obedient, fast and smart. If it is nervous, stubborn or lazy, the whole team is poor. A good leader is the pride of every musher. The next in importance is the wheel- or butt-dog. Its job is to keep the sleigh on the trail, steer it around trees and stumps and bends, and start it with a jerk when it has stopped.

When not working, the dogs are kept tethered. At the main camp one has houses for them, but on the trail a bed of spruce boughs is made for them on which they curl up into round balls of fur for the night. They are comfortable there even in sixty-below weather. I have owned dogs that spurned even that luxury and preferred to sleep in the snow, no matter how cold it was.

When working they are usually fed only once a day—at night. A meal in the morning makes them sluggish. The ration is about five to six pounds of fish or caribou meat a day each. When resting or when it is very cold they are given all they can eat. In the middle of the winter my team ate about two caribou a week.

In the north dogs are a necessity. Without them it would be impossible to cover the vast distances of that roadless land of snow. It is almost unbelievable what a dog team can do. For it to pull a load of three hundred pounds in deep snow, sometimes several days without food, is not unusual. On a good hard road they can pull three times that much. Dogs also have an amazing reserve of strength and stamina. They can seem absolutely exhausted, so that the sleigh hardly moves. And then they see game. It is as if an electric shock goes through them; all tiredness is blown away. They are off at a gallop in a second, so that the driver has to jump on the back end of the sleigh to avoid being left behind when they speed over the trail howling and barking in wild pursuit, mile after mile, with the sleigh bouncing and dancing over the drifts like a piece of cardboard. Once I had driven ninety miles in three days without the dogs having a single bait. Then we saw caribou, and the team ran headlong after them until I shot one.

But when the team takes a notion to become contrary there is nothing more trying to the mettle of a tired driver. Without warning the dogs may leave the trail and run after caribou, and one has to flounder in the deep snow after them. Or, when one is fixing a trap, they suddenly hit on the idea of starting for home and run away heedless of curses and orders to stop, forcing a man, dead tired after a hard day, to walk several miles home, to find them contentedly lying in front of the door, wagging their tails, with a spiteful expression in their faces that can provoke him to murder. Then he has good reason to try his proficiency with the whip, because the rule about sparing the rod and spoiling the child holds true about dogs also.

But on those days when the sun is shining, the sledding is good, the lead-dog goes straight as an arrow from point to point, and the team seems to love loping over the ice, then one is content with life and the world. It is a pleasure to ride when the toboggan slides over ice like glass, the wind whistles past the ears, the dogs run well and even break into a gallop at times.

Dogs also have their pride. Chum, one of my lead-dogs, was very proud. He was the best lead-dog around the Cannery when

I bought him from a half-breed one Christmas. He was used to being the first in a train of dog teams, and he could not stand running behind another sleigh. He would lead his whole team into a cluster behind it and constantly try to sneak past it, until one just had to let him take the lead. Then he was happy; he would increase his speed and lope proudly away with a long elastic gait, his tail high like a flag of victory. And as long as he had any strength left nobody would pass him. He would rather have pulled the whole load alone, the rest of the team included.

A dog's memory and sense of direction is also remarkable. When I bought Chum I drove back to my trapline over a sixty-mile trail that was completely unfamiliar to him. But three months later, when I again went to the fort, Chum led all the way and found every portage and bend in the trail that we had not used since Christmas, although all signs of it were snowed over and blown in. He had a map in his head. Another time, when I was driving through unfamiliar country and crossed a lake, I noticed that Chum trotted on purposefully as if he knew where he was going. I let him have his head, and he took me from lake to lake over old, well-cut portages. Later I found out that he had been there with his former master on a hunting trip a couple of years before. He still remembered the trail.

It is hard for an outsider to understand how much company dogs are to a man alone in the bush. When he sits by the camp-fire on a cold winter night and the dogs interestedly follow his activities, it gives him a wonderful sense of companionship. He speaks to them and they seem to understand every word. Maybe they do, too; at least they understand the tone of voice he uses.

'Jack, you old son-of-a-gun, are you hungry again, you mutt?' Jack sits up, wags his tail, moves his paws expectantly and—if he really wants to be ingratiating—bares his teeth and grins at me. Wapush, who also wants to be remembered, whines jealously, and when I call him a lousy pooch or something equally agreeable he squirms and his one eye gleams like a green jewel in the fire-light. Then he wrinkles his nose, sneezes and grins. He is the one who has taught them all to laugh. When they feel like it the whole bunch will sit and show me their teeth and wrinkle their noses, laughing at me.

Chum had one bad habit. He wanted to sleep warm. Ordinarily he could be tied with a string and would stay where he was supposed to be. But when I camped out he would wiggle out of his collar no matter how tight it was. In the morning I would find him sleeping either in the ashes of the burned-out camp-fire or on the bottom of my sleeping-bag. And when I reproached and scolded him for his weakness he knew I was just fooling. He opened one eye a little, hit the ground with his tail—*dunk, dunk*—and slept on until we broke camp.

Jack was the caribou specialist. When a wounded one was about to escape I let him out of the harness. Like a shot out of a gun he galloped after his prey. When the caribou saw that it could not get away, it turned and faced the dog. But Jack continued straight for it until it reared up on its hindlegs and chopped at him with its hoofs, so that the snow flew in a white spray. But when the hoofs hit the ground Jack was not there any more. A split-second before he jumped nimbly to the side and in one sweeping movement he reached over its neck, grabbed its throat and pulled it down in a half-nelson of sorts. Then he hung on until I arrived, when he would move aside to let me shoot. The surprising part was that the caribou usually, after a few futile efforts to rise, quietly resigned itself to its fate and lay still, even when Jack released his hold, for just as long as he remained beside it. But when he moved away I had to be quick with the rifle, because then it would try to escape.

Then Jack received a 'Good Dog', a pat on the head and some scraps of meat as his reward. And, of course, he licked up some of the warm, red blood that had poured out on the white drifts.

Dog-food is an ever-present problem. Summer or winter, the dogs have to be fed, and one never gets enough food stored up. No matter how many fat caribou one kills or how many shining fish one pulls out of the lake, the day always comes when one is without dog-food. And so a trapper is forever hunting, and his rifle is always loaded and loose in its case on the top of the load, where he can grab it the moment it is needed.

Probably the worst fate to befall dogs is to be owned by Indians. Then they are beaten and kicked by one and all. In the winter they must pull and struggle with heavy loads, be whipped and poorly fed. And in the summer they starve. Most Indians own countless dogs that they never take care of. When they are not needed they slink about without food, thieving, and lean as skeletons. When they are old and worn out they are simply taken out of the harness and left to starve to death by the side of the trail. They are old before their time. Often they are blind or crippled by abuse.

Once an Indian came to my cabin. One of his dogs, left untied, fumbled around the yard butting into everything. When I asked the brave about it he said that the dog was blind, as he had beaten it with his rifle butt . . . 'no good for work now'. I urged him to shoot the animal, but he refused. Next morning he departed, leaving it behind. I had to take it out in the bush and end its misery.

One of the hardest things to do is to put an old hunting pal to death, although it is often necessary and the kindest thing to do —better than letting a bad master own him. For that reason many trappers prefer shooting their dogs to selling them.

Old Wapush, whom I had for years, became quite feeble, but I put off killing him as long as I could. Finally, one spring, it had to be done. I gave him a big fat trout and, while he ate, I pointed my rifle at his head. Wapush died happy.

However, to put a stone on a dog's grave, like Bill did, is perhaps to go too far. But Bill wanted to honour his best lead-dog, so he did just that. The stone bore the following wording: 'Here lies Dog Jack, Born ——, Dead June 16, 1932. A True and Faithful Servant. R.I.P.'

Many a dog in the north has deserved such an obituary, because a dog who loves his master is never false or deceitful. The will to serve is the one great passion in his life. And he whom even his dogs do not like is a poor man.

# CHAPTER IX

## *The trapping begins—Minks, foxes and a stray dog*

TOWARDS the end of October we started trapping. Our outfits had been ready for a long time, and shortly after the caribou-run we caught an ermine which was already white, and a few days later a winter-prime mink. It was time to begin.

Long before that we had decided how to hunt to best advantage. Karl was to go up the Porcupine and the Nest Rivers and I up the Grease River and down the Porcupine. By flipping coins we had also divided the dogs between us. I had got Wapush and Queenie as my share.

One morning I started down the Porcupine with the sleigh loaded high with traps, provisions and other gear. The river was still open and I had to travel on shore, where the going was tough, until I reached the first frozen lake.

Mink tracks were numerous along the river, especially by the rapids. I set my traps with great enthusiasm and high hopes. Mostly I made so-called 'pen' sets. Two lengths of wood about four feet long were laid, about six inches apart and parallel on the ground. Spruce boughs were placed on top and one end of the pen closed. The trap was set about halfway in the pen, where drifting snow would not cover it, and the bait was placed behind it. Then a little bait was scattered around the pen.

Bill had shown me another set that he assured was the best of all. The trap was laid on a little platform about a foot above ground, and a stick leaned against it like a gang-plank of sorts. The idea was that, in this way, the trap would not become buried in snow and thus would always be in working order.

The mink, which belongs to the weasel family, is about a foot long and dark brown in colour, with white blazes under its chin and chest. Its natural habitat is running water and it seldom wanders far from it. In winter it lives mostly in rapids, or narrows with open water, and wanders from one such place to another along the ice. It is a ravenous hunter and lives mostly on fish, which it catches as expertly as the otter. But it does not spurn meat, and it is the scourge of the muskrat, although mice, moles and squirrels also find a place on its menu.

The mink is very curious and investigates every hole, nook and cranny that he passes. A hollow log, for instance, is therefore a 'natural' to catch him. Hence, also, the artificial tunnel of the pen set. In country where he has been left unmolested one does not have to hide one's tracks; when he sees that somebody has been there he just has to investigate the hole. The more signs one leaves, the better.

His silky, soft fur is very valuable, especially when it is dark. When one considers that it takes sixty to eighty skins for one fur coat, it is clear that only a millionaire can afford to buy a coat of wild northern mink for his wife or mistress.

On the lakes there were fox tracks. In early winter, when the snow is not deep, the fox loves to run on the new ice. Points, and especially islands, which he has not been able to visit in the summer, are good places to catch him. The trap is fastened to a pole or tree-stump, snow is heaped into a mound, on top of which the trap is set in a hollow about two inches deep. Then the trap is covered carefully with new snow, which must not be stirred so that it freezes hard. A piece of sheet tin is used to transfer the snow intact on to the trap. Later in the winter a thin piece of snow crust can be used. The bait is scattered on and around the mound. Then everything is covered with snow, and all signs of man obliterated as well as possible, to make everything look natural. The trap must not be touched with bare hands, and to spit or drop tobacco ashes around the set is folly.

Rotten fish or eggs, the rottener the better, are good bait. A spot where a caribou or other game has been killed is also a good place to set a trap. And a trap in which a fox has already been caught is a very good one in which to get another, for then his scent will attract others, and no bait should be used.

Another good way to catch Reynard is to take advantage of his little weaknesses. He has the same habit as most dogs; he just cannot pass by an object that protrudes out of the snow without cocking his leg against it and sprinkling it. Whether this is his signature, a way of marking his domain, or just a friendly greeting to his fellow foxes, is immaterial. The fact remains that he cannot refrain from marking a stump, a stone or a tuft of grass. The deceitful trapper places a trap a few inches from the tempting object. If Reynard already has been there, all the better. Then he surely will return. Or else some other fox will come and put his foot in the trap. This set is good especially in January and February, when Reynard's thoughts turn to love. But even then all tracks and signs of man have to be destroyed. He is a clever fellow, who quickly suspects foul play.

There are two species of foxes in Canada: the red fox with its mutation, the silver; and the arctic fox, white and blue. The cross fox is an offspring of red fox and silver.

The arctic fox is found chiefly on the barren grounds and the Arctic islands, including Greenland. Some winters droves of them range south into wooded country, but never very far. The wild blue fox is very rare and mostly really blue-grey, not brown like the farmed animal. About one blue fox is caught to each hundred whites.

The red foxes are very common some years; they increase in cycles, closely following those of the snowshoe rabbit, their principal food. The winter following one when the plague has killed the rabbits the foxes are half starved and go for anything edible. They are then very easy to catch. Then a trapper can easily catch a hundred or more. Of these usually about thirty per cent are silvers and crosses.

The price of foxes is now very low, but it has not always been so. Before 1920, when there were few fur farms, a trapper could get up to a thousand dollars for a living silver fox, and several hundred for a pelt. The black fox is very rare—I have only seen two skins—and were at one time worth a fortune. Then it was every trapper's dream to catch one. But today, with fur farms and diverse methods of processing rabbit, calf and sheepskins, genuine furs have become cheap.

As I continued I found some marten tracks in a valley between two high hills. With something approaching awe I followed the track of this freebooter of the wilderness, for which an Indian forgets all other fur-bearers, and which has been almost exterminated. Marten, the scourge of the squirrel, grouse and ptarmigan; marten, the insatiable, bloodthirsty hunter, who kills and kills out of pure lust; but who has himself been relentlessly hunted almost to extinction.

The marten likes high hills and high trees. A family can live in a very restricted area for a while, but every so often they range far from home. When one sees a track it is wise to set a trap, because sooner or later he will return, although it may take months. The trap is set in a small hut of spruce boughs. For bait one uses fish or small game and something with a strong odour, like oil of anise or oil of catnip, which is sprinkled over the lure. Most old trappers have their own secret concoctions by which they swear. The fur is very fine and valuable, and the darker it is the better.

The ermine or weasel, kid brother to the marten and the mink, is caught in the same way as these. It lives mostly in rock heaps and among wind-falls. An ermine pelt is worth little, and few professional trappers bother setting traps for them; they get caught in mink and marten sets, anyway. The ermine of the far north is very small, its skinned body being about the size of a man's index finger. He is easy to tame, and if one has mice in the cabin an ermine often appoints himself house cat. That winter we had one that soon became so fearless that he ran all over the cabin in the evenings while we read or worked. He ran across our beds at night and finally climbed up on the table when we ate. He just hissed angrily when we chased him off. He became quite a nuisance after a while, gnawing our food and dirtying everywhere. And then one night, when he started chewing on Karl's ear, our patience was at an end. Karl set a trap in front of his hole and a few minutes later he was there. But he had put an end to all our mice. Our flour and meal bags were left alone from then on.

On a lake I crossed a wolf trail; there were enormous prints, big as saucers. I could hardly cover one with the palm of my hand. There had been nearly a dozen, and I set two of my biggest traps by the carcass of a caribou they had killed and partly eaten.

Just below a rapid a family of otters had been tobogganing down a smooth rock, and their peculiar tracks, resembling those of a ski-runner, crisscrossed the ice. I built a fence in the shallow water where most of the tracks led into it. In a gap in the fence I set a trap.

Steel traps are of different sizes, and numbered accordingly. 0 is for small game like squirrel or ermine; number 1 for mink, marten, muskrat and animals of similar size. For fox one uses numbers $1\frac{1}{2}$ and 2; number 3 for coyote, fox and lynx, beaver and otter. It takes a 4 to hold a wolf. The biggest sizes, 5 and 6, hold anything, including grizzly-bear and lion, but few trappers have any, as they are of little use to them.

A trapper usually sets from one hundred and fifty to three hundred traps in a winter, although some use twice that many. Karl and I had only one hundred and fifty together. We could have used more, but by setting them in the most favourable spots we could find, and building dead-falls besides, we expected to catch our share of the fur-bearers in a district where they were plentiful. Besides, we were green and would not have been able to handle many more to full advantage. We also set snares for foxes in rabbit trails in the willow thickets, and built dead-falls for marten.

During my first trip I did not get far in a day. I had to cut trail, look for tracks, and set traps in likely spots. And so I only travelled about one-third of the distance I later covered in a day. I camped for the night wherever darkness overtook me, cutting spruce boughs for my bed and a lean-to, and building a fire in front.

One night I had an amusing experience. I had left the dogs untied; they were very tired and fell asleep on their spruce boughs as soon as I had fed them, and so I did not want to disturb them, thinking that they would hardly get into any mischief.

After supper I crawled into my feather robe and fell asleep, leaving my camp-fire burning. Suddenly I was awakened by a noise. I lay still and listened. The camp-fire had burned down; only a few glowing embers threw a faint light. Then, only a couple feet from my head, I saw the outline of a sharp-eared dog silhouetted against the glow. It stretched its head hungrily towards some meat I had placed near the fire.

'You damn thief!' I yelled, and made a grab for the dog, but it was too fast; it was gone like a shadow. Soon enough I discovered that it had not been just a bad dream, because a piece of meat I had cooked for breakfast was gone. This made me angry. The dogs had got all they wanted to eat, so much so that they had lots over when they fell asleep. There was no need for that damned Queenie to steal my food. I walked over to where she lay to teach her a lesson, and found her peacefully sleeping. This made me angrier yet. The wily bitch pretends to be innocent, I thought, and started beating her. She got up, yelping and whimpering for all she was worth. When I thought she had had enough, I stomped back to bed, while Queenie, whining, curled up on her spruce boughs again. Although I told myself that the dog needed chastisement, I still was not quite satisfied with myself when I fell asleep.

In the dawn, when I hitched up the dogs, I caught a glimpse of something moving among the trees. A sharp-eared yellow bitch! About Queenie's size and much like her otherwise. Last night's marauder. I started towards her with a piece of meat and tried to call her with soft words. But no matter how I tried, I could not get closer than twenty feet. She was shy as a fox and probably also bothered by her conscience. After half an hour's vain attempts to make friends, I had to give up. But it was exasperating, as I needed an additional dog badly, and there was one almost within reach. I was angry over my poor luck, and felt guilty, besides, for beating up poor innocent Queenie, who had enjoyed her well-deserved sleep after a day's hard work.

I never saw the strange dog again. But a week later Karl caught one that answered its description, in a trap. But it was so badly injured that he had to shoot it.

It took almost a week to get all my traps set, because the days were short and the dogs tired quickly. The load was too big for them, soft as they were after a summer's idleness. Queenie had an injured paw, besides, where she had probably been caught in a trap at some time. The last days of the trip she began to limp and her paw became swollen. Although she tried, she could not pull much. The last day of our trip she could hardly walk, and Wapush pulled the load alone. We got home, but I was in a spot. Queenie needed a rest. None of the other dogs could lead, except Jack, whom Karl was using.

After my return we discussed the problem and decided that Karl would take Wapush while Queenie was sick, and I would trap on foot meanwhile.

Queenie's paw never did get well again, and the rest of the winter I pulled the toboggan myself. Walking on snowshoes, and with the sleigh loaded high with bed-roll, traps, food and tools, some days I made fifteen miles in deep, loose snow. Many a night I was so tired that the last mile seemed endless, and I stumbled along, and sat down every few hundred feet for a rest. And when I finally reached camp I was hardly capable of cooking a meal before going to bed. This gave me a healthy respect for the strength and endurance of a sleigh-dog.

Bill's way of setting mink traps proved completely wrong. When I went over my line the first time after setting my traps I saw where the mink had been sniffing around the base of the stump on which the trap was; but not one had used the gang-plank. Swearing savagely, I took away the traps and set them in the old manner. I had lost several mink because of credulity and inexperience.

'Oh hell, anybody should know that mink don't climb trees,' was all the consolation I got from Karl when I complained over my loss.

Our small overnight cabins also proved to be no good. When it was cold they took too long to heat, and the fire-places we had built did not heat much, but smoked instead, so that our eyes smarted all the next day. Once I was almost blinded.

After a night in the hut I went out on my line, and as I walked along the shore of a rapid I broke through the ice and got soaked to the skin. The weather was very cold, but I could not stop to light a fire, because my matches were wet, too. So without much hesitation I turned and ran back towards the hut, which was three miles away. The only thing to do was to get there before I froze.

But although I ran as fast as I could the cold was creeping through my clothes, which froze so stiff that they crackled at every step; and my feet stopped aching and became numb, as if cut off. The last half-mile I ran over a lake and my hard frozen moccasins clattered on the ice like two sticks of wood. When I got to the cabin I grabbed a box of matches, thanking my lucky stars for the kindlings I had ready, and soon had a huge fire going. Then I opened the door wide to let out the smoke and started getting out of my clothes. They were all frozen together, so that I had to take them off practically in one lump. I wanted badly to slash my moccasins with a knife, but could not afford to, since they were my only pair; so I just had to flex and bend until I finally got them off. My feet were badly frozen. I rubbed and pounded for hours to restore circulation, but both my big toes and the second toe on one foot would not thaw. And so I sat there naked the rest of the day and part of the night, rubbing my feet, and also my eyes, which were now smarting from the smoke. I also dried my clothes.

When I started homewards in the morning my eyes were so inflamed that the strong sunlight made them burn like fire; and I could see only by squinting between the swollen lids. And they remained sore for several days.

That taught me a lesson. I abandoned my huts altogether, and hereafter spent all the nights that I was away from the home camp out in the open. In some sheltered bluff I built a lean-to of spruce boughs, which reflected the heat from the camp-fire and gave some shelter from wind and snow. It took a lot more wood, but dry wood was plentiful, and I was much warmer and more comfortable than in any hut even during the coldest nights. But some mornings when I woke up I found several inches of snow on my sleeping bag.

Some of my toes turned black, and the nails and skin peeled off. On one big toe I had an open sore that did not heal until the following August. And that taught me another lesson. After that I never went out without having some matches, in a waterproof container, in my pocket.

After returning from a long trip we usually stayed at home a few days and rested; we skinned and stretched our furs and prepared for the next day. We tried to time our trips so that we were home at the same time. In the evenings we told each other of our experiences and discussed our plans.

That first night at home always seemed very short. It was hard to tell everything one wanted to—there was so much to talk about and to listen to. It was wonderful to be able to unlimber one's tongue after several days' silence, and so one hardly had time to listen to the other. We often found we were both talking at once, quite unintelligibly.

Karl had much to report these days. He had penetrated far east with the dog team, and after every trip he could tell about some new and large lake, some new river or creek, an old Indian camping-ground, or perhaps a beaver-house or an old tumble-down cabin that he had found. By piecing together the information we gradually got a pretty good picture of the land and our grounds.

We were camped just on the western edge of a great plateau-like rolling land, with long reaches of lakes connected by winding creeks and short stretches of river. Some twenty miles up the Nest River there was a big, almost triangular lake with many islands and points. Judging by the number of old stages on the shores, the surrounding country was rich in caribou and the lake itself in fish. In the sand country beyond, Karl had found numerous signs of wolves and lynx. And mink continued to be plentiful.

So the first part of the winter passed. In spite of my unfortunate mistake in using Bill's trapping methods, the trapping was even better than we had hoped. We had come to a veritable paradise for mink. There were many on all our lines, and the best of all was that we had not encountered a single track of other hunters. We were in undisputed possession of our domain. We praised the superstition of the Chipewyans, and the fewness of white trappers, and the vastness of the land.

Although mink were our main catch, we also caught a few foxes. My first one was a so-called 'full silver'—one that was covered with silver hairs from nose to tail. We got some crosses and reds as well. Karl caught a pair of lynxes and some grey wolves way east, and I had two martens in my dead-falls. Our bundle of furs in the corner of the cabin grew steadily in girth for each trip over the lines, and we started considering ourselves trappers.

But our store of provisions was steadily getting lower and towards the middle of December it started to give out. We had gone more and more on a meat diet and rationed our other supplies, but, in spite of that, first the sugar, then the beans, then the dried fruit, and then almost everything else came to an end, until we finally had only a few pounds of flour, some tea and salt left. For some time past we had made our own candles from caribou tallow and cotton string. It was high time for somebody to go to the fort to replenish our larder.

We flipped a coin and this time I lost. I was to start the next day, with Wapush and Jack pulling the sleigh. While I was away Karl was to look after our traplines as well as he could with the remaining dogs. I was to hire a couple of Indians to help freight our stuff back.

It was about the fifteenth of December when I departed. We were not quite sure of the date. We had probably lost a couple of days during fall and winter.

# CHAPTER X

## *The Christmas journey—On the trail with Indians*

THE trip down the Porcupine was one that will always remain in my memory, because it proved that a crazy greenhorn can do things that would make an old-timer's hair stand on end, and that the Lord holds his hand over children and idiots.

We knew that the Indians had their own winter trail into our district and never followed the river. But, as we had not found it and had no maps of the area, I was forced to follow the same route we had come, which was down the river.

The first day, when I followed my trapline, went by without event and I camped for the night just above a fall.

On the second day I entered that part of the river that was practically an unending series of rapids and falls. Here the river, from which the fog rose up in the cold air like steam from a boiling kettle, frothed forth through its canyon, confined between high banks of ice that succeeding overflows had built up on both sides of the channel. Sometimes these rose more than ten feet above the water. In places the ice hung along the canyon wall like a shelf, which occasionally was only a few feet wide. Somehow I had to get through here. On one side I had a ten-foot drop straight down into the foaming rapid and on the other a sheer wall of rock. To get past the place through the bush was just about impossible. I would have had to climb over several high ridges, and with my big load that would have been so slow that I would have run out of provisions. Weighing the risks, I decided on the river.

With my heart in my mouth I had to go on along the ice-shelf. Occasionally, where it was narrow, I left the dogs behind and broke trail carefully with snowshoes, keeping as close to the wall as possible and gingerly testing my footing. Then I returned, and drove the sleigh past the dangerous stretch to a place where I could leave the dogs while I negotiated another nerve-racking spot. In this manner we edged past the worst canyons. But a couple of times I was almost kaput.

I had just worked myself past an especially bad spot, where the canyon wall made several sharp turns and the shelf-ice, sometimes only two feet wide, followed it closely. I had successfully cleared some jutting rocks and got to where I could see easier going ahead. Then I turned to go back for the dogs, and walked around a bend that screened them. Then I saw them approaching on a dead run, following in my tracks, with the sleigh swinging behind. On a bend the sleigh slid in towards the canyon wall which was fine, as the dogs had taken a short cut, but the next instant they ran past a projecting point and the back end of the sleigh slid out over the edge of the shelf in a way that made me shiver. I felt weak as I stood there and yelled 'Whoa, whoa!' as loud as I could. But the dogs paid no attention. They just saw me and increased their speed. Several times I thought the sleigh would slide too far out, but each time it righted itself. Only inches saved the sleigh, and with it the dogs and everything else, from plunging over and disappearing in the swirling chasm. But the dogs were in luck. When they finally reached me they looked so satisfied and whined in such plain expectation of a pat and a word of praise that they got them. I was too happy to do anything else.

A little later I got a still worse scare. I had broken trail past another risky spot, gone back to the dogs and was driving them along the fresh trail past a point where the shelf was only two feet wide and where I had tramped the trail right next to the rock. Jack and Wapush had already passed the dangerous spot, and the toboggan was following, when the snow under it started sliding on the slick ice out towards the water. I yelled 'Mush!' at the top of my voice, the dogs dug in quickly, and just managed to pull the sleigh to where the ice was a little wider and the snow stopped sliding under it. But there it hung, like a seesaw, with the whole back end dangling over the rapid. I dared hardly breathe when I edged over, grabbed the head rope and crawled up the rock, which luckily was not as steep as in other places, and managed to reach a birch growing in a crevasse and snub the rope to it. Then I helped the dogs to pull the sleigh to safety. But I was pretty well done in then. I sat down on the sleigh, rolled a cigarette, and hoped earnestly that such incidents would not be too numerous.

I had to experience one more shock that day. I was forced to cross the river in a place where it had overflowed so recently that there was no snow on the new ice; only enormous frost flowers were spaced evenly over its blank surface. As I crossed I heard the water rumble hollowly underfoot, giving me such a nasty feeling that I could not even admire the lacy white roses I walked over. And then the ice broke! 'Good night!' I thought. I fell, but only a few inches, and had firm ice under me again. It was only the thin shell that had formed on the latest overflow which had given way. But I stood there a few seconds with outstretched hands, breathing hard, before I hurriedly scrambled for the shore.

So the trip continued, past one rapid after another, and it was with relief that I, in failing daylight, passed the last one and saw the widening frozen river in front, unbroken by open water. There I camped for the night.

The next morning, a few miles farther on, I found a dog-trail. It led down the river and soon joined a well-travelled road at the junction of the Porcupine and the Black River.

The dogs seemed to gain new life as they smelled the many interesting tracks and we moved along at a good clip. In the afternoon we arrived in an Indian village near the mouth of the river below Burr Falls. Jack and Wapush must have smelled it quite a way off, or else heard the bark of other dogs, because the last few miles they ran full speed although I was riding.

I drove up to the nearest cabin and stopped. A middle-aged fat squaw came out and welcomed me in a friendly fashion, smiling from ear to ear. Using sign language and all the Chipewyan I knew, I tried to find out who lived in the village. But when she opened her mouth, embellished by a smile over yellow fangs, she almost blew me over. Literally. I nearly fainted from the horrible vapour. That woman suffered to a high degree from that insidious complaint which, according to some magazine advertisements, makes an otherwise delightful person a social pariah. However, braving asphyxiation, I gathered that Joseph Beau was one of the inhabitants, and proceeded to his cabin, where I was also greeted by smiles, although of a less terrifying nature.

About half a dozen families in the village. The fishing was good in the Black Lake, and here, in the mouth of the river, there were about ten more or less inhabitable cabins.

Joseph, with his squaw and papooses, lived in a cabin perhaps ten feet square. The little room had several windows, but was bare of all furniture except a large stove. The family lived, ate and slept on the floor, which was made from hand-hewn planks and surprisingly clean. Although I wondered how there could be room for everybody, Joseph invited me to stay there for the night.

For supper a piece of canvas was spread on the floor and the food piled on it. Then the whole company squatted on their haunches around it. The utensils consisted of a big pot, some enamel mugs and a number of big, sharp knives. These were used expertly by young and old. I have never become quite accustomed to Indians eating meat. They grab a big piece out of the pot with their fists, stuff as much of it into the mouth as they can, and then cut off the rest, even with the lips, with a lightning-fast slash of the knife. This was the first time I saw it, and the procedure looked very risky. I stared fascinated when they ate, at any minute expecting somebody to cut off his or her nose. But it never happened. Even Joseph's four-year-old girl handled her one-foot butcher knife with surprising dexterity. Here again I observed the efficiency of Nature in providing the Chipewyans with small flat noses and thus lessening the danger considerably. Or perhaps the short-nosed just had outlived the long-nosed through natural selection.

In addition to the meat there was a piece of bannock, intended obviously for me only, because nobody else touched it. Then came strong black tea. When I say strong tea, I really mean it. Two fistfuls of tea-leaves were dumped in a couple of quarts of water and boiled for five minutes. Then the concoction was stirred vigorously, poured and drunk, leaves and all.

Tea is the passion of all Indians. All day long the kettle simmers on the stove, cup after cup is poured from it, and more leaves and water added. It sounds unbelievable, but one fall a family took a whole plywood chest containing about fifty pounds of tea with them into the bush, and were out of tea before Christmas!

When the meal had been cleared away we rolled out our sleeping-bags, lit our smokes, and talked. I then hired Joseph and a friend of his to freight our supplies back.

In spite of the fact that it had been a good year, these Indians had caught only a few pelts each; Joseph, for instance, only a fox and a couple of minks. 'No traps,' was his excuse. Later I heard that he had lost them all in a poker game in the fall, and then borrowed half a dozen or so from his friends.

But some of the other members of the band had not done much better. They had plenty of meat and fish, and some tea and tobacco. As long as there was food in the house other things did not matter. One lay and smoked and played cards and let the women and children cut wood and carry water. Only when the food was gone did the average Chipewyan remember that he had traps in the bush that maybe needed tending. Then he went out, and if he caught something he immediately went to the fort to trade it for tea, tobacco and shells. Then he would lie around until there was a shortage again.

One reason for their indolence is their almost communistic system of sharing everything they have with the other members of the tribe. As long as one has food everybody else also eats. This custom is, of course, necessary at times, and has been developed through their age-long struggle against nature. When one man kills a moose or a caribou he is entitled only to the best parts, allotted to the hunter by old custom, and his tribesmen and their families get the rest. This applies to almost everything else also. Consequently the good hunter supports his indigent and less fortunate tribesmen, but himself benefits little from his work—

which is no inducement to undue industry, if one does not consider the honour and position due to a good hunter.

In spite of this, there were some notable exceptions—men who were as good as most white men. Old Joe Bullet, who brought in a good catch every winter, and had made many trips outside in the summers, was one. There were a few others. But the majority were shiftless and lazy.

In the early dawn I left the village. From here on I followed a hard, well-beaten road that became wider and better the nearer Stony Rapids I came. From all directions new tracks joined it; the bush people had gone to the fort to trade. Now we were travelling at a good speed, because I was able to ride in the sleigh a good part of the way.

It was already pitch-dark when I rounded the last point on Stony Lake and saw the lights of the Indian settlement twinkle in the distance. The few scattered dots appeared to me like the neon lights of a metropolis, and the feeling of loneliness, of which I had been only partly conscious, seemed to vanish as I approached them. Even the dogs came to life. They increased their speed, and soon we passed the cluster of cabins and started on the last short stretch to the fort.

When I drove into the police yard I was greeted by the wild barking of a score of dogs. Jack and Wapush forgot their tiredness as they stalked up to the door, doughty and growling proudly, their tails stiffly in the air.

A few minutes later I sat in a comfortable chair, smoking a 'tailor-made' cigarette, while a big steak sizzled in the frying-pan, and Red emptied the contents of various cans into a saucepan. Both he and Les welcomed me in the best northland manner, trying to make me as comfortable as they could. They told me news from the world outside and from our own environment. I found out what had happened in Stony Rapids since the summer, how good the hunt had been and how much the various trappers had caught. While I listened to this the radio played. And then I received mail: letters and newspapers, the freshest two months old. It seemed as if I had suddenly been transferred to civilization again.

The fur prices were low, but the price of supplies had risen. That is something that always happens in the northern forts as soon as the even ordinarily sketchy communication with the outside world is broken, and the customer is left at the mercy of the local trader. The business methods in the north are as they always have been. Furs are worthless and supplies expensive when the trapper has little chance to take his business elsewhere.

It was not so long ago when an Indian, who wanted to buy a shotgun, had to pile beaver and marten pelts in a stack as high as the length of the gun to get it. Those guns had been made with especially long barrels, with just that purpose in mind, and had cost the trader ten shillings and sixpence. In our day it is not quite that bad, but the old spirit survives. One tries to sell the Indian as many glass beads, silk handkerchiefs, yards of ribbon and lace as possible, and as little as one can of foodstuffs that are comparatively cheap and bring less profit. If a customer thinks that he gets too little for his furs, the price is raised after much bargaining, but the price of the merchandise rises in proportion. Hard cash is paid reluctantly. The trader wants the customer to take trade goods in exchange for his fur.

A white man is a less-favoured customer than an Indian, because he usually has a much better idea of value, and is harder to fool.

Although I knew I was getting the worst of the deal, I sold our furs. I had to buy provisions.

Bill was still in the village. He stayed right there and ran his trapline northwards. He was a little surprised that we actually had succeeded in reaching the Porcupine Forks, and just a little bit annoyed when he heard how many pelts we had caught. We had more than he, and that a couple of greenhorns had surpassed him was *lèse-majesté*. But I managed to soothe his feelings by telling him about the awful lot of fur that we had in our parts, and that it of course depended more on luck than skill that we had done so well. But when I reproached him for his advice regarding mink trapping, Bill just grinned and invited me to stay with him while I was in the fort.

Two days of rest and visiting passed, and then Joseph Beau and Jean Lafleur arrived to freight our supplies.

Jean Lafleur was a little hunchback of about thirty, with a pair of bright, smoky eyes set in a wrinkled monkey face, and he weighed less than a hundred pounds. In spite of his infirmity, he was as tough and agile as any of his more robust tribesmen. According to Joseph he was also a good hunter and provider. He was married to the largest squaw in the band, a woman who weighed about three times more and was quite a few years older than her man. The following summer, when I again saw Jean, his wife had just given birth to a son, and no prouder Indian than Jean existed.

Jean had a good dog team and good equipment, that contrasted favourably with Joseph's. It was with some misgiving I eyed the latter's outfit because it was something the like of which I have never seen since. The toboggan was old and homemade, the cariol was a patchwork of moose hide and canvas, and the harnesses consisted of pieces of rope and strips of canvas, augmented by hay-wire and rawhide. They naturally broke frequently on the trail, but it was still a wonder that they held at all.

Joseph, I found out then and later, was something of a black sheep. 'Too much school,' the chief, Jeremy Crow, once said to me, and there was much truth in that statement. For seven or eight years Joseph had gone to a mission school, where he had lived almost secluded from his people, except for his short summer vacations. When he returned to his tribe at seventeen he had learned little more than to read and write, but the life and customs of his people, the bush and lakes, had become strange to him.

He once told me himself that the first winter he was with his father and had to go alone out on the trapline or hunting, he was so afraid of the bush and the dark that he often sat by the camp-fire and cried. Everything that the other Indians had known since childhood he had to learn anew, because he had forgotten even what little he had known before going to school. He was severely handicapped. As green as any white city-dweller, Joseph lacked the latter's energy and knowledge. He became a burden to the tribe. And there were others like him.

What surprised me was that he usually was fairly well dressed. Apparently he was just clever enough to buy clothes for his family and himself when he had money; for other things he depended on others.

I had never been on the trail with Indians, and now I learned a lot about their ways. Their mode of travelling differed a lot from white men's. They drove their teams at top speed for a couple of hours; then they would stop, boil tea and sit by the camp-fire for a while. Then they were off again for another ten miles, and then a new rest. We stopped for tea about three times a day. One circumstance that maybe prompted these frequent stops was that, according to our agreement, I provided the food, and that there were many good things to eat in the sleighs. At any rate, I learned a few words of Chipewyan these days that I never shall forget: *suckah* for sugar, *bis* for knife, *shluss* for spoon and *tjetue-clishee* for butter (literally cow's-milk-grease). I thought that *bis* was a very appropriate name for knife, because the knife went into the butter repeatedly and so often that the butter disappeared like snow on a hot day.

But it was a pleasure to watch these fellows make and break camp. With axe in hand they ran in and out among the trees on their snowshoes, as if they had nothing cumbersome on their feet. In a few minutes the fire burned under the kettle, the snow had been shovelled away and spruce boughs had been spread out to sit on. Those boys certainly knew how to handle their axes with snowshoes on.

From the mouth of the Porcupine we travelled the way the Indians used to get up to The Forks. Some miles below the first rapids we turned to the right and followed a creek for a while. Then we turned off again, and drove through some hilly country to a string of small lakes, and came in the second evening to a large lake, where we camped for the night on a point covered with tall, sheltering spruce.

Far into the night we sat by the fire and talked. Jean and Joseph drank gallons of tea; they made it a real feast. Again and again they filled their kettles with snow, and cut down trees for firewood. They talked incessantly. From their gestures I understood that they discussed the surrounding country. They drew maps in the snow, stuck hands in the air, counted on their fingers and grunted 'Yes' or 'No'. Sometimes Joseph turned to me and explained something about some lake, 'So big—beaver-house near creek—long lake no far—this way', and made motions with his hands. He and Jean did not have any maps, but apparently they did not need any; so well did they know every landmark, lake and hill we passed. They seemed to have complete maps in their heads.

That was one of the coldest nights of the winter. The sky was clear and the stars shone as big as marbles among the tree-tops. The smoke rose straight up, the trees split with sharp cracks, and out on the lake there was an almost constant rumble, as the ice was rent from shore to shore, with loud thunder claps. But we were warm, the fire burned brightly and a wall of spruce boughs behind our backs reflected the heat.

It was very late when we went to bed, and it seemed that I had hardly fallen asleep when I heard Jean's voice and saw him start the fire again. When I asked what the idea was, Joseph replied: 'Pretty soon day, must start.'

In reply to my question as to how he knew that, he pointed at a star that shone brightly just above the bush in the south-east and explained: 'That star—morning star—show himself one hour before day come. Clock for Chipewyans.' I had to admit that it was a pretty reliable clock, and crawled out of my sleeping-bag.

He was right; soon it became lighter, and when we had finished breakfast and harnessed the dogs it was almost day. We had not travelled far out on the lake when the sun rose over the horizon, so red and angry as it can be only on a really cold winter morning.

This turned out to be the same lake that I had found in the fall, where the old Indian camp was. Joseph said it was about twenty miles long and was called Cracking-stone lake. The name probably came from the shattered sandstone and quartzite hills that surrounded it. On a sheer rock wall in a sound I saw old carvings of canoes full of men. They were so old that the black lichen had almost covered them again, making them hard to distinguish. They were possibly a memento of an old feud or a successful hunting trip.

Here the Indians discovered a herd of caribou way out on the lake; and in a moment I and my dogs were left as though standing still. Yelling and swearing, Jean and Joseph drove their teams in hot pursuit. 'Mush, taishlini beasee'—'Go on, you goddam devils'; their voices sounded shrilly, followed by a flood of other, unknown curses that echoed in the distance as they sped away and disappeared behind a point. Shortly after I heard a couple of shots and the excited barking and howling of their dogs. Then all was quiet.

I drove after them as fast as I could, but when I rounded the point the lake was bare, with nobody in sight. But out on the ice I found two caribou, skinned, cut to pieces and covered with snow. It was at most half an hour since the two Indians had left me. In that time they had shot the two animals, dressed them and driven to the next point, as I saw by their tracks.

I followed, running behind the sleigh, when my dogs suddenly turned and rushed off at a full gallop towards the bottom of a bay, where a herd of caribou stood calmly observing us. The smell of fresh blood had awakened the dogs' hunting instinct, and they tore off, heedless of my yells and curses. The caribou ran off into the bush, of course, and the dogs after them. Then the heavy sleigh bogged down in the deep snow so that the dogs could no longer move it. Swearing and wading in the deep snow, I trudged after them. My snowshoes were in the sleigh, because on the hard trail I had not needed them. I was warm, sweating and mad when I got there and, after giving Jack and Wapush a good hiding, I turned the sleigh around and we continued in the tracks of the Indians.

Soon we came to a strait that, owing to the strong current, was open in the centre. Keeping close to the shore, I drove towards a pillar of smoke which rose up some distance ahead. The Indians were probably cooking an early lunch there.

Then a caribou suddenly ran out on the ice a scant hundred

yards away on the other side of the narrows. In a flash my dogs were off again, paying no attention to my angry cries: 'Whoa, you dirty so-and-sos such-and-suches. Stop!' Away they tore, making a little detour around the open spot, but passing so close that the ice was heaving and shaking, causing waves in the calm water. But luck was with them, they got across and up in the bush. And there they were stuck again. The caribou was of course gone.

Cursing and almost weeping from anger, I ran around the weak spot in a wide circle to the other shore. When I got to the dogs they lay comfortably stretched out and wagging their tails, obviously very satisfied with their feat.

This enraged me so much that I took a ten-foot leap and with a roar of fury hurled myself on Jack and bit him in the ear. Jack let out a howl and yelped in a manner that I never had heard before. Now his last moment had come for sure. Now master would eat him, hair and hide. He had received beatings before, plenty of them, in fact, but never before had a man bitten him. There was such a deathly terror in his howl that I had to sit down on the sleigh and laugh, while Jack still yelped with fright. I laughed both at the dog and my now vanished anger, and thought that it was lucky that nobody had seen me or he would certainly have thought me mad.

But when I looked around I discovered Jean and Joseph by their camp-fire only two hundred yards away across the river. That nothing that had passed had gone unobserved was plain in their faces when I reached the camp-fire. There was fear in their eyes and a certain respect, and, although they said very little, they followed all my movements warily. And all afternoon I observed that they watched me furtively. They had evidently calmed down a little by that night, but it was morning before they began to treat me as a normal person again.

The next afternoon we came to my trapline, and although it would be late we decided to go on until we reached our cabin. It was already dark when we came to the upper fork, but the tired dogs got new life when they struck a fresh trail.

When we, stiff and tired, drove up the trail towards the cabin I yelled and received a weak 'Yahoo' in reply. Karl stepped out, his face one great smile.

I had been gone for ten days, and it was Christmas Eve when I was home again with three sleigh-loads of food. Karl had maybe a pinch of salt and a pound of flour left in the bag. But that night we feasted.

# CHAPTER XI

## Cabin fever—We receive company—
## The tea-kettles

ABOUT this time the cold really set in. With only a few short breaks, the temperature all through January, February and way into March hovered between twenty and sixty degrees below zero. The snow was so dry and powdery that the toboggan dragged, squeaking and screeching, over drifts that were about as slick as sandpaper. And our snowshoes sank more than a foot into the fluffy flakes.

This cold, almost paralysing at times, drove all living things into their dens or shelters, and hardly anything but caribou moved abroad; even the partridges stayed in their burrows in the snow. The trapping became poor, and there was little use in visiting our traps as often as before Christmas. Now we went over our lines only to see that the traps were in working order; and came to stay at home much more than before. We repaired our outfits, patched clothes, dried caribou meat, and cut and hauled wood home, against the busier spring season. But, in spite of that, we had time to read or just loaf. Too much time— because now came the cabin fever.

Cabin fever, next thing to being bushed, is an insidious disease, which creeps unnoticed upon people who are forced to live together for a long time in cramped quarters. The continuous presence of another person breeds a loathing for him that eventually develops into hate. And idleness aggravates the malady tenfold. A gesture or mannerism frequently repeated; the way the other person cuts a slice of bread, rolls a smoke or turns a leaf in a book, his opinions and expressions, irritate past all reason.

Karl and I had heard about the sickness and had agreed to fight it tooth and nail if it attacked us. But that was easier said than done, because one's wily brain refused to believe that one suffered from it, and tried to find perfectly legitimate reasons for sulking and bad temper. Karl had a way of methodically stacking up tins on the shelf when he was cooking that made my skin creep. And if he lay on his bunk it irked me. 'Now the so-and-so lies there, doing nothing again. If he was up and about, busy with something . . . Oh yes, now he pretends to work like hell again, but he doesn't fool me.' No matter what he did or did not do, it displeased me. Everything about him irritated me unreasonably.

Sometimes we were inside for a whole day without exchanging more than a dozen words; we just glared at each other angrily across the table or from our bunks. The few words we uttered came huffily or with studied indifference. We banged with pots and pans more than necessary, and slammed the door when we went out. And our gestures were jerky. It never came to an open quarrel—we were aware of what might result; but both of us enjoyed being as unpleasant and offensive to the other as he dared. The best cure was, of course, to go out and work or hunt, but in the bitter cold one did not want to be outside very long.

Cabin fever has resulted in many tragedies. It has made friends enemies for life, it has caused murder and madness, and is probably itself a form of madness.

As the winter wore on the cabin fever got steadily worse. But then we received visitors. Six dog teams drove into our yard one night. The chief from the Selwyn Lake, with some members of his band, stopped on his way to Fond du Lac. By moccasin telegraph the news of where we lived had already spread abroad.

Their visit was a heaven-sent diversion. We saw new faces and new voices, and heard the latest news about the events in the district. We talked all night and next morning, when the Indians left—the back of the cabin fever was broken.

After that we had many other visitors. Indians from both the Black Lake and the Selwyn Lake came calling. Without knowing it we had travelled all the way up the Porcupine River and built our cabin right smack on the old Indian route between the two places. Had we only stayed ten miles farther down or gone a few miles past The Forks we would have been out of their way.

But now we lived about thirty miles, just a nice day's journey, from the Selwyn Lake. Our cabin became a popular stopping-place for all travellers. Now that we had opened the road and the evil spirits had not destroyed us, the Chipewyans again ventured into the land in increasing numbers.

We also got competition on our traplines. Karl's pride in our catch had prompted him to show some Indians our pelts, and that resulted in an invasion of our grounds. The hunters followed our lines and set their traps at the same rapids as we. But as they did not tend to their traps well they caused less damage than we first expected. But they thought it fine to visit us, get food and drink and feed for their dogs, then, after a good night's rest, go out and set their traps alongside ours.

Some soon became a regular nuisance. They were always in need of something, and some were forever begging, sometimes tea, sometimes tobacco. One of them had his own system. First he asked for tobacco; then, if he got that, for something else; if he got that, for something else again, and kept on begging until we refused him anything more. But he just had to beg. With him it was a matter of principle, or perhaps pride, not to leave our cabin empty-handed.

There were some exceptions, though. Joe Kaskawan, a lone wolf, who lived and hunted by himself with his family, was a notable one. He was a real hunter; his outfit was as good and his catch as big as any white man's. Although he was a full-blooded Chipewyan, he liked to keep company with whites and considered himself their equal. Which he was. He certainly had energy enough for five of his tribesmen. Karl met him once on his trap-line out east, and when Kaskawan found out where we lived he came visiting. Once, when he had borrowed a pound of tea, he came thirty miles out of his road to pay it back, just to show that he was not like the rest of the band.

Towards the end of February some families of the Black Lake tribe came to our cabin on their way out to their winter camps. Joseph Beau was with them and was very depressed. He told us that he was forced to go with the others because he had no rifle—it had broken.

He wanted to stay with us. In exchange for caribou meat he could be useful to us in many ways, he said. He could haul wood and meat, show us a lot of country that we did not know, and his woman would mend and wash our clothes and look after our camp and belongings while we were away. The proposition did not appeal to us much, but as Joseph seemed very wretched we let him stay. And so he pitched his tent in a bluff a few hundred feet away.

It was a lot better than we expected, though. Joseph's squaw really washed for us a little, and his company compensated for the trouble he caused us. He got meat for himself and his dogs from us, but in other respects his wants were quite modest. When he got some tea and tobacco and a handful of dried fruits for the children he was quite happy. And we learned a lot from him about the bush, Indian camping and trail methods. His outfit was as ragged as before, but he owned six lean dogs.

Since I lacked dogs and Joseph a rifle, we often went hunting caribou together. Here I learned to dress a caribou Chipewyan style. The skinning only takes a moment when you know how. With a few cuts and yanks the hide comes off. The whole secret is to know just when to cut and when to pull.

To cut a caribou to pieces using only a knife is equally easy, if one knows the animal's anatomy, and a Chipewyan knows the caribou as well as any surgeon the human body. A couple of slashes with the knife and the front quarters fall off; the hind quarters follow almost as easily. One just cuts at the joint, bends a little and cuts again. One takes advantage of all joints and other weak points, and in fifteen minutes the carcass is divided into its simple components. The wizardry with those caribou on the Christmas trip seemed less astonishing to me now.

Even the bony head of a caribou can be taken apart with just a knife. This is something of a trick, though, and no Chipewyan maiden is considered eligible for marriage until she, among other requirements, can do it. To watch a squaw cut a little there, and tap a little there, until the jaws come off or an eye falls out, makes one realize that it is an accomplishment with a lot of study and work behind it.

Joseph also knew surprisingly much about the land around us. He showed me many a short cut, and many lakes that I had not even suspected were there. He had been in the district before, but most of his information came from other Indians, who knew every creek and every beaver pond.

Many an evening when we sat by the camp-fire Joseph told tales about the great feuds between the Crees and Chipewyans in bygone days, when part of the latter tribe had been completely annihilated and the rest driven farther north. He also knew much Indian lore and much about the life of the wild animals. A lot of it was superstition, but I still gathered some information when I learned to distinguish between fact and fantasy. Some of his fairy-tales were both entertaining and instructive. I still remember the one about the bear and the hunter:

'Once upon a time a she-bear lost her cubs, and abducted a little boy, and, taking him away deep into the bush, raised him there. The boy learned all the bear's tricks: how to watch for the beaver, how to fish in the creeks, and how to find stumps with fat ants. In the fall she showed him how to prepare the den. She gathered dry grass and spruce boughs, breaking only the lowest branches from the trees, where it would not show. But during the winter, when the bear hibernated, the boy roamed the woods alone. Then he also came to know other humans. But in the spring he always returned faithfully to the old she-bear, and so he stayed with her until her death. Just before she died the old bear taught the boy all her "medicine", even how he could catch bear. When he wanted one he was to climb a high hill, light a fire and throw secret herbs in it. Then he would see smoke rise from the spot where the bear was. But he must not tell this secret to anybody, because then the "medicine" would turn bad. After the old bear's death the boy joined the humans and became a great hunter among them. In his tee-pee there was always beaver, fish and caribou, and, whenever he wanted, also fat bear meat. And so a great chief gave him his daughter for his woman. But the woman was very curious, and one night she heard him talk in his sleep about his "medicine". She then started to ask him about it, and badgered him night and day trying to make him tell her his secret. But he told her nothing. Then she made herself sick, and told him that she would die because he did not love her, and that the only way he could prove his love and make her well again was to tell her about his "medicine". He then told his secret, and she was contented. But now the curse of the bears was on him, because now, when he had lost his power, they revenged themselves on him. He got no more caribou, the bears chased them away; no more fish, they scared them off and broke his nets and traps; but he never saw them. Now, when he had to live on the charity of others, the men insulted him for his weakness, and finally drove him and his foolish woman out into the woods.'

The one about the whisky jack (Canada jay) and the squirrel is also amusing:

'The whisky jack and the squirrel were always quarrelling over food. When there was plenty the whisky jack gorged himself until he was sick and cached all he could in the trees. The gluttonous squirrel ate what he could and carried away and hid in the ground more than he needed for the winter. One day all the food was gone. Then they quarrelled more violently than ever, accusing each other of hoarding, but neither would admit that he himself had cached anything, and both starved rather than use their stores. The Great Spirit, who heard their quarrel, became angry then, and put his spell upon them. From that day on they were both compelled to steal and cache all the food they could, never getting enough. But they never found what they had hidden. And so it has been to this day: both the squirrel and the whisky jack always steal and hoard all they can, but in spite of that never have enough food.'

Very few of the Indians that visited us spoke much English. One had to resort to sign language, especially with the older ones. My astonishment was therefore all the greater one night when I offered an old white-haired man a smoke, and he replied in the best King's English: 'Could you roll one for me, please? My fingers are so stiff that I mostly smoke a pipe nowadays.' I nearly fell over backwards. When I had collected my wits, I deluged him with questions and got his story piece by piece. As a boy Fred Mackenzie—that was his name—had been raised by a Hudson's Bay factor, who had sent him to school and then secured a job for him with the company. Fred had worked for them for many years, but then his Indian blood had called him back to the life of his fathers. Since then he had lived among his kind and exactly like them, without regrets or longing for the life he had once known. 'I am poorer, but also happier now, than when I was a fine clerk with the company,' he said simply.

We talked late that night. He was both clever and well read, but it was difficult to connect the civilized accents with the wrinkled, smoke-brown visage and the ragged clothes. I came to know Fred much better later, and always found him equally pleasant; and his reputation among the white settlers was the best. He had repeatedly been offered jobs as clerk and interpreter by the traders, but always declined. He really preferred to live with his people.

In March trapping became good again. The mink were mating and were running around more than ever. The foxes had already been rutting in February, and were now so badly rubbed on the flanks that their skins were worthless. Consequently we picked up all our fox-traps and set them again for mink and lynx. As the days became longer and warmer, the sledging also became better, and we could go much farther in a day than before.

Karl and I now extended our traplines, especially as mink were getting scarce near the cabin. And, as we were getting short of provisions again, we made a trip to the fort along the river; and at the same time we set traps by the numerous rapids beyond my line. This time, however, we avoided taking such risks as I had taken before Christmas. When necessary we broke trail through the bush, and that was easier now when there were two of us and we had enough food. We set traps all the way down to the last rapids and proceeded to the fort. When we returned we had nearly twenty mink in the traps we had just set.

In Stony Rapids we had bought new tea-kettles; the old ones were badly battered from long use. So that we would not have to melt snow for our tea we usually stopped for lunch at some open rapid. Once, when it was my turn to make lunch, I stretched myself out on the ice below a fall and hooked my new tea-kettle on a stick and dipped it into the water. But I fumbled in some way and the pail slid off the stick and, although I made several lunges for it, it was sucked under the ice by the current.

Karl, who was tending a mink set on the opposite shore, watched the performance and, grinning derisively, shouted something about foolish fumbling blunderers. It rankled, but I just swallowed my chagrin and dug out my old kettle and hung it over the fire. During the rest of the day I had to stand many more remarks and digs on the same subject; but they were easier to take then, because the day had been a good one in other ways. We had caught several mink, and a cross fox, that also had fumbled—into one of our mink sets.

At sunset we arrived at a rapid just below the big lake west of our cabin and had only about ten miles left to reach home. Instead of camping out that night, we decided to continue until we got there, especially as there was a full moon to light our way. It was Karl's turn to cook supper, and he went ahead with the dogs, while I remained behind to fix a set in which we had caught a mink. While I worked I heard Karl yell a couple of times, but paid no attention, thinking that he just shouted at the dogs. I covered the mink set with spruce boughs and went up the trail. There I suddenly came on a set of most peculiar tracks. They looked as if made by a great big wet bear and came right out of the open rapid and up the trail. Then I realized what they meant, and hurried on, grinning, to our camping spot. Long before getting there I heard the sound of furious chopping. There Karl was cutting wood at top speed, very wet, and looking very angry.

Without a question I lit the fire, and then I, too, started cutting wood. Then we searched our bags for dry clothing; and while he changed by the fire I finished the wood-cutting. When I sat down he told me what had happened.

He had driven the dogs up to the camp, and then walked out to the edge of the shelf-ice. He had taken off his snowshoe, hung his kettle on its upturned nib, and leaned over to dip water out of the rapid. Just then the ice broke under him, and so, together with snowshoes, ice and tea-kettle, he fell into the drink and was swept down by the current. Luckily the rapid was shallow on our side, and after floating down a hundred yards or so he found bottom and managed to crawl up on the ice again. But had he fallen in only a few feet farther up he would have landed in the main current and been swept away without a chance to save himself.

'And I lost one of my snowshoes and the tea-pail, too,' he concluded and looked angry.

'Yes, it was too bad about that brand-new kettle,' I said solemnly.

Karl looked angrier yet, if possible, and then grinned. And so we sat there and laughed about our tea-kettles.

# CHAPTER XII

## Beaver-hunting—Indian signs—The three rapids —Hunger march

SPRING was near. It was a time when the sun burned all day long, the snow started melting, the rivers began to swell, and the rapids opened up more and more. But the nights were still bitterly cold, and in the early morning the drifts were covered with a crust as hard as a floor. Daylight came early, and often we rose at three o'clock and made our trips while the crust still carried our weight. Those were wonderful mornings. The sun shone dazzlingly bright from a sky of clearest blue, the air was as though washed and invigorated by fresh ingredients; it forced one to breath deep and hard. Even the dogs seemed to have got a new lease on life and ran eagerly over the drifts on which the toboggan slid as though on polished glass. In two hours we now covered distances that formerly had taken a day.

Now also the caribou migrated again. But these were not the stately animals that had arrived in the fall. Now they looked moth-eaten and shaggy, and followed their trails over lakes and muskegs with slow dragging steps in long wavering rows. The great bucks, who had lost their horns during the winter, seemed to hang their heads in shame as they ambled behind the does and fawns.

In addition they coughed like consumptives in the last stage. The reason was that at this time of the year the throat, larynx and nose were full of parasites, the larvae of the nosebat-fly that in summer lays its eggs in their nostrils. During the winter these develop into yellowish white grubs about the size of a small bean. I have found as many as fifty in the larynx alone. Although they are not fatal to the caribou, they are very irritating.

The caribou suffer from another parasite also—the warble-fly, that burrows into their hide and lays its eggs there. The larva develops in a bag in the skin tissue, so that the caribou are quite lumpy on the back in the spring. These maggots do not penetrate the flesh, but live in the hide itself, and come along with it when a caribou is skinned. There can be a thousand or more of them on a single animal. In spite of all these parasites, the caribou are quite fat in the spring.

According to Joseph this was our last chance to get fresh meat, because after the spring-run the caribou would be gone all summer. So we had to get our supply for the spring now or go without. This was not easy, though, because we were almost without ammunition for our big rifles. As usual, we had not been able to get shells for them.

But we still had plenty of ammunition for our .22-cal. rifles. With a lucky shot from a .22 one sometimes could kill a caribou at a hundred yards. Fortunately I was a better marksman with a .22 than with heavier rifles. But if one wounded an animal one had to keep shooting at it until it dropped. It often required a lot of shells, but then no injured animals would escape to die later. Joseph also had a shot-gun for which he loaded his own cartridges, using brass shells and 'treaty powder'. With all this armament we managed to get what we considered a sufficient number of caribou before the run ended.

Joseph's squaw was very busy these days. She cut the meat into great flakes and dried it with slabs of back-fat over smoking fires; and broke large bones and made marrow butter. She also powdered dry meat with a wooden club on a flat rock, and mixed it with rendered fat and berries, packing it in lard pails and baskets made from birch bark.

Now the time had come also for beaver-hunting. There is something special about the beaver. It has traditions back to those far-away times when it, together with marten, was the only furbearer that was worth trapping. Because the beaver is stationary and has fixed habits it is easy to kill and therefore is almost extinct today in large areas. Even in the far north it is becoming increasingly rare. Its worst enemies are bear and man.

When beaver come to a lake where they intend to stay they first build their home on a steep shore or an island, as near the outlet as possible. The lodge is built of poles and branches, intricately interwoven, weighed down with stones and cemented together with mud. The mud is slapped on with the fore feet and not with the tail, as popularly believed. When the house is ready, a dam is constructed to regulate the water level in the lake and to facilitate the floating of feed. There are often several dams, one behind the other. In the lodge there are sleeping quarters, with dry grass on the floor, above the water level. From these several tunnels lead into the water. The dining-room consists of a platform, even with the water level in one of these tunnels. Dug into the banks all around the lake there are breathing-holes, with entrances under water, and in swampy land they build canals for floating logs and poles.

Trapping beaver in the winter is a slow and laborious process. First one has to search for lodges and make sure that they are inhabited. Almost in every lake there are beaver-houses, but most of them are abandoned. The most reliable sign of a 'live' house is the pile of fresh brush in front, partly visible above the ice, and fresh mud and sticks on the house itself. A creek that has overflowed, so that the water has formed a sheet of ice among the trees, is a good sign of a dam higher up. The beaver allows the water to seep through the top of the dam, over its whole length, and the water freezes before reaching its channel again, thus forming an expanding ice-sheet that soon covers the whole valley.

A hole is cut in the ice in front of a live house, and a long dry pole, to which the trap has been fastened, is pushed down to the bottom, so that the trap lies horizontal about ten inches below the lower surface of the ice. A piece of green poplar, with the bark on, is placed above the trap for bait. The trap must be left undisturbed for several days. By then the ice has frozen thick in the hole and there is much chopping before one can look at the trap. Usually it is empty. In spite of much hard work I caught only two beaver in this way.

The Indians have a different method. Early in the winter they walk along the shore of a lake and hit the ice at frequent intervals with a heavy club. By listening to the changes in the sound they locate the breathing-holes which the beavers have in the banks. When they have found and blocked them all with sticks and stones, they break open the house and block all entrances but one. The beavers leave the house, of course, but are forced to return for air, since all their other holes are plugged. After throwing flour in the water of the remaining hole to make it turgid, the Indian sits there on guard, holding a large hook, tied to a pole, just under the surface. When a beaver comes up for air he hooks it, pulls it out and kills it with a club. In this manner he catches every beaver in the house. This method is, of course, one of extermination and strictly forbidden, but that it still is in wide use is proved by all the broken houses that can be found in the northern lakes.

A much easier method than trapping beaver under the ice is to shoot them when the water opens around the house. Especially that year, when each trapper was allowed only a limited number, it was easy to get our quota that way.

In the spring the first opening in a lake is usually in front of a beaver-house. The beavers like to come out in the daylight and crawl up on shore for a bite of fresh bark, after months of living on soggy, musty stuff. The hunter goes there. He can sit in the open quite close to the house if he remains motionless and to the leeside of the beavers. The beaver cannot detect a man as long as he does not move. If the hunter is lucky he may shoot several in one evening.

The snow had already started melting; on the southerly hill-sides there were bare spots, and rivulets of water were running under the snow, when one day I passed a beaver-house and saw open water in front. The beaver had been out and felled a birch on the shore.

Joseph and I had agreed to hunt together. He had experience and could teach me a lot; I, on the other hand, knew of several beaver-houses and was able to shoot them at a longer range than he could with a shot-gun. And so we teamed up.

The next afternoon we went to the house I had visited. The opening near the house was already much bigger; the creek that fell out there had enlarged it rapidly until it now was two hundred feet across. We sat down, one on each side of the house. The wind was right—the beavers would not get our scent. We had been sitting there perhaps half an hour, when a branch that moved a little brought my attention to a small brown object that slowly rose to the surface. First I saw the beaver's nose, then the head, and then, gradually, the whole body. Only the slight movement of the branch as it was pushed aside revealed the beaver's presence. Although still hard to see among the surface debris, I realized that it was a big brute. It lay quiet for a moment, then it slowly swam towards the place where I sat with my rifle cocked. When it stopped about fifty feet away I fired. Simultaneously Joseph's shot-gun roared. The beaver jerked spasmodically a few times, rolled over on its back and was still, after some weak slaps with its tail. The water around it turned slowly pink.

But out there, more than a hundred feet away, something splashed and there I saw another beaver that rolled over and over, while Joseph stood on the shore tensely raising and lowering his gun. He waved me over, and I ran there with my rifle ready, but did not have to shoot. When I got there the second beaver also lay still.

Joseph told me that his beaver had surfaced far away almost out of range of his gun. He had waited for it to come closer, but when I shot he also fired before the beaver had time to dive.

We had two beavers, but had made so much noise that it was useless to expect the others to show themselves. It would be too dark to see before they would come out.

So after tying a string to a stone we threw it out several times, until the string landed across one beaver, and pulled him ashore. Then we did the same with the other. We had been lucky. Both were big. 'Blanket,' said Joseph, after inspecting them critically. 'Blanket' meant that they were of the largest size, and it is the size that sets the price of a beaver hide.

When we returned home with our spoils Joseph said: 'Leave here, my wife she skin.' And after a few words flung over his shoulder to her he marched into the tent and lay down. I looked on while she skinned the beavers and scraped the hides. It took her a little more than half an hour to get them perfectly clean.

I had three hours' work with one I skinned later, and cut a couple of holes in it besides.

In its natural state a beaver pelt looks much like muskrat, but before it goes on the market the long guard-hairs are removed, and it is then called plucked beaver.

Like the muskrat, the beaver has a pair of castorium glands above the vent. These are removed and dried and sold. Joseph did not know what white people wanted them for, but he told me that the Indians use them for medicine and for bait to catch lynx and marten. When I told him that they were used for perfume that fine ladies douse themselves with, both he and his wife laughed so heartily that the tears were running down their cheeks, and Joseph said between fits: 'If white man's woman know where come from she not use!'

Soon the snow had melted so much that we left our sleigh at home and roamed through the land from lake to lake, with gun and packsack. Even now the dogs had to work; they packed their share. Twenty to thirty pounds were loaded in a pair of bags that were hung over their backs, one on each side, and made fast with a so-called squaw hitch.

I let Jack pack my bed-roll. I thought it was safer to carry the food and beaver hides myself. But not even the bed-roll could he be trusted with, because on a warm day he would plunge into a bay or a creek to cool off. There he would stand up to his belly in water, cooling himself, lapping away and, incidentally, also soaking my bed, without paying the slightest attention to my angry yells and curses. Finally, when he was good and ready, he came out leisurely, looking innocent and reproachful. His mien said plainer than words: 'Here I slave all day, and when I want a drink the master just bawls hell out of me!' But the result was that most nights I slept in a wet bed that smelled horribly of dog.

On our trips we often ran out of food, and then we had to live on what we shot. Now I had to eat beaver-steak, fried in beaver-tail grease, every day. But luckily we ate some more delicious food also.

Grouse and ducks roasted by the open fire tasted wonderful.

After skinning and cleaning them, we split them open, spread them out flat and skewered them on a stick, salted them, and roasted them, with the flat side to the fire, while they were still warm. Never over the fire where they would burn or become covered with soot, but beside it, where one could move them closer or farther away as needed. The reader should try that some time.

In this region there is a route used by migratory birds, especially waterfowl. It is not nearly as important as the Athabaska-Mackenzie River route, but it is still used by thousands of fowl, including geese, ducks, cranes and many other species. Their route probably follows the string of lakes that forms the basin of the Grease-lip, and continues up the Porcupine to the Selwyn Lake, and north along the Dubawnt River. The marshy flats and sloughs around The Forks offer them good resting-places. This route is probably unknown to ornithologists, because I have not seen it marked on any maps; though it may perhaps be that it is not considered important.

Geese rested on the edge of the ice wherever there was open water. Most of them slept head under wing, but one sentinel always stood with neck straight up and head erect, vigilantly watching for any sign of danger.

In this case Joseph showed me the Indian way of hunting them. Walking or crawling on all fours, and with head down, he approached through the bush. Even if he broke branches or made other noises the guard would not become alarmed so long as he kept his head down. The guard probably took the man for a bear or caribou, and so it was easy to get within range. But if one just lifts one's head long enough for him to recognize man the whole flock would be off in a second.

We got many a goose in this manner, and many an evening we eyed it greedily while it roasted and the fat fizzled as it dropped in the fire.

Sometimes we shot jack-fish in the shallow water near shore. A certain amount of experience is needed here, because the surface deflects the light rays so that the fish appears to be higher in the water than it actually is, and so one has to aim a bit below where one sees it. The Indians just skewer the fish on a stick and roast it whole. If cleaned first they will fall apart before they are cooked.

The dogs ate mostly beaver—except Jack, who sometimes got a partridge. He was an incorrigible thief when he was hungry, and that was always. When I shot a partridge there was always a mad scramble over who was to get the bird. If it was Jack, the fowl disappeared in a wink, and no amount of beating or scolding helped.

Between trips we stayed at home and hunted muskrats. But the rats, of which we had expected to get hundreds in the fall, had died during the winter. The mink had probably accounted for most of them, but many had been killed by caribou. This sounds unbelievable, but it is nevertheless true. In early winter, when the rats build their push-ups or breathing-holes on the ice, the caribou come along and kick them apart from pure curiosity. The breathing-hole then freezes quickly and the rats die. I saw sloughs with a hundred or more push-ups that had been kicked to pieces. Overflows probably accounted for some also. At any rate we got only some thirty muskrats instead of the five hundred or so that we had expected.

Spring had now really come. The woods were full of songbirds; in every pond and bay frogs were croaking; grouse walked almost underfoot, quite unafraid, and were drumming everywhere. They started slowly, *tom—tom—tom*, speeded up, *tomtomtom*, and ended in a flurry. The cocks, that spring had given a red spot above the eye and a comb of bright feathers, were duelling all over, and strutted bravely and with measured steps in my path. Scared? No, not they.

In bays and open lakes ducks and loons splashed in pairs, while wedge after wedge of honking geese and calling cranes made their way northwards overhead. The deciduous trees seemed to compete in producing new buds and leaves, and the scourge of the land, the mosquitoes, filled the air in clouds. They were out even before the ice had melted from the lakes—in fact as soon as there were some bare patches of ground. As Matt Philipson said, 'the first ones came on snowshoes'.

It was wonderful how they knew to attack a man just when he was unable to defend himself. When I was sitting by a beaver-house, and a cautious beaver, just out of range, was sniffing the air suspiciously, they would light on my nose. There they would feast, and gorge themselves, and grow big and full, and finally, loaded to the gills, fly away, while I watched helplessly, unable to move a finger or do anything else about it.

The spring is short but concentrated in the north. Everything grows and turns green—overnight it seems—and then summer is here.

About a week after the ice had left the river we had visitors. Two Indian families, who were hunting beaver as they followed the river, stopped overnight, intending to continue up Grease-lip River the next day. Now Joseph also caught the travel fever. He wanted to leave right away with his friends. The next morning, cooking utensils, bedding and clothes were packed in bags and bundles. So off they went. Joseph had stowed his squaw and children in the already overloaded canoes of the others, and he followed behind in his fourteen-footer. It was heaped high with baggage, so that only a couple of inches of free board remained. Most of the dogs followed, running along the shore as best they could. Long after the Indians had left we heard frantic barks and howls as they tried to keep up with their masters.

The Indians were going to follow roughly the same route to the Black Lake that we had taken before Christmas. From the Cracking-Stone Lake they would portage into Sandy Creek, which fed into the Porcupine near its confluence with the Black River. They urged us to use the same route when we left. It was a much easier one than the Porcupine, they said; there were 'only three real rapids on it'. They also promised to leave plain marks for us to follow along the route.

When they had left, Karl and I took stock of our supplies. There was not much left, but as we still were six beavers short of our permitted number we decided to hunt another week before leaving. Besides, the ice would probably still be strong on the Black Lake and keep us from crossing it, so there was no hurry to leave yet.

We went, each our own way, on a week's hunting trip over ground that had not yet been visited, hoping to find new beaver-houses. I was lucky and found two quite close together. There I stopped for a few days and succeeded in getting four large beavers. That was all I needed, and so I retraced my steps home-wards again. My food lasted only two days, so I lived the rest of the time exclusively on beaver, grouse, fish and last year's cranberries. I also tried mushroom morels, but they were no delicacy without cream or butter to cook them in.

On the last afternoon on my homeward trip I walked across a wide muskeg and came to a marshy spot, where I had to hop from tuft to tuft, keeping my eyes on the ground, to get over dry-shod. When I had passed the marshy part I looked up, and—stopped on the spot. There, only twenty feet away, stood a huge jet-black bear. He eyed me calmly and steadily. Jack, who had followed in my footsteps, stopped also and sat down beside me and looked, too.

And there we stood, all three of us, and gazed at each other; and the more I looked, the larger and squarer Bruin loomed. At the same time I was eager to shoot, but not too eager. Here was a mountain of food, of meat that we sorely needed, and here was I with a single-shot .22, with a long shell in the breach. True, a black bear is supposed to be pretty harmless; but wounded—well, one could never tell. And this one was a massive brute. I didn't know what to do. . . . But while I stood and argued with myself Bruin had finished his inspection and come to the conclusion that retreat was the best policy. With a snort he made an about turn and galloped away. He was gone in a moment.

On my way home I figuratively kicked myself in the pants and called myself a coward and a fool and everything I could think of. I should have shot. But the curses did not improve matters. We were still without meat. And to this day I have not been able to decide whether I should have shot or not.

Karl was already at home, and he also had the beaver pelts he needed. We now had our full quota. Only food was getting scarce; and, what was worse, we were out of smoking tobacco, too. Only a few plugs of chewing tobacco remained. I had tried kani-kinik and other substitutes used by the Indians, but they tasted awful and burned on the tongue like fire. Then I tried tea—with the result that I still today get sick just from the smell of burning tea-leaves. We finally hit on a satisfactory substitute. We mixed leaves of the baked-apple plant with our plug tobacco, cooked them and dried them. That tasted a little like the real stuff.

It was high time to leave. The next day we loaded our canoe and headed up Grease-lip River, and then over the lakes. True to their promise, the Indians had left marks for us along the route.

After only a few hours' travel we heard the howl of some dogs that had been marooned on a point. The yammer of abandoned dogs is the most lonesome heart-rending sound that can be imagined. While we rowed across a lake we heard their long-drawn-out wail echo over the water. There was such utter sorrow in the sound that we went ashore, intending either to take them with us or put them out of misery. But when we got there they stole away, and although we called we did not catch a glimpse of them. But as soon as we had moved a few hundred yards farther they again started a lament that almost brought tears to our eyes. Karl growled: 'Those so-and-so damn redskins, they should be hanged, every last one!' And on this point I agreed heartily.

That sort of thing happened every year. Why should one worry about dogs? It was summer now. One did not need any dogs any more. They were just a problem and a nuisance. They needed care and feeding. Queenie, Bear and Jack had been left behind the year before to starve in just that way. They had survived, but how many others were there that had not?

In April Queenie had become a proud mother. But the pups, all four of them, were something of a problem now when we were moving. They crawled all over the canoe, scrapped and tore things, and fell overboard when one was not looking. We rescued all of them at different times, and then they would reward us by shaking water all over us. I finally solved the problem by putting them all in a big box and nailing a couple of slats over it to keep them in when we travelled. They did not like that much, and kept up an ear-splitting katzenjammer for a few days, sometimes almost upsetting the box in their efforts to escape.

When we came to the portages we found that the Indians had not marked them in any way. It was only by using instinct and common sense that we found them. From the west end of the Cracking-stone Lake we packed across to Sandy Creek.

There we found out what the Indians had meant when they talked of three rapids. Their arithmetic was very poor. Sandy Creek was full of rapids. If there was one rapid per mile on the Porcupine, there were three per mile on Sandy Creek. One hundred and three was the approximate number. One could not have crowded in an extra one there without shoving the others together to make room for it. There were only three big falls, but innumerable small ones that they had forgotten, and all so shallow that our canoe did not float in them. We were forced to unload and portage, load again, and unload again and portage again; and if we were really lucky we could pull the empty canoe over the rocks where the creek did not disappear completely underground for a way. This we repeated *ad infinitum*. We swore, sweated and worked.

Meanwhile the mosquitoes feasted on us, and our food gave out completely. We had only some tea left. We drank that as strong as possible. The last days on Sandy Creek we lived solely on suckers caught with our bare hands in the shallow rapids, which sometimes teemed with them. The sucker is not particularly toothsome fish, especially when eaten without salt, but we thought it was better than caviar when we devoured it after roasting it on a stick. And they kept us alive.

On the shore of a little lake we found one more sign of our Chipewyan friends—a beaver that had been wounded and had crawled ashore and died. It was already so far decomposed that we could not even save the skin.

Late one evening we pitched our tent just above a fall, past which led a well-beaten portage. We followed the path for a way, until we saw the water of a lake glitter between the trees ahead. Then we turned back and went to bed.

In the morning we picked up our first loads and started across. We had come only part way over when we saw smoke, and soon we found ourselves in the middle of a small bush-fire. A big patch of timber had burned, and the fire still smouldered here and there in the moss. Luckily the night had been calm, and the fire had not got far before it was stopped at the edge of a muskeg. Otherwise we might have been awakened from our sleep by a full-size blaze. As it was, we had only to put out some smouldering logs and stumps and patches of dry moss. At the lower end of the portage we saw signs of recent campers. From the signs we concluded that our friends had been there the day before and left their camp-fire burning when they departed. A widening V-shaped strip of burned lichen and pine-needles led from the camp-fire to a clump of small spruce. From these the fire had jumped to surrounding trees. That was the third mark that our helpful friends had left for our guidance.

The same day we reached the Porcupine again. We recognized the place at once. We were below the last rapid. Only twelve miles remained to the Black Lake, and there we could set our net below Burr Falls and get a big feed of fish. We might also find people there. We rowed briskly downstream, and at dusk we came to the portage. Taking only the canoe and the fish-net, we rushed across to set it in the eddy where we had caught so many trout and pickerel the summer before.

Before we got to the other side we saw the glimmer of a camp-fire among the trees. There Ed was sitting and cooking his supper. We ran past with only a short 'Hi Hi!' and put the net in the water before giving ourselves time to talk to him. Then he invited us to sit down to a cup of tea. We accepted the invitation deliberately and carelessly, as if we had just eaten a hearty meal. But our tongues were almost hanging out and we swallowed hard when we inspected his larder with covetous eyes. He treated us to bannock and butter, sugar, dry meat and even jam. We masticated slowly and methodically, and then when we had finished we asked Ed offhandedly if he could spare a little flour and such, as we had run a little short of some things. Oh, sure, he could; he could spare some flour, butter, sugar, lard and dry meat. When we had thanked him and talked for a while, we said we were pretty tired and were going to bed.

But if Ed had seen us half an hour later his eyes would have popped open, because there we were sitting gorging ourselves with a large, fresh bannock covered with a thick layer of butter, and drinking several mugs of tea with lots of sugar in it.

But the next morning we received some bad news. Ed told us that the ice still covered the Black Lake. It had started shifting, but it could still take a week to move away. The road to Stony Rapids was blocked. For that reason Ed intended to stay right where he was until the way was clear. He had lots of time. He advised us to do the same.

But we did not have lots of time; we were short of food and had to get to the fort as quickly as possible. We wanted to try, anyway, and so we left. When we came to the lake we discovered a narrow strip of open water that was stretching as far as we could see along the south shore. We followed this channel for several miles expecting at every bend to see it end. And so it finally did, too. Starting at a long point of land that jutted out in the lake, the ice lay jammed on the shore for miles ahead. We could go no farther. After looking vainly for an opening, we gave up and camped on the point. All we could do now was to wait.

In the night we were suddenly aroused by a pounding, grinding noise from the shore. While we looked, the ice, pushed by a strong north wind, moved slowly but relentlessly up on the shore. Big blocks weighing tons broke and fell over with a crash and piled up in great heaps. The heaps grew before our eyes and kept on advancing, uprooting trees and pushing large boulders before them.

It was a fine spectacle, but we had no time to admire it, because immediately the ice threatened our camp. Working hard, we scrambled to save first our canoe and then carry our stuff farther into the bush. The advance finally stopped, but then the ice was stuck on the shore as far as we could see each way. And there we were caught in the middle; we could not move either way. And we were without food again, too. Discouraged, we returned to bed to ponder over the problem. But there was no answer; we just had to wait until the ice left.

The next day we shot a jack-fish and a grouse, and picked berries left from the year before. We went to bed with the ice still blocking the shore, and it could remain there for a week.

I woke up early the next morning. As I walked to the lake to wash, I stopped in my tracks and stared. Then I shouted to Karl. The ice was gone; beyond the heaps on the shore the water was open. The wind had turned during the night and moved the ice away so silently that we had not even been awakened by it. Beginning perhaps a mile to the east there was only open water. But now the whole east end of the Black Lake was blockaded instead.

Hurriedly, hardly believing our luck, we loaded the canoe and were off. That same day we came to the Elizabeth Falls portage. Now nothing could keep us from reaching Stony Rapids the next day. We had been very lucky, we found later. The ice remained in the east end of Black Lake for a week, and Ed and a couple of other trappers had to wait ten days before they could get across.

In the eddies of Elizabeth Falls we shot arctic grayling for supper. Karl, who was the better marksman, did the shooting, and I jumped in the river and retrieved the fish before they were swept down by the current. It was a wet but thrilling sport. The water was ice cold, but I preferred jumping in to starving. We got a dozen fish that way, and ate two apiece ourselves and gave the rest to the dogs. And how good they tasted! And so off again. One more day and we would have lots to eat.

But not even that last stretch was to be passed over without event. We had just arrived at the Middle Lake portage. There we loaded all we could on ourselves and the dogs, and started over, decorated like Christmas trees, when the dogs, howling in unison, suddenly galloped away into the bush, their big loads pitching loosely like feather pillows. There was a breaking of branches in the bush, and something grey-brown ran across the trail. 'A caribou!' shouted Karl. We stopped, dropped our loads, grabbed our rifles, and started running. In full cry the hunt went down towards the lake. When we reached the shore the caribou was already far out in the water swimming away, with Wapush and Bear, who in some way had got rid of their packs, close on its heels, while Jack, yelping as if possessed, waded around belly deep along the shore with my soaked sleeping-bag on his back and tried unsuccessfully to swim after them. Queenie and the pups paraded back and forth and did their best to add to the confusion.

Quickly we turned, ran to the canoe and pushed out. I grabbed the oars and rowed for dear life, and Karl paddled so that the handle was bending. The gap between us and the caribou was closing rapidly, when Karl asked if I had any shells left, as his were all gone. Hurriedly I searched my pockets. Three 'shorts' was all I found—our last shells. Then I grabbed the oars again. We were only thirty feet from the caribou when Karl fired, but it only speeded up more. We were almost on top of it as he shot again. It still did not take effect. Karl cursed and grabbed the paddle again. And, using his last shell, he almost stuck the rifle barrel in the animal's ear before he shot. It turned over on its flank and became still. 'Well, if I had had to bite it I wouldn't have let it go!' he said.

We had a feast again. The largest kettle was hung on the fire, and we skinned the beast, with the dogs in a tight ring whining around us, excitedly pawing the ground and growling at each other. The animal was quite lean, but we took the best parts and put them in the pot, and threw great big chunks to the dogs.

Then, after licking our chops for an hour, we sat down to our meal. I speared a big chunk with my fork and started eating. But after the first bite I stopped and looked at Karl. He had also stopped, and then he spat out the piece in his mouth. I did the same. The meat had a nauseating, sickly, sweetish taste. We could not eat a single piece of it, although we were so hungry that our stomachs rumbled. At this point we noticed that not a single globule of fat floated on the broth, and that even the dogs ate their rations reluctantly. The caribou had been sick—of tuberculosis probably. For that reason it had remained behind the others. Of all the tough luck!

But there was nothing we could do about it. We hung the meat in a tree, in case somebody wanted it for dog-food, shouldered our packs again, and marched across the portage to the Stony Lake, our stomachs complaining worse than ever.

When we landed at the shore above Stony Rapids we hardly gave ourselves time to unload and tie up the dogs before we walked to the settlement.

Bill and Joe welcomed us like two prodigal sons. Joe had a bottle in one hand, a glass in the other, and a wide grin on his face. When he wanted to treat us to one more, I said: 'Thank you, but we'd sooner have a bite to eat first, if you happen to have something handy.'

Bill took one look at our hollow faces. Then he placed a frying-pan full of bacon and another full of eggs on the stove, while Joe put butter, cheese, bread, jam and other civilized food on the table. They had seen hungry people before; they knew the sickness and also its cure. When we sat down to eat, Joe laughed as he placed the bottle in front of us, and uttered the only word of Swedish he knew: 'Skoal!'

# CHAPTER XIII

## *Summer vacation—Indian festival in Fond du Lac—Out again*

IT was the middle of June when we arrived in Stony Rapids. Our summer vacation had begun. The first few days we did hardly anything but rest and eat copious amounts of fresh eggs, oranges, potatoes and vegetables, and all the other things that we had gone without and longed for those many months, although the prices would have appalled people who lived outside.

And then we talked—all day and far into the night. It was wonderful to tell one's experiences to people who had not heard them before, and who seemed to enjoy listening, besides, and to listen to what others had to tell. All of us enjoyed company after many months of solitude. The subjects discussed were many and varied: last winter's hunt; how it had been in Chipewyan, Fort Smith or Reliance; what the boys in the different districts had caught and how much money they had made; then the fur prices and the traders' deceitfulness—a very popular subject—and the morals of the Indian girls—a yet more popular subject—and especially the chances of those present to lower them.

A fire in the open, as on the preceding summer, was the meeting-place. Gradually, as the evening wore on, the male element of the settlement gathered there in an ever-widening circle; it became a club. Tea-kettles hung on the fire, and sometimes mugs, containing even stronger stuff than tea, were passed around.

The first great event of the summer was the arrival of the steamboat. It brought mail and supplies. When it left, some of the boys, who felt rich and in need of a fling, went out with it. They went to Edmonton to 'buy their supplies cheaper', as the saying was—but really to live a few weeks in riot and revel with wine and women, and perhaps to dissipate the fruits of two years' backbreaking work. Some never got any farther than McMurray before going broke.

Art Englund was perhaps the worst of the lot in that respect. Normally he spent two years in succession alone out on the barren lands east of the Dubawnt Lake without even coming to Stony Rapids for the summer, and he lived under conditions impossible for ordinary people to grasp. Then he went to Edmonton with the two or three thousand dollars he had made. There he took the most expensive suite in the best hotel, hired an automobile with chauffeur, a sweetheart by the week and stocked his room with liquor. He lived like a king for two or three weeks, drove from bar to bar, and had his rooms full of people that he mostly did not even know, all eating and drinking at his expense. Then when he was broke he headed north again. Often he had not even bought any supplies, but had to take them on credit from the Hudson's Bay in Stony Rapids before he left for his trapping grounds.

Do not feel sorry for him, though. During those short weeks he was happy. They compensated him for years of hardships and loneliness. They were all he wanted for his money. 'A thousand dollars a week, that's my style,' he said once, with a smile; and added: 'I just wish I had a couple of thousand now. I'd go right back to Edmonton.'

Karl also went outside with the boat; but although I, too, wanted to, I could not afford it.

The second great event of the summer was the 'treaty'. Then the Indians all gathered in Fond du Lac to receive five dollars a head and some provisions from the government. They also had a pow-wow with the Indian agent and made various complaints, to him.

Many of the trappers also went there just to have fun and visit friends. I went along with Joe, who had bought a new canoe and outboard motor, and took my canoe in tow. The motor was humming steadily as we travelled over the calm, sunlit lake, and I enjoyed not having to row but to just sit in the stern and steer. Our canoes were loaded and the dogs were stretched out on top, panting in the heat, but not daring to move. If one by chance did he immediately looked guiltily at the boss, expecting a harsh command or a slap with the paddle. But out here they at least had a little peace away from the mosquitoes. I almost dozed where I sat.

Then I discovered something in the lake away over by a point ahead—something that was swimming. A dog? No, not a dog— a moose! I yelled to Joe, who was fiddling with his brand-new kicker, the apple of his eye, and hardly had eyes for anything else. He looked up, startled by my hellish holler, that aroused the dogs and could be heard even above the puttering of the motor. I gestured wildly, grabbed my rifle and pointed at the moose. Joe took one look in that direction, then put on full speed and started feverishly digging into the load for his gun. We speeded on at an angle to cut the moose's way ashore as it crossed the narrows. I sat on pins and needles. We had dreamed about a fat moose steak for a long time now. Would we get this one? Would we get in range in time? Four hundred yards—three hundred and fifty—three hundred—now the moose was almost at the shore. I rose, but could not shoot. Joe was right in the line of fire. Then, at the last moment, he stopped the motor and turned his canoe, just as the moose rose out of the water. . . . We sent a shower of bullets at it. The animal shook itself, took a few long strides and disappeared in the willows. Holding our breaths, we speeded the last few hundred yards. Had it got away?

No, there it was on the shore just behind a clump of willows— a big bull, a mountain of meat. Now we would not lack meat, we thought, as we started to skin it. But we had hardly begun, when a canoe, loaded full of Indians, arrived at full speed around a point. We had not seen a single one all day, but as soon as we had game they were there. They, like ravens, seemed to be able to smell fresh meat for miles. They offered to skin and dress the animal, so we just removed the tongue and the liver and let them do the rest. We did not have to touch it after that. Grateful for part of the meat, they took our share to Fond du Lac, where Jerry Bear's squaw made a big sack of dry meat for us out of it. That night we ate boiled tongue and fried fresh liver.

In Fond du Lac I met Albert, an old-timer in the north. He had lived and trapped there for nearly thirty years and had become one with the country. Although he was over fifty, he looked and acted like a man of forty; he was tall, broad-shouldered and an excellent bushman and trapper. He was kind to everybody and generous to a fault. No one needed go hungry as long as Albert was around. He expected anyone in need to turn to him for help, and was almost hurt if one did not. In the store he always had a flock of children around him eating candy and looking at him with worship in their eyes. He was their friend and hero, something of an everyday Santa Claus. Although he was a good hunter, his earthly possessions were few. But Albert was always happy and kind, just the same.

His greatest fault was perhaps that he was a bit careless with his person; not so fussy about shaving or washing himself or his clothes. He had lived alone so long that he simply had not noticed that he gradually had become negligent, especially when there was nobody near him who would point it out or to whom he could compare himself. It was nothing deliberate. He washed himself every day, only the area was small; many parts went untouched and remained so. He also intended to do his laundry every week, but it was always put off because of some more pressing business. Instead he bought new clothes and the heap of unwashed laundry grew steadily in the corner of his cabin. This also made it hard to sweep more than the middle of the floor. But Albert did not consider himself dirty and would indignantly have denied that he was.

With regard to cleanliness old-timers in the north can be divided in two groups: the ones who become more fastidious as the years go by, and those who go in the opposite direction. The former finally become as particular as old spinsters, the others like old Martin. This gradual sinking into sloth and indifference is, together with cabin fever, one of the greatest dangers that threaten a lone man. Both are the result of isolation and can be described by one word: 'bushed'.

I had become a bit careless myself in some ways, but Albert's example came as a warning at the right time and put a fear into me that lasted all through my years in the north.

Joe and I camped in a bay at the outskirts of the settlement, where we had some privacy and were less bothered by prowling dogs. As a precaution against these we tied our own dogs in a circle around our tents so that they could reach any unwelcome visitor who tried to get through.

One nice evening in June we were sitting on the shore satisfied after a good supper, smoking and looking out over the lake. It was like a mirror. The houses on the south shore were silhouetted against the dark bush beyond and reflected in the water, and the howl of countless dogs in the village blended with the subdued tinkle of dish-washing that went on behind us. Paul Cook, an old Indian, who had come to enjoy supper with us, was washing pots and pans in exchange.

'Look, there comes a beaver!' said Joe, and pointed with his pipe-stem to a point. Something was swimming there all right— it was a beaver, no doubt about it. How did it dare come here? We stood up to observe it better as it crossed the bay.

'No beaver—dog,' assured Paul Cook's voice suddenly behind us. But when we looked around a minute later he had disappeared and left the dish-washing half done.

'Now he has gone to tell the others. Just wait—now there's going to be fun. They are going to kill it,' said Joe, while the beaver disappeared towards the settlement. We followed slowly along the shore. I doubted that the Indians would dare kill it out of season and in the middle of the village.

But I had hardly said it, when the first canoe, full of bucks and boys, all armed to the teeth, left the shore. It was followed by several other skiffs and canoes, and along the shore walked a yet bigger crowd, with squaws and papooses trailing. Paul Cook, who was in the leading canoe, had alerted the whole tribe, and there they came loaded for beaver. But the beaver had dived.

Then it showed its head above the water for a moment. The squaws and children yelled and pointed; there was a cracking, banging and thundering from guns, rifles and muskets of all kinds and descriptions from the shore and the boats, and lead whistled and whined through the air in all directions. But the beaver dived unscathed.

'You mustn't shoot a dog, Paul,' I yelled. 'Don't you know it means bad luck?' But my words were drowned by the din.

'To hell with it! I'm leaving. I don't want to get shot,' said Joe. I agreed. It was really dangerous to stay near that crowd, which fired with abandon as soon as it caught a glimpse of the beaver, not caring what or who was in the way. But the beaver was wise. It always appeared quite close to some boat and escaped. For a long while after we left there was a heap of ammunition wasted, probably as much as the beaver was worth. They finally got it. It never really had a chance to get away.

But that nobody was killed or wounded by all the shot and bullets that flew around, although both the lake and shore was crowded with people, was a real wonder.

Who really shot the beaver was never established, although the police tried to investigate. But a few days later Paul Cook sold the Hudson's Bay a beaver pelt that was badly bleached by sunlight and not quite prime.

More and more Indians arrived in Fond du Lac, and one day the R.C.M.P. motor-launch came, with the Indian agent aboard. The treaty was about to be signed. As it was a new experience to me, I followed the proceedings with interest.

It was a very formal affair. All the Chipewyans from the Black Lake, the Selwyn Lake and other points east had met up in Fond du Lac. Their tents, standing in rows on an open field near the Hudson's Bay store, made a fair-sized town. Here indescribable noise and confusion reigned. Shrieking squaws and dirty papooses dressed in their Sunday best, and countless lean dogs were running among the tents, while those dogs that happened to be tied up kept up an unceasing howl from hunger and thirst.

The men were primping and preening themselves for the solemn occasion. The height of elegance was a pair of blue serge trousers, a shirt—that at least was white on this day—and beaded moose-hide moccasins. Those garments are the pride of a Chipewyan and the proof of his success in life.

A few hundred feet from the village had been pitched the great tent in which the conference was to take place. The Union Jack was flying from a tall pole, and inside, under portraits of the King and Queen in heavy gilt frames, were table and benches for the councillors.

Then the great moment arrived. In the tent door stood the government agent flanked by two Mounties in parade uniforms —scarlet tunics, wide hats and blue breeches—stiff as ramrods; and modestly, a step behind, the interpreter, a local half-breed.

The chief and his councillors, in recognition of their rank dressed in blue coats with shining brass buttons, approached in dignified procession, followed by the other men of the rank and file. Squaws and children came behind them at a proper distance in a disorganized flock, with a few stray dogs at the fringes. Slowly and deliberately the delegation stopped and greeted the Indian agent, and then listened to his speech of greeting. On his invitation the chief and councillors deigned to enter, and the conference began.

This is the yearly pow-wow and signing of the peace treaty between the government and the Indians. Although a mere formality, all the pomp and ceremony possible is maintained to give the Indians, who love it, a chance to show their importance. The government has shown great wisdom in making the occasion as impressive as possible.

Inside, the conference lasted for hours, in fact long enough to make any parliament proud of itself. Sitting on the ground, the multitude waited patiently outside. When full accord had been reached and peace was assured for another year the meeting was adjourned. As a gift of friendship from the government every Indian, regardless of age or sex, received five dollars and some provisions—flour, lard, nets, black powder, lead shot and other articles.

When the money had been received one and all went to the stores, where the merchants, who for days had been preparing for this chance to make some quick money, stood ready, rubbing their hands. Soon business was in full swing. As long as the money lasted they bought all they wanted and could afford.

Now the Indians started their special festivities that lasted for several days. In the evenings they danced to mouth-organ and accordion. But for the men, gambling was the chief attraction. The Chipewyans have their own game that is played individually and by teams. Blankets are spread on the ground and the teams squat down on opposite sides facing each other, the captains at the ends. The stakes are piled on the blankets, and in front of each player five short sticks are stuck in the ground and five in front of the captains. Then the play begins. The captain and each man in one team take a pin in one hand and start wagging and pitching back and forth and nodding their heads in time with a wailing song and the beat of several tom-toms belaboured by some half-grown youths. Simultaneously the sticks are moved from one hand to the other behind the back or under a cloth draped over their knees, all in time with the singing and drumming. The tempo gradually increases. The gestures and contortions become increasingly violent, the players' hair is flying, and the sweat pours off their faces, until the drumming suddenly stops with a bang. Then the gamblers extend their clenched fists, and the opponents have to guess in which hand the stick is. If his guess is right, the pin is stuck beside his own; if not, one of his is given to his opponent. The play goes on until one man has lost all his sticks. The same goes for the captains and the bets of the teams. The bets consist of shells, packages of tobacco, matches and so on. As the time wears on, the motions become more violent and the song wilder. In spite of admonitions from priest and police, the play goes on day and night until one or two men have all the tobacco and shells in the band.

The priest was a very busy man these days. He absolved the sinful, published bans, married and baptized, sometimes all at once. One had not always had time to wait for the priest and the order sometimes became jumbled, but the main thing was that the sacraments were honoured. The priest also collected tribute in the form of mink and fox pelts. And frequently the tolling of bells called the faithful to mass.

The Indian agent, who also happened to be the doctor for a district bigger than some provinces, was another busy man. This was also his yearly tour to inspect the health of the settlements, the time when he vaccinated, doled out pills and pulled teeth.

L

I happened to be present once at a tooth-pulling. It was a simple affair. The doctor sat in his tent, armed with a pair of huge forceps, with a stocky interpreter for assistant, and received the patients, who had formed a line outside. As they entered one at a time the interpreter grabbed hold of the patient's head and told him to open his mouth, whereafter the doctor, without anaesthetics or other ceremony, pulled out the offending snag, swabbed the hole with a strong-smelling disinfectant, gave the howling victim a couple of aspirins and kicked him out.

Big, grown-up men came out of the tent howling with pain and grey-faced and flopped in the grass. One fainted.

It is a widespread belief that Indians endure the most bestial torture with the utmost stoicism. But my experience, confirmed by many others, including the doctor, is quite the opposite. The average Chipewyan is more of a sissy and more afraid of pain than the most pampered society lady. At the least ailment he promptly believes that he is mortally ill and lies resignedly down to await the grim reaper. If he, against his own belief, improves, he attributes it to a miracle. He dotes on medicines, herbs, wizardry and pills, especially if they are administered by the priest or the medicineman, no matter which.

But when it comes to hygiene he never learns anything. The doctor told me that he had for years preached about isolation of consumptives and the importance of washing, and the usefulness of a varied diet and a vegetable garden. But with slim results. The tubercular Indian still sits in a crowded tent and spits among the children. Scrofulous diseases, caused by the monotonous fish and meat diet, lower their resistance and make the Indians an easy prey for epidemics. Here was positive evidence of their squeamishness. I do not think that the average white, even after a cure like the doctor's, would have shown one-tenth the brand of stoicism exhibited here.

There was life and there was noise in Fond du Lac these days. There were drums and song, and the howl of hundreds of dogs night and day. It could be relatively quiet at times, but then a thread-thin wail was heard far away. It grew in strength as it approached and as more dogs joined in; it undulated back and forth through the encampment; it swelled to a chorus, passed and decreased, and finally died far away to the south-east. It was still for a moment, and then it started again somewhere else. Some nights one could hardly sleep.

We also had to guard our belongings carefully, because there is hardly anything a hungry dog cannot eat, or at least steal. All food had to be kept in stout boxes, and it was risky to leave a greasy frying-pan or a dirty dish outside. I even lost the leather strap to my rifle. How they managed to get past our own dogs was a mystery, but they did.

Not only the dogs but also their masters stole. They started filching fish from our nets at night. When we had had only a few fish and a lot of seaweeds in our nets several mornings, and our dogs had been almost without food, Joe became angry. He made me a proposition.

Around midnight, when dusk had settled over the sound, most people had gone to bed. The mist shrouded the shores and willows in downy clouds. We stepped into the canoe and paddled silently to the point near which we had our nets. There we pulled our canoe out of sight among the brush, rolled into our bed-rolls and lay down, with our rifles beside us. Here it was quiet, but over in the village the dogs howled and the sound of a tom-tom carried across the water. I soon fell asleep.

It was around three o'clock and almost daylight, when Joe grabbed my arm. I heard a faint splash from the lake; somebody was paddling out there. The sound grew stronger, and then we saw the outlines of a canoe with a lone paddler appear in the mist. He stopped at our net-buoys and started to lift our nets.

Joe grinned maliciously from ear to ear and took careful aim. The man sat in the stern, and the bow of the canoe, high in the air, offered a perfect target. Just when the thief took the first fish out of the net Joe fired. Three shots in quick succession ripped through the bow of the canoe, so that splinters flew in the air. With a shriek the man dropped the net, grabbed the paddle, and spurted away with unbelievable speed. Long after he had disappeared in the mist we heard him alternately paddle, bail and curse. 'Daishlini, daishlini!'

Joe laughed so that the tears were rolling down his cheeks. 'That no-good so-and-so! Oh, oh! Did you see him go?'

In the afternoon we sauntered along the shore as if by chance, until we found what we looked for—a freshly patched canoe. The shots had hit nicely, all three on the water-line—fine round holes that had been neatly covered with canvas and painted. 'There, you can see that I've been in the navy,' said Joe.

When the boys who had gone to Edmonton returned, the summer was drawing towards an end, and it was time to start thinking about our return to the traplines. But before leaving we were going to have a farewell party.

When the boat arrived all helped to unload it. Then the party was to start. But for some reason it began a little early. We carried sacks and bales ashore, and between trips we were given refreshments aboard, so that Bill fell in the lake when he was balancing along the narrow gang-plank with a flour sack on his back.

With the boat Karl also returned; and with him he had a boyhood friend, whom he had met in Edmonton. His friend, who had come to Canada on the same boat as Karl, had been broke and jobless, and so Karl took him along north.

We talked this over. Karl felt obliged to take his friend out trapping with him; a greenhorn would hardly be able to get along alone in the wilderness or catch any fur all by himself. And three men were too many in one spot, as there would not be enough territory for us all. And so Karl and I agreed to split up, and I decided to try my luck alone in a new spot the next season. We parted with a handshake.

In the evening the dance started. Fred executed drills and cadences on his accordion, and the fiddles were crying, and the trappers were whirling around the floor, with the ladies, some white, some more or less dusky, tenderly pressed against their palpitating bosoms.

The older men were celebrating in their own fashion. They sat by the fire and sampled the real stuff that had arrived on the boat and told hair-raising tales about their experiences. Joe told about an awful thing that had happened to him. 'You know Birch Rapids? Well, I came down there a couple of springs ago and almost went straight to hell. I shot the falls on the wrong side and went over a three-foot sandstone shelf. There is a trough below them, as you know, and beyond that a high swell. Well, my canoe stuck just on the edge of the shelf and slid down so slow that it didn't make it over the swell, although I paddled my arms off. I was stuck in that trough, with my bow pointing up and water coming in over the stern. I was in a helluva fix. So I quickly turned the canoe broadside to the fall, and paddled ashore in the trough. There I had to get out and pull the canoe over the swell before I could keep on going. . . .'

It was very quiet for a while; nobody dared look at Joe, who had a challenging look in his face, as if he dared anybody to comment. Then Albert said slowly as if not sure of himself: 'That was pretty bad, Joe, but nothing to what happened to me when I came down McFarlane River once. You know yourself how those shelves are. You can't see them before you are right on top of them, and then it's too late. You just go down, that's all. Well, that's just what happened. I hadn't travelled down that river before, so I wasn't familiar with it, so one day I came right down a fall before I knew it was there. I tried to stop with the paddle, but it was no use; but the back end of the canoe struck the edge and bounced, and at the same time I went over the brink. The canoe turned end over end as we went down. I just had time to think that's the end of me, before I hit bottom, dizzy as a coon. But when I came to I didn't believe it. Do you know what had happened? I had landed right side up behind the fall. The shelf was hollow underneath, and there I was in calm water, with the water coming down like a curtain in front of me. But in one end it was open, so I just paddled around the edge of the fall and kept on going.'

Joe looked suspiciously at Albert's innocent face, but nobody said a word. Somebody took a drink and spat in the fire. Then Matt asked: 'That must have been a horrible experience. How come you didn't get any water in the canoe when you went through that fall?'

'Didn't I tell you?' said Albert. 'The canoe turned over and was upside down, when we went through the water. So that's why. And it turned around so fast that nothing fell out either.'

Joe still eyed Albert with suspicion, not sure if Albert expected to be believed. He never found out either, because old Paul Cook, the Indian, came to the fire and complained that he had broken the amber stem on his pipe. Albert consoled him by saying that it was not much of a loss because it wasn't real amber, anyway.

Joe, who still felt disbelief in the air, said: 'Sure it's real.' When the others still voiced their doubts, Joe bristled and snapped: 'I should know genuine amber when I see it. I onced worked in a mine, where they had a solid layer of it three feet thick! I know what I'm talking about.'

Mike started laughing. 'I think you foolish it, Joe,' he said with his strong Slavic accent. Joe walked away, offended.

The celebration continued far into the night, and it was already daylight, when I heard a canoe being paddled towards our shore and Karl's voice rose happily in song: 'There's a husky, dusky maiden in the Arctic. . . .'

The next day some of the trappers flew out to their traplines. Joe was one of them. He was a bit careless in his habits, and always flustered when he had to hurry. We all helped to load his stuff while he scurried around gathering up all his belongings. Then he was off. The plane was about halfway out to his cabin, when Joe suddenly started, cursing: 'Damn it, damn it, damn it!'

The pilot turned. 'What's the matter, Joe?'

'I forgot my goddamn rifle. We got to go back for it.'

'O.K. by me, Joe, but it'll cost you thirty dollars extra.' So they turned, Joe cursing all the way in.

When they landed, Bill stood on the dock. When he saw Joe, he yelled: 'Hey, Joe. You forgot your fish-net.'

Joe exploded: '—— the goddamn fish-net! I want my goddamn rifle.'

It is difficult to name two things more important to a trapper than his fish-net and his rifle.

# CHAPTER XIV

## *I fly out—A happy time, and an accident—Reynard*

ABOUT sixty miles north-west of Fond du Lac, near the border of the North-West Territories, lies the Ena Lake. It is twelve miles long, has many deep bays, and is dotted with islands. There I decided to go for the winter. From other trappers I had found out that nobody hunted there, and that my nearest neighbours lived thirty miles to the west. I could then go there without fear of encroaching on anybody's grounds or of having other trappers too close for comfort.

This time I, too, intended to go by plane. A gold-rush that had started farther west on the lake had brought commercial aeroplanes into the area, and they could now be chartered easily and much more cheaply than formerly. One could go in a few hours to places that before had taken weeks or months of back-breaking toil in rapids and on portages to reach. One saved both time and work, and even money, if one took into account wear and tear on clothes and outfit, and outlay for gas and oil for motors.

I talked to Bill W., one of the first pilots to fly in the north.

'Sure, I'll take you out, Erik,' he said, 'but you must not have more than eighteen hundred pounds, yourself included', was his ultimatum when he heard how far it was.

These northland flyers are fine fellows; they are also excellent pilots and good bushmen. They really deserve a whole chapter, but since I have no room for it I must limit myself to just a few words to describe their importance for the north country.

Commercial flying in the north had been the dream of many, but it was only about 1930 that it really started, primarily because of improved planes, mining, and greater experience in bush-flying.

All planes in the bush are equipped with floats in the summer and skis in the winter. The wilderness is dotted with innumerable lakes, large and small, that provide natural landing-places and make flying safer than in most other areas. In case of trouble there is always a place to go down on, within reach.

But dangers still lurk there. Large areas are still unmapped, and the risk of getting lost is therefore great. It has happened that pilots who have been forced to land because of engine trouble or run short of gas have had to wait for weeks on some lake before search-planes have found them and brought aid. Weather forecasts are also very unreliable, as the stations are few and scattered, and a pilot never knows when he will run into a snowstorm or fog. Occasionally a plane's crew and passengers have to sit patiently by a camp-fire waiting for the weather to clear. But such things are taken with great calm. And rightly, because commercial flying in the north has an enviable record for safety. Fatal accidents have been very rare, although most pilots have broken through thin ice or damaged their floats landing on rough water. Many have had to land in pitch darkness without the aid of beacons or radio beams. Also most of them have at some time braved snowstorms or fog to bring sick people to hospitals.

But then, the conditions in the north have changed drastically owing to aviation. To many places, where formerly mail arrived only a few times a year, it now comes once a week, even every day.

More and more goods are transported by air every year. Fresh fruits and vegetables, fish, furs and even pieces of machinery weighing tons are moved by plane. Some gold-mines have received most of their machinery by air. The greatest achievement of all is perhaps that the rich radium ore from the Eldorado mine at the Great Bear Lake, beyond the Arctic Circle, was transported by air to Fort McMurray. For many years more freight left by air from Edmonton than from any other airport in North America. And what air transport means for mining cannot be easily estimated.

All this means that whoever wants to go anywhere in the north quickly and comfortably flies there. Regular air traffic is maintained by many companies; and Eskimos and Indians who never have seen a train or an automobile are perfectly familiar with the aeroplane.

Today the role played by the aeroplane is totally different from what it was when I first went north. But the years I lived there marked the transition from steamboat, canoe and dog-team to aeroplanes.

The people of the north are proud of their pilots, and the feeling of mutual liking is deep. I know pilots who have flown miles out of their way just to bring a lone trapper his mail or a can of tobacco, or just to see how he is getting along. And I also know trappers who, right in the busiest part of the season, without a thought of payment, have gone with messages or driven a pilot in trouble to the nearest settlement.

A bush pilot must also be a woodsman. He handles axe and gun and makes camp as expertly as he flies his plane, and sometimes has to make his way on snowshoes through uncharted wilderness. I admire him.

While I waited for Bill I completed my outfit and discarded everything I did not need. Still the pile was too big. With aching heart I eliminated a lot of things that I did not consider absolutely essential. Luckily my dogs did not weigh much. Only two were full grown and the other four were pups, not weighing more than a hundred pounds together. But I still had more than the eighteen hundred pounds Bill had set as the limit. When I resolutely had thrown away a few more objects I judged that I could not cut my outfit any further and resolved to try to get away with what I had.

Then came the longed-for day when we were to leave. Bill's mechanic and I loaded the plane. Sacks and crates, bundles and rolls were stowed into the cabin, from which the seats had been removed, and my eighteen-foot canoe was lashed to the outside struts of one float. That is the way canoes are transported in the north. A little corner was left in the cabin for the dogs, who were crowded in there whining and growling, and I was to lie on top of the load to quieten them if they became restive.

Bill came down to the plane and took one look at the floats that rested dangerously deep in the water. Then he looked at me and shook his head. 'Oh, yes it's the same old story,' he said with a grin. 'Trappers' pounds are always a lot heavier than common folk's. You've got at least a ton aboard. I'll try it, but God only knows if we can make it, calm as it is.' Upon which he climbed into the cabin.

It was a splendid fall morning. The lake was a still and glassy mirror. The sun was shining brightly from a cloudless sky on the blue water. The shores were fringed with yellow birches and still shrouded in a light mist. We taxied slowly out onto the open lake. Bill speeded up; the engine roared louder and louder; faster and faster we rushed over the water that flew around us as if from a hose, and the craft shivered and shook. But it did not lift. Bill rocked it up and down and from side to side trying to lift it on the step, but we did not rise one inch. He turned and shook his fist at me and muttered something that I could not catch above the roar. But the meaning was plain. My heart sank down into my shoes.

Then Bill pointed east. There a breeze made a grey stripe on the calm lake. 'We have to catch that one,' he yelled, and speeded up again. When we hit it he succeeded in jerking one pontoon up on the step. We went a little faster—another jerk, and up came the other. We were on the step. The speed increased. We skimmered along faster and faster. The plane suddenly stopped bouncing, the water turned to spray, and the shore that had been approaching alarmingly fast dived under us.

When we had climbed five hundred feet and were heading north-west Bill yelled: 'We made it, but, damn you, you have at least five hundred pounds over-weight. I only hope this kite stays together.'

Higher and higher we rose, and, map in hand, I watched our progress, as we first passed well-known territory and then flew over strange lakes and rivers. After half an hour's flight Ena Lake glinted ahead of us.

'Will you make a circle around the lake if I pay extra?' I asked.

'I'll see if I have gas—O.K.,' replied Bill.

Now I had to do many things: look for a good place to build, with a clean shore and a harbour in front; observe where the country was burnt and consequently poor for trapping, and where it was green, and see what it looked like up north. There were no maps of that part, and I had to see quickly where lakes and possible routes through the land lay.

Yes, there were several large lakes, probably connected by a river or creek. West of the Ena Lake the land was all burnt and desolate as far as I could see, but to the east and north-east it was green all the way to the horizon. And by a strait in the Ena Lake itself there was a fine sandy point with a bluff of tall pines.

'Let's land there,' I pointed. 'That's where I want to go!'

'O.K., boss,' grinned Bill and nosed the plane downwards. A while later we landed and coasted towards shore. I stepped on the float, with a paddle in my hand. The pontoons scraped in the sand and I jumped ashore and moored the plane to a tree.

And then out with the stuff. Soon my outfit was in a pile on the shore, the canoe pulled up alongside, and the dogs tied to nearby trees. 'Nice camping spot,' mused Bill. 'Wish I had time to stay here a week with you.'

But soon he pushed off. 'Come and see me sometime,' I shouted.

'You bet. Take care of yourself,' answered Bill, and gunned the motor. The plane sped away, lifted and disappeared on its way south. I was alone.

When the hum had died away I explored the surroundings. They were beautiful. To the east of my point a white sandy beach stretched in a shallow bend all the way to a rocky point; to the south it continued to the mouth of a little creek. The point itself, and the land beyond, was a gently sloping flat with tall pines, the bigger ones evenly spaced, as in a park. And on the point was a bluff of trees that were tall and straight and just of the right size to build with. Just inside the point there was a little cove, sheltered from most winds and making a good harbour. From the north shore a point came out to meet mine, leaving a narrow gap where fishing probably would be good. I was satisfied with the spot; here I would build my cabin.

The first job was to set a net. The dogs needed food, and I thought a fresh white-fish would taste very nice for supper.

That afternoon I was busy cutting logs for the cabin. It was wonderful to feel the sharp bit of the axe sink deep into the soft wood with every stroke, to inhale the aromatic smell of fresh resin, and to watch the straight pines fall to the ground with a crash. At night twenty logs were piled up beside the four pegs that marked the corners of my future home.

In the twilight I paddled out to the narrows and examined my net. In the few hours it had been in the lake it had caught several fish. I picked out a fine white-fish, which I cleaned in the deepening dusk and roasted by the camp-fire when the dogs had been fed.

The evening was quiet and the stillness of the wilderness reigned. Not even the dogs stirred. They had eaten and slept peacefully, rolled into furry balls, with their noses under their tails and their heads towards me, so that without moving they could open one eye to see what master was doing. The hill on the west shore of the lake contrasted sharply with the still light evening sky, their reflections in the calm lake a deeper shade of lilac and orange.

I was tired but happy when I sat by the camp-fire and smoked my last cigarette before bed. I was again out in the wilds without a soul in the vicinity. All the land I could see was mine, and around me lay my six faithful servants, who never questioned my authority and always were ready to obey and to work. With a sigh of contentment I took a last pull, threw the butt into the fire and went to bed.

The next day I continued to cut logs. While I wandered around searching for suitable trees, I suddenly saw several caribou on the open sunlit shore, approaching the point at an easy trot.

Quickly I doubled back, trying to run for my rifle in the shelter of the bush. But the caribou discovered me, turned and galloped away. A couple plunged into the lake, making the spray fly and glitter in the sun, and started to swim across the narrows.

Taking my rifle, I jumped in the canoe and paddled after them, and succeeded in coming within range just when they reached

the other shore. I laid down the paddle, scooped up the rifle and
fired. One dropped on the spot, the other staggered, but disappeared in the shelter of the bush. Panting, I jumped ashore and
followed. A hundred feet farther it lay on the ground trying to
rise when I arrived. One more shot and it fell like a sack.

Hooray! Two fat bucks! Fresh meat for the pot and dry meat
for a month ahead. That day I cut no more logs, but in the evening
a stage loaded with strips of meat stood far out on the point,
where the wind and the smoke, from a fire of rotten stumps
under it, would dry the meat and keep flies away. And up in the
trees, so high that flies would not find them, hung sacks of fresh
meat, and over the fire by the tent simmered a pot full of tongue
and ribs. Life was fine. Again I was living a trapper's simple,
hard, but, in spite of its loneliness—or perhaps because of it—
happy and peaceful life.

Fall passed. By and by the cabin was finished. It took three
weeks to build, because the floorboards were made of split logs,
the walls were hewed smooth, and door-frames, bunks, table and
other furniture were hewed from dry logs. A pile of firewood
had been gathered from the bush, and a row of dog-houses stood
a hundred feet from the cabin. And down by the shore stood a
stage on which fish for dog-food hung skewered ten on each
stick, suspended between poles to dry.

I had not eaten white-fish since that first night, because a
serpent—or rather a worm—had invaded my paradise. The white-
fish were all wormy. I had not noticed that when I cleaned the
fish in the dark that first evening. But the next day, when I
cleaned another, I found a lot of worms in the flesh. I threw it
aside and tried another. It was equally bad, and so were all the
rest. I almost retched when I thought of the one I had eaten.

While I was building I took time off and rowed around on
the lake and explored the long bays east and north-east, picked
cranberries, and cut trails for the winter. And then I started feeding
the foxes in the neighbourhood to keep them there until they
became prime. I transported fish-heads and guts to suitable places
on the lake shore and buried them in the sand, where they spoiled
and lured Reynard to come and eat. I also placed closed traps

beside the baits to make him get used to them and the smell of iron. They soon visited the feeding-places and ate the guts, so that I had to replenish them regularly. When Reynard became prime I would only have to set the trap to get him. By then he would have become careless of it. But that at least one fox was not satisfied with the board I provided and wanted something better became apparent a while later.

One night after dark the dogs were very restless; they barked and growled and would not stay quiet although I yelled at them repeatedly. Finally I lost my patience, took my whip and a flashlight and went out to chastise them. But when I walked along the trail I saw a pair of red spots shine in the beam of light down by the fish-stage. They appeared for a few seconds only and disappeared again. But as I went nearer I saw them again, and a reddish shape scurried through the beam and was swallowed by the darkness. A fox.

He soon became a steady visitor. To begin with, he appeared with the dusk and foraged only by the fish-stage, then he dared to investigate the garbage dump, and finally, when he had lost his fear of the fettered dogs, he came right up to the cabin. One night, when I sat on my bunk reading, something scratched on the window. There stood Reynard, with his front paws on the sill, looking curiously into the room.

Soon he was there all day long. He ran around the yard smelling at everything, chewed pieces of hide and bone, snapped up eggshells and bacon rind and carried away fish-heads. By now he paid no attention to the dogs, and they barked at him more or less only from jealousy, because he was allowed to run loose and not they. He often came to the door, jumped quickly inside to grab some morsel I threw him, and just as quickly out again. He now let me come within a few feet, showing no fear, and sometimes he followed me down the trail.

The peak of his daring came one day when I had rowed back from the nets. I was hanging a fish up to dry, when I spotted Reynard. While I had had my back turned he had taken a trout from the canoe and was making off with it, quite unconcerned, his neck stiff and tail proudly in the air.

With a yell I went after him, but he just scampered away faster, without letting go of the fish. I just about caught him, but then he started to dodge under a bunch of windfalls and brush. But when he got through that I gained on him again, as his load was so heavy. I was only a few feet from him when he finally dropped the trout and ran for it. But not more than fifty feet; there he sat down on his haunches and looked at me reproachfully. And a little later he snooped around just as brave as ever.

Reynard stayed around almost for a month, providing me with much fun and diversion, but just when he was getting prime and I started thinking of relieving him of his coat he was gone. He had found better food than I provided. The caribou had arrived.

Later I heard that some other trappers in the district also had had tame foxes, and that those who had killed theirs had found them very lean and half starved. Some of the older men said that disease had killed the mice that year, and there were few rabbits. There was famine among the foxes. Starvation had made Reynard tame.

Some animals quickly become tame, if they are not molested. As soon as they see that one bears them no enmity they pay as little attention to a man as to the rocks or trees. Almost every trapper has at one time or another had a weasel for a house-cat, and many have kept bear cubs or fawns for company in their loneliness.

Ptarmigan, that arrive in great flocks from the barrens in the early winter, are often so tame that one can pass them a few feet away when they sit in trees or on the ice, and they do not even move. Or else they amble calmly around the tent or the cabin, like tame poultry. Grouse can be just as tame. That winter a whole flock stayed near my cabin. Every morning they aroused me by pecking around the stove-pipe on the roof. The snow had melted there, so that they were able to pick sand for their craws. They were a bit of a nuisance at times; for instance the time they sent a cloud of sand down into the frying-pan through the crack next to the stove-pipe. But that was compensated for by the homey feeling of having them around.

When I was away on a trip they roosted in the dog-houses, and often when I came home and was going to tie the dogs I would be met by a flock of half-awake grouse that flew out of the houses and, blinking and clucking, settled in nearby trees. On sunny days they would sit in the pines around the cabin picking needles or sleep in their burrows in the snow. One cold morning, when I was carrying wood home, one was feeding on a low branch and did not mind me at all when I passed only a few feet away with logs on my shoulder. I went for my camera and snapped several pictures of him as I walked closer. Finally, when I was a yard away, he became a little worried and walked a little higher up on the branch. But he still did not fly away. Because I had plenty of other meat and never disturbed them, they stayed with me all winter.

About the end of September my cabin was ready, and the most important chore now was to put up enough fish for the winter. But one morning I had a serious accident.

I had gone out to cut a dry pole, from which I intended to make floats for my nets. While I was cutting, my axe slipped, and I cut my left foot just ahead of the joint. I hopped to the cabin as best I could, pulled off shoe and socks and tried to stop the flow of blood.

The cut had gone right to the bone, but fortunately no large blood vessels or tendons had been severed, and the bleeding was not great. I tried to close the wound by stitching, but the skin kept slipping, and the pain was so great that I stopped. Now I made an unpleasant discovery. I had no plaster with which to draw the edges of the wound together and no disinfectant. My bottle of iodine had been cracked sometime and was empty. The only thing that could possibly be used was pine tar; I had heard that lumberjacks sometimes put that on cuts. I did have some bandages, though, and also some white shirts from bygone days that could be used.

And so I bandaged my foot as well as I could, and manufactured a pair of crutches, with which I hobbled around quite nimbly after a few days.

However, I was very lucky to have my cabin built and most of my wood up for the winter, because a few days later there was snow on the ground. But the fall fishing was a worse matter. The few hundred fish that I had stored would not last long and had to be saved for the winter. It did not do to feed them to the dogs now. Whether I wanted to or not I had to fish. After I had lain in bed for a few days I realized that I could not afford to decimate my scant supply. If the caribou did not come I would be in a bad spot.

And so I got up, fixed up all my nets and set them. Luckily there were lots of fish in Ena Lake. But in late fall, when the weather was below freezing, and storms, with rain and sleet, lashed the lake almost continuously, as it seemed, fishing was no sinecure. Then I had to kneel for hours in the bow of the canoe and pick fish out of the net with swollen red hands, aching from water so cold that it froze on the canoe. To be able to work at all I had to keep my hands in the water; in the air they would have frozen in a short while. But, even so, I had to stop and slam them together every so often to restore circulation.

When I cleaned the fish I laid the livers aside and put them, together with rotten eggs, in a tight can, which I placed behind the stove in the cabin. There they rotted to an atrociously smelling mess, which almost drove me outside although the lid was tight. But it had to be kept there until ripe, because the foxes loved it. In the winter they would come clear across a lake to find the source of the enticing odour. After a few days in the cabin the tin was placed on the roof to await the trapping season.

Then another complication set in. The wound that had been healing well began to fester. It turned green and began to smell. When I fished, a lot of water mixed with fish slime collected in the canoe. Several times my injured foot had been soaked in it, and this was the result. My bandages were also finished, and I had to wash and boil them and use them over again. Now I really became worried. There was no way of getting help. I could not get out, because I was unable to portage the canoe or wade in rapids. And freeze-up, after which I could go by dogteam, was still weeks off. What was I to do?

Then I suddenly remembered. Hot salt water was supposed to be a good disinfectant. I put pots and kettles on the stove and added salt to the boiling water. Then I cut off some of the discoloured flesh around the wound. It was painful, but not as bad as I had expected; some of the nerves must have been destroyed. Then I soaked the foot in salty water, as hot as I could stand, for several hours, repeating the procedure every day. The cut started to mend surprisingly fast. In ten days it had healed, and the dull pain that had kept me awake at nights was replaced by a healthy itching.

It was a great relief. After a couple of weeks of restrained worry I was calm again, even hopeful. Perhaps my foot would be well again by the time trapping started, after all.

Soon I again hobbled around with the aid of a stick, managing to do my work, although I had to be careful how I stepped. And now I enjoyed life more than ever.

Late fall is for him who lives close to nature the best season. One never tires of being out in the woods, when the air has a crisp foretaste of winter, the feet tread lightly on the frozen ground, the moss crackles underfoot and the muskegs carry without yielding. Mosquitoes and blackflies are not there any more to torment one—the frost has long since gathered them in. And when it is calm and sunny one can paddle on the lake and enjoy the colours, the clean air, everything.

Fall resembles the evening after a day of hard work, in that a feeling of contentment is mixed with a longing for rest. Fall is far better than the over-publicized and over-estimated spring, the time of wet feet, flu and mental aberrations, or summer, with its stifling days filled with perspiration, flies and hot, sleepless nights.

Let the pavement poets bemoan autumn as the dark era of rotting leaves, death and decay as they see fit, but nature sees in it promise of well-earned rest after an exhausting season.

But for me fall was a time of preparation, of expectancy before the coming of the harvest. It was a time of waiting for winter and the start of trapping.

# CHAPTER XV

## *The caribou come again—An abortive hunt—Unexpected visitors*

ONE cold October morning, when hoar-frost sugared the trees white, icicles glittered on the willows along the shore and the mist was drifting over the water, I was fishing my nets. It was bitterly cold, and I froze and shivered, though I was swathed in clothing like a mummy. My fingers ached, so that I frequently had to stop to swing my arms.

While I did this I saw something resembling a floating brush-pile in the narrows. But it moved. I looked closer. The mist thinned for a moment and I saw that it was no brush but the horns of caribou. A big herd was crossing the narrows.

Even while I looked a stately buck rose out of the mist and shook water from its coat, so that the drops glistened like ice in the sun, and the wide horns trembled. Then it ran off among the trees. The rest followed ten or more abreast. The fall run was there.

I let the net slide back in the lake, paddled ashore and, throwing my fish in a heap, hopped to the cabin. The fishing could wait; now was the time to get meat. I took my rifle and also a spear that I had made and went back to the canoe.

Before leaving Fond du Lac I had as usual not been able to get enough ammunition for my Mannlicher carbine. It was always the same story: when I ordered shells they were promised, but when I needed them part of them had been sold to somebody else and I had to be content with just a few. Now I had only forty, which I would need later in the season when the caribou were shyer and had to be shot at long range. Now, when the run was on, I had to get them by other means; primarily with the .22, for which I had bought plenty of high-speed, long rifle cartridges. This is a much more effective weapon than commonly believed. A good marksman can kill even moose at a respectable range, and I have seen hunters perform miracles with it. Just because I often lacked shells for my other rifle I had often been forced to use my .22 for caribou, and had become quite proficient with it. Now, when caribou were plentiful, my experience with it helped a lot.

I also intended to try spearing them. One evening by the camp-fire, old Joe Bear, an Indian of the old school, had instructed me in the use of the spear. The Indians used it mostly when the migrations were on and caribou were abundant. Two hunters in a small, fast canoe would lie in wait by an island or point where the caribou crossed the big lakes. When a herd had swum about halfway over the sound they overtook it and paddled up on the left side of the last animal. The man in the stern navigated the canoe while the bowman killed the caribou. He made a swift thrust, holding the blade of the spear parallel to its ribs, and quickly pulled it out again. The blade was held in that position so that it would not stick in the ribs and give the animal a chance to upset the craft. One stab was usually enough, then one could go for the next caribou.

In days of old, blood-crazed Chipewyans had massacred hundreds of caribou by this method, killing every last animal in a great herd. Often, after cutting out only the tongues, they left the carcasses adrift to pollute the water. For that reason the practice had been forbidden, but rumour had it that four Indians only a couple of years before had killed hundreds of caribou in the narrows of the Selwyn Lake. This case was an exception, however, as education has made the Chipewyans conscious of conservation, and today they seldom kill more caribou than they need for themselves and their dogs.

Although the method was forbidden, the wilderness knows only the laws of survival and necessity, and most Indians still use a spear when conditions allow. Joe Bear showed me a blade two inches wide and eight inches long that he always carried with him.

Intending to try the method myself, I had fashioned a crude spear from an old file and lashed it to a birch handle. Now my chance to try it had come. Armed with rifle and spear, I paddled to the point and sat down to wait. Not long afterwards a score of caribou ran into the water from the other shore and started swimming towards me. I let them come about halfway before I paddled out to meet them.

The caribou saw me, turned and swam away. I paddled after them full speed, and, passing them with the idea of turning them back, stopped in front of them. But they did not turn. The herd split in two and swam past on both sides. A big buck was close to my left. Quickly I turned and manœuvred up alongside him. I grabbed the spear and got ready for a thrust, when the canoe suddenly received a violent bump from the buck's horns and nearly upset.

Surprised and believing it just a coincidence, I grabbed the paddle, righted my course and tried again. But the bump had been no accident. The buck deliberately swung his horns and delivered another resounding thwack, sending the bow of the canoe spinning off course. If I had not had my paddle ready the canoe would have turned over. I just managed to prevent it by a quick stroke.

This sort of aggressive behaviour was not at all what I had expected. Discretion was apparently called for. I let the buck go unharmed and decided to try a less formidable prey and sidled up to a less dangerously armed doe instead. That worked fine. But just when I thrust, the doe veered, my spear went into the water and I almost fell after it. Damn it! Up alongside again. This time I succeeded in spearing the doe, but the spear stuck and held fast. I hung on and stabbed and tugged, the caribou swam and pulled, the canoe rocked wildly and finally turned around and was towed towards shore, stern first. Because all the weight now was in front, it ploughed through the water, zigzagging from side to side. I could not let go or I would lose the spear, and I couldn't reach my rifle; and so I hung on, shifting my weight to keep from capsizing. Then the caribou tired, and I managed to stab a couple of times in quick succession. It worked. The animal turned over on its side and lay still.

I was now able to recover my spear, but the other caribou were all gone. I tried to feel elated over my successful hunt and my fine prey, but the feeling would not come. A small voice inside insisted that it had been a pretty poor and botched performance, and nothing to be proud of. This method struck it as filthy butchery.

Trying not to listen to the small voice, I started to lift the caribou into the canoe, but slipped on the icy bottom and almost pitched overboard for the fourth time. I then tied a rope to the animal and started towing it. It was a slow job. The caribou's horns and legs braked effectively; but I could not leave it, because the wind would have taken it across the lake.

When I finally reached shore I was thoroughly disgusted. I had bungled the job completely, tired myself out and lost a lot of time on the so-and-so harpooning. Of course, I had many excuses; the canoe was too big, I was alone, the wind was wrong, etc. etc. Anyway, the result was that I decided to use more humane hunting methods, and, although I did not throw away my spear, it stayed unused in the corner of the cabin for the rest of the winter.

Instead I took my .22 and hopped over to the point, where most of the caribou had landed. My luck improved. As the caribou streamed across the sandplain I picked the fattest and largest. Usually I had to fire several times before one dropped. But no wounded animals escaped to die slowly in the bush. I would not have been able to trail them, as my foot was still too much of a handicap.

The migration continued for about ten days and I soon had all the meat I needed. The butchery—one could not call it hunting—lasted two days. It lacked completely the thrill of the chase and that feeling of triumph over outwitting the quarry that is the essence of a successful hunt. This was not pleasure, but a chore. I needed meat and this was the only way to get it.

When I had enough for dog-food, I shot only an occasional fat doe. Most caribou are pretty lean right after the rutting season, but in the herd there are some does that have not been bred and they are fat.

Joe once told me a good rule to follow: 'That caribou which is the liveliest when it is cold and the laziest when it is warm is the fattest in the herd and the one to shoot.'

The run was the greatest I had ever seen. Day and night the animals streamed past. Some were quite tame and would stop only fifty feet away and calmly inspect me or poke around the fish-stage until the dogs barked, when they would suddenly come to life. A little fawn happened to stray in among the dog-houses and barely missed being bitten in the ham by the suddenly awakened Wapush. I have never seen anything move as fast as that fawn. It literally flew over windfalls in its haste to escape. If the cabin had happened to be in the way I am sure it would have sailed clean over.

That fall I also saw something I had heard Indians and trappers tell of: caribou bucks that, exhausted after the rutting season, lay, dead to the world, and slept. I really thought they were dead when I found two lying side by side. They did not even wake up as I came up to them. But they were safe. Their musk smell protected them from the fangs of their enemies.

After I had stopped hunting I still caught an occasional one in rope snares that I hung in their trails. When one was caught the dogs would sound the alarm. They heard it struggle and pitch in its effort to get free.

With the migration came the winter. The little lakes froze over first, and so one morning the Ena Lake was covered from shore to shore by a sheet of glass. Soon trapping could begin. But one important chore still remained. The pups had to be trained to pull the sleigh.

Although brothers, the pups were all dissimilar in looks and showed features of all the strains from which they descended. Mike was light-grey, sharp-eared and looked much like a wolf. Jim was almost black, with all the markings of a husky including 'spectacles', dark rings around the eyes. Bear had the build of a St. Bernard but the curly hair of a spaniel, and Buck resembled a long-haired hound. But they all had long powerful legs, big paws and broad, deep chests.

Ever since birth they had been very shy, and although they were very attached to me, and almost tried to eat me in their enthusiasm when I came near, they feared and avoided strangers. They were typical one-man dogs. Mike let nobody touch him, and if a stranger caught him he would bite and growl. And Bear, who was cocky enough in harness, would run away and hide in the bush if a stranger came near when he was loose. It was amusing to see him hide behind a spruce and watch the visitor, or sneak about from tree to tree at a safe distance. Then he would not come out even when I called him; he just crawled out of his hiding-place, lay down and waited for me to come and fetch him.

In spite of that they were no cowards. They would fight among themselves almost too readily, and any strange dog that made insulting faces or growled provokingly was in for a rough time. It was probably the wolf strain that showed itself there. Mike had both the eyes and the general physiognomy of a wolf.

I had great hopes that they would make a good team. When the first snow came I hitched up Jack and Wapush and one of the pups behind, intending to train them one at the time. Mike and Jim thought it great fun and pitched in from the start like veterans, and when we finished the lap and came back to the cabin they tried to pull the sleigh alone. They understood what was required of them right from the beginning. It was as easy as falling off a log for them. But Bear did not like the set-up at all. He looked perplexed and uneasy when he had been harnessed, and was taken completely by surprise when I yelled 'Mush!' and the other dogs started pulling. He held back at first all he could. Then when he noticed that it was easier that way he went along unwillingly and stiff-legged. But his whole attitude expressed plainer than words: 'I don't like this at all.'

But Buck! He was deathly scared; he howled, yelled and struggled, with his legs sticking out in all directions like a spider's, and was hauled along the ground on his belly for long stretches. It took patience, time and many placating pats to make him understand that his life was not in peril. Finally, panting and his whole body shaking from fright and exhaustion, he consented to pull.

Then I got the bright idea of hitching them all up together. I thought that it would look grand to see them all six in a row, and drive a little way with them. Off we went. But oh, ye gods, what a racket and mess! Jack and Wapush started on my command, and Mike and Jim, who thought it great fun, jumped after them barking, but Bear held back, stiff-legged and growling, and tried to pull his head out of the collar, while Buck, terrified, leaped straight up, landed flat on his belly and dragged along either on his stomach or his side, with legs extended as if he were dead. Still it went fairly well until Bear went on the wrong side of a tree and was thrown and ended up facing backward in the harness. I stopped the train, but while I straightened Bear out Mike and Jim walked up to Jack, started playing and entangled themselves, so that when we started again the traces became looped around their legs. That hurt, and they yelped and growled, and then Jim grabbed Mike by the neck, probably under the impression that Mike bit him. That started it. A regular free-for-all began. Jack hurried to get in on the fun, and the others piled in. They bit, shook, howled, growled and whined, from fear, fury and pure enthusiasm, and the result was a complete mess of whirling, fighting, angry dogs and tangling traces. I yelled myself hoarse and plied my whip, but without any result. Then I tied the sleigh to a tree and started after Jack and Wapush with a big stick. They tried to escape and stretched out the whole tangle into a long rope, in which the pups resembled balls of woollen yarn on a string. They had woven themselves in so that they could hardly move. It took a lot of work to straighten them out again one at a time, and it was a sorry parade that I drove home. Mike lifted his paw and hopped on three legs and whimpered, Jim shook his head and yelped every time he did it, and Buck dragged on behind as before, now whining and yelping. Only Bear still walked on all fours. But he growled, just the same. He still did not like the set-up.

But in spite of the poor beginning, the pups learned in a few days. Northland dogs are born to the harness; pulling is in their blood. Quickly they learned to keep their harness straight, and before long even the last finesse of walking off the trail to defecate—this so the stuff would not freeze under the sleigh, making it rough and heavy to pull.

Only Buck still gave me trouble; he absolutely refused to pull on clear ice. Then he just lay down and dragged along like a sack. He was so impossible that I had to leave him tied up at home when I went on a trip. When I approached the cabin after a long journey, it was sad to hear his dismal howls, hoarse and monotonous, and with long intervals between in the distance. Only when the ice became covered with so much snow that it did not show through could I start to use him. But in spite of all the trouble in the beginning, Buck eventually became the best dog in the team.

In less than a fortnight after the first heavy snowfall it was full winter. The season was so far advanced that the furs were prime, and my foot had healed so well that I could start to trap, if I was careful with it. While I waited for the ice to become thick enough for a long trip to the north I ran some short lines over the little lakes south-east, and set traps along the lakeshore near home, opening the ones I had kept near my foxbaits.

'Only a couple of days more,' I thought one day, when I tested the ice on the Ena Lake. Then suddenly I heard a faraway howl. I froze in my tracks and listened. There it was again, a chorus of howls far to the south-west. 'Damnation! Dogs. Now the Indians are in the country,' I thought. 'They are on the other side of the lake and can't cross the weak ice.' So I reasoned. I heard it again; no doubt about it. I had company on my hunting-grounds. I went home grumbling.

The next afternoon I had been visiting my traps along the shore, caught a red fox and was on my way homewards, when I suddenly heard an infernal racket from the cabin. My dogs were barking like mad.

With the fox over my shoulder I hurried homewards, thinking that one of them had got loose and started a fight. But when I came up the trail from the lake, just about winded, there were two dog-teams in front of the door, and two black-bearded men, whom at first I did not recognize, came out.

'Oh, it's Big Erik,' said one. 'How are you?'

'Well, I'll be damned,' said the other, grinning and shaking my hand.

'Hi, George! How are you doing, August,' I answered, when I recognized them through their hirsute disguise.

They were the trappers who, as I had heard, were hunting west of me. I asked them in and put the tea-kettle on the stove.

They told me that they, too, had moved to the lake that fall and built a cabin at the south-west end. We had arrived almost on the same day, because when they were on the last portage they had seen a plane pass over. It might seem odd that we had not met during the fall, but our cabins were far apart, and I had no interest in exploring the burned-out south end of the lake. The brothers, August and George, had run out of gas for their motor, and knew the lake, besides. They had been too busy to paddle around.

As I knew, they had trapped farther west the year before, but, as the country had burned and the trapping was poor, they had moved. Besides, the fishing was good in the Ena Lake.

They had been on their way to a cache where they had left some traps, when they came upon my tracks on a lake to the south. They cursed heartily, as they did not like Indians in the country any more than I. They followed the tracks to find out who it was.

But when they came to the spot where the trail left the lake they immediately realized that a white man and no redskin had invaded their territory. 'There were trees that big that had been cut down,' laughed August, showing the size with his hands. 'No Indian would do that,' he added.

One look at the cabin confirmed this; and then they had studied the dogs to find out who the owner might be. But they did not know them. So they sat down to wait, knowing I could not be far off.

August and George had homesteaded in northern Alberta some years before. The land was good and everything had gone well for them. But the depression came. They had very little money and it hit them hard. They stuck it out for a couple of years because they had put a lot of work and money into their land and did not want to lose it all. But finally they had to.

One of their neighbours who had once trapped in the north had fascinated them with his tales and persuaded them to accompany him to Camsell Portage. From there the three of them had gone into the hinterland to trap. The third man had moved on after one winter, but the brothers had stayed. This was their third winter, and they liked the life, although it was so different from anything they had done before.

And now we were here practically in each other's laps. It was too late for anyone to move, and so we had to do the best we could—divide the hunting-grounds so that we would not be in each other's way. There was still plenty of room, and no other neighbours to worry about.

George and August had been trapping on some of the lakes to the north, but had not gone far north-east or east, and so I decided to extend my lines as far as possible that way. The boys gave me a lot of valuable information and descriptions of trails, portages, lakes, rivers and creeks. In complete amity we agreed on the limits of our grounds and sat down to eat.

I mentioned in passing that I had known that somebody was in the country because I had heard their dogs howl. They looked a bit surprised, and August said: 'It wasn't our dogs, they never howl. It must have been wolves. We heard them too, eh, George?'

They told me that wolves usually were plentiful in the area, and that they had seen more tracks than ever this year. All signs showed that they were more numerous than before. The winter before, the wolves had arrived in great numbers just after the caribou.

This was good news. For some reason the price of wolf pelts was very high that winter—higher than it had ever been. Here was my chance to make something.

We talked for a long while, and it was getting dusk when the boys got up to go. Though it was late, they would not stay for the night.

'Harvest-time is here for trappers, and we have to get our lines out,' said August. 'You have set a lot more traps than we have already and we've got to hurry.'

'Listen!' said George, and held up his hand, when they stood outside ready to leave.

Out there, far away in the north-west, sounded the thread-thin howl of a lone wolf. Even as we listened others joined in, and, rising and sinking like organ music, it swelled and died. Like an omen, a promise of a good hunt, we heard the blood-curdling chorus of a wolf-pack on a fresh track.

# CHAPTER XVI

## On the trapline—The wolf trek—Unwelcome escort—An unwary lobo

THE morning was cold, calm and clear when I, with the sleigh loaded full of provisions, traps and bait, drove northwards over Ena Lake. The toboggan slid easily, and the pups, six months old almost on the day, ran like old, seasoned sleigh-dogs, with tails curled high over their backs. Their ears pointed straight up, and their heads were thrown from side to side, as they looked with curiosity at all the new things that came into sight ahead. Only poor Buck was left at home. Tied to his house, he sat, with a whole caribou beside him for food, and his mournful howl escorted us on our way. He was still so afraid of thin ice that he had to be left behind. This trip would take at least a week, and I had left him plenty of food until my return.

We drove to the nearest point. There I saw a fox track and stopped the team. Then I pulled a trap out of the sack, fastened it to a root, set it, covered it carefully with fresh snow and sprinkled pieces of rotten fish and a few morsels out of the can around it. Afterwards I obliterated my tracks and resumed my journey.

A mile farther I ran across the first wolf tracks, huge saucer-sized prints made by a pack of at least a dozen beasts. I set two of my biggest traps nearby and kept on going. We were now almost at the north end of the lake, but before we got there I saw the tracks of yet another pack.

A small river fell into the north end of the lake. There was an open rapid, and there a mink had hopped along the shore, gone in for a swim and come up again a little higher up. I built a pen and set another trap.

After a couple of small lakes with short portages between them, I came out on the first of the large lakes which I had seen from the plane in the fall. Here I travelled through beautiful country—wide lakes fringed with long, winding sandbeaches growing tall pines, many islands big and small, with birch on the shores and dark spruce in the middle, divided by shallow narrows and here an isolated, dark hill. A river, that flowed calm and wide in broad curves, connected the lakes. The land consisted mostly of sandplains occasionally broken by steep eskers or dark spruce growing in muskegs. What wonderful country that would be to spend a summer in. Such bathing beaches, and probably millions of mosquitoes and blackflies too.

The sandplains were crisscrossed by caribou trails, and the snow was pitted by holes which they had made to get at the lichen and reindeer moss. I saw a herd running away, their white rumps bobbing among the tree-trunks.

And only now I really saw wolf tracks! Never would I have believed that one could see so many in one day. Trail after trail, made by great packs of twenty or more wolves, crossed mine. Sometimes they were behind each other in Indian file, sometimes spread out as if made by a platoon of soldiers in battle formation. He who never before had seen the tracks of a full-grown wolf would hardly have believed his eyes. They were five, six inches in diameter; and when one sees thirty or more abreast at once and crosses the trails of new packs every so often, and then tries to visualize the beasts that made them, it almost makes one shudder. Hereabouts wolf signs were as numerous as caribou tracks, and all of them pointed south-west. But although I saw the tracks I did not see the wolves themselves. They were too shy and alert to show themselves.

But instead I heard them. To begin with only occasionally, but, as I went on, more and more often, and finally I heard them continuously. Far to the west ululated one pack, and straight ahead another. And presently this devil-concert sounded on all sides. At times I had to stop to really listen. I could hardly believe my ears. But it was true—they seemed to fill the land with their howling. I felt surrounded and insignificant, and got a creepy feeling up my spine.

So I continued north-east for two days, and day and night the chorus of the wolves followed me. Especially at night, when I camped, they seemed set on entertaining me. Every pack that came near my tent seemed to stop to sing for me. At first my dogs joined the choir, but soon quit in shame; as singers they could not compete with their wild cousins. And some nights, when they came close, the dogs were very quiet; they lay rolled up tightly, as if a little afraid.

One night the howl came so near that I rushed out of the tent with my rifle ready and peered out over the moonlit lake. Any moment I expected the wolves to hurl themselves at my dogs. But although I stood there for a long while, silent and unmoving, I did not see any, and when the howl had retreated somewhat I crawled back in bed and listened to the song until I fell asleep.

In the morning I walked down the ice to see how close they had been. The nearest tracks were well over two hundred yards away, although I could have sworn when I heard them that they were within a hundred feet of us.

So far I had been unlucky with caribou; the wolves had scared them so badly that they stampeded long before I came within range. But that day I surprised a herd behind a point and got two before the rest escaped. One I dressed and put in the cariol, but the other I served to Mr. Lobo. I dragged it out on the open lake and gutted it. Then I cut some deep, parallel gashes in the liver and poured dope in them, laid the liver on the bare ice and covered it with guts and snow. Finally I pulled the carcass on top. Here were some tit-bits for Lobo, if he would just taste them. I covered the liver so that the ravens would not find it. There were plenty of ravens around also, and they lived the life of Riley on all the half-eaten caribou the wolves had left. Flocks of them flew overhead and I heard their bell-like *cling-clong, cling-clong* as they called their friends to fresh plunder.

As I went I also set a lot of traps on points and islands. Most of them were too small for a wolf, as I had expected to catch mostly fox when I bought them. But I set them in pairs, in the hope that a wolf would step in both of them and stay put. Two should hold a wolf.

One wolf-pack took a notion to follow me. When I drove over a lake they ran along the shore in the shelter of the bush, but when I came to a portage they closed up behind me and ran at my back but a little to one side of the trail. At times the howl seemed to come very near, but no matter how I scanned the bush, tense with my rifle cocked, I never caught a glimpse of them. As many trappers had told me, wolves are good ventriloquists; they seem to be able to throw their voices so that they sound closer than they are, or vice versa.

Although I knew that wolves never attacked man unless desperate for food, I still got that creepy feeling down my back, as if the hair that was not there was trying to stand on end. That blood-freezing savage song made some hidden nerve in me tremble; it was perhaps a heritage from the long-forgotten past, when wolves were a real danger. Therefore I was relieved when the pack decided to leave me and the ululation died away and blended with more distant choruses.

For two days the wolf trek continued around me. I had landed in the middle of one of those runs of which I had heard other trappers tell but until now believed to be pure nonsense. A week before, I would have laughed if somebody had told me there could be so many. But now I had to believe my eyes and ears. How many were there? I did not know, but there must have been thousands.

Soon most of them were gone. They followed the main caribou herd. (The wolves were numerous all winter, but although they trekked again in March I never again experienced a run like this one.)

After two days I turned and travelled east and south-east in a wide arc, setting my traps on the lake shores and in the mouths of creeks where mink or otter lived. Mink *or* otter, because they do not get along, and their tracks are seldom seen together near the same spot.

The territory I travelled through was unmapped. For that reason I now made my way on a general south-east course, knowing that I would soon encounter Tazin River, which flowed south-west and passed very close to Ena Lake. When I reached it I could find my way home again, because I had a rough map of that country.

N

In the twilight I would pitch my tent, make a fire in the stove, and put on the tea-kettle. While the water was coming to the boil I would cut spruce boughs for the dogs, and feed them, if I had fresh meat. Otherwise I placed the frozen fish behind the stove to thaw. Then I would drink tea, which would be my first refreshment since breakfast; during these short days I was too busy to stop for lunch. Then I would pick a standing dry pine, fell it and cut it up for firewood.

By now the fish would have thawed. For a long time the dogs would have been looking expectantly at the tent, pawing the ground impatiently. When I went to feed them they would break out in a flurry of whining and barking and strain excitedly at their chains.

Then I would cut a chunk of ice and place it in the coldest corner of the tent. From that I could melt water when I wished, without having to go out for it. Then I would prepare supper. It usually consisted of a fresh caribou steak, over one inch thick, filling the whole pan, and beans that had been cooked and frozen into cakes, from which I could break a piece and heat it whenever I wished. For dessert a handful of raisins and a mug of strong, hot tea.

After supper I maybe skinned some game, mended clothes or read a little by candlelight. And so, when kindlings for the morning had been cut and placed near the stove, and I had taken one more look at the dogs, I would crawl into my sleeping-bag and blow out the candle. The stove would still glow red for a while, but soon the fire would die, and it would be as cold in the tent as outside. But my sleeping-bag was filled with eider-down, and under it there was a caribou hide. Even when it was fifty below I slept warm. It was often midnight when I fell asleep.

Gradually I found my way from lake to lake south-eastwards. The terrain became hilly again. Sometimes I discovered an old trail, cut and blazed long ago by some other hunter. The stumps were black and rotten and the blazes mere gum-covered slits, overgrown by new bark. In a valley I saw the tracks of lynx. They had walked in single file, stepping in each other's tracks. They were probably made by a female followed by her litter; sometimes one had left the others to investigate something interesting, but had soon returned to the trail, and the tracks continued, one behind the other, in a straight row.

And here was the track of a marten. He is the fearless scrapper who does not hesitate to attack the many times larger fox if necessary, and who does not run even from forest fires, plunging ferociously into the advancing flames, but whose cruel being is swathed in wonderfully soft and silken fur, which after his death adorns the soft, and not so soft, shoulders of another being, sometimes equally cruel: woman.

Turning straight south, I came to a large lake. A river ran out of its south end. It must be Tazin River. I followed it, and the following day I came to a region that vaguely resembled the map I had. Here the river should part in two channels, and the portage should go across the island between them. Yes, and there, in the little lake between the two rapids, was the little island with the lone birch, where Joe Bear had forgotten a No. 3 trap when he left the place four springs ago. I stopped and scraped away the snow. Yes, here it was. There were some bones, part of the front leg of a fox, still in it. I lifted it out of the snow, set it again, and sprinkled bait around it. The place was good; I left the trap there. Then I drove to the west shore, because here the trail that led back to Ena Lake was supposed to start.

It was easy to find. It had been well cut and blazed once, and both caribou and wolf had used it this winter. That same night I was home again, after an absence of ten days. There I was greeted by Buck, hoarse, but almost beside himself with joy.

Buck had had no fun while we had been away, and now he was so glad to have us at home again that he barked excitedly, played and romped around his brothers, and whined pleadingly for me to come and pat him. But he had not lacked food, as there was still lots of meat left on the caribou I gave him. And he had not been alone, either. At least not all the time. Only fifty feet from the dog-houses I found fresh wolf tracks.

Oh, how wonderful it was to sleep in a cabin again for a few nights, to wash and shave thoroughly and to change clothes. It was real luxury. And now my traps were all set and I had only to visit them.

The next time when I intended to go out on one of my short lines and laid out the harnesses on the ground Buck went absolutely wild. He tore around his house like a shuttle, howled, barked and whined, and stood on two legs pawing the air. 'Oh, don't leave me at home; oh, please don't leave me,' he said, plainer than words. And when I loosened his chain he almost dragged me over to the harness. On the trail he pulled like a tractor, and even forgot to be scared when we drove out on the ice. Buck was cured, he had become a sleigh-dog. Soon he was the best in the team.

In one of my traps I had a wolf. He had been there a long time, because when I approached he lay asleep curled up like a dog, and only woke up when we were quite near. He looked tired when he got up, and just sat and looked at me until I shot him.

I caught one more wolf that day, but he was made of different stuff. He pulled on the chain and howled and bit the trap when he saw us. But when we came closer he stood his ground stiff-legged, with neckhair bristling, and growled, his long white fangs bared.

The dogs took that as a challenge and a personal affront. They were not going to stand for that sort of an insult, they were going to teach their uncouth relative some manners. They did not stop at my command, and although I yelled and cursed, they just pulled until I upset the sleigh and sat on it. And even then they had to jump and lunge in the harness, spoiling my aim when I tried to shoot. Finally I got out my whip and with a few cracks and some harsh words quietened the team. We were then only thirty feet from Lobo, who still stood his ground all set to welcome us. I did not dare leave the sleigh, and, sitting on it, I put a .22 bullet through his head.

He was a magnificent brute, almost white, only along the back there was a dark stripe, and the tip of his tail and his claws were black. The front legs were the size of a man's calf, and the bared fangs almost two inches long. He must have weighed a hundred and twenty-five pounds. A pleasant fellow to come to grips with if he took a notion to attack!

I also caught a fox and a mink that day. The season was off to a good start.

But that was all it did, because now came a Chinook, a balmy south-west wind, with rain and mild weather in its train. The snow melted, the ice became bare. I was forced to remain at home in idleness because I could not travel before the weather became cold again, and it would have been a waste of effort, besides, to touch the traps. They would have to be set all over again, because when it froze they would freeze, too, and be out of order. To pass the time I roamed around in the vicinity.

Because of the wet weather I dressed in rubbers that made very little noise as I walked along the ice. One day when I rounded a point I suddenly came eye to eye with a full-grown wolf. The surprise was mutual. Lobo, who, drowsy from the heat, had been loping along in the sunshine, his tongue hanging out, sat down on his haunches fifty feet away to gaze at me and figure this thing out. I just stopped and stared. But I was the first one to collect my wits. I raised my rifle and fired.

The wolf jumped, growled and spun around and around biting his shoulder, where the bullet had hit. I fired again. That one got him in the head, and he fell over, legs kicking. As I approached him gingerly with rifle cocked, his eyes shone with a greenish light as intensely full of hatred as a devil's. The pupils became pinpoints of hell's fire. But while I watched, the light suddenly went out and he went limp. It was as if somebody had pulled a blind over his eyes. He died not knowing what had hit him, but ferociously fighting it to the last breath.

This one was also white; only a few black hairs were sprinkled through the fur that shone like silk where the blood had not sullied it. It is not often a wolf will let a man come so close as this one. The reason this one did was probably that he had been sleepy and sluggish from a full stomach and the hot sun as he trotted along. Anyway, I skinned him on the spot and walked home again, with the pelt on my shoulder.

There I found my neighbours again, who also had found time heavy on their hands and had put steel runners under their sleighs and come visiting. They had been overtaken by the thaw out on the trail and forced to return home. On the way they had passed some of my traps, killed a fox in one, and seen three wolves at one of my baits.

'Your sugar sure works,' said George. 'They had not gone more than twenty feet before they died. We covered them with snow, but you'll have to hurry there before the ravens cut them to pieces or the heat spoils them.'

Good show! Three more. The brothers laughed when I overwhelmed them with questions about the size and colour of the wolves. They had been lucky, too, as they had got more than twenty pelts, and they also had surprised a pack, shooting two wolves, and had seen more wolf signs than they had believed possible.

From their talk I understood that there was going to be a race as to which of us three would get the most pelts before Christmas. I was still a few skins ahead, but would I be able to keep the edge on them?

When the boys left the next morning it was a little cooler, and that night it started freezing again. I prepared for a new trip over the line.

## CHAPTER XVII

### *A lucky day—Feud with a coyote—Wolves, caribou and 'experts'*

M Y next trip over the line proved profitable. The first day I got one wolf, besides those the boys had found, and a nice silver fox as well. Numerous wolves had hung themselves up in my traps, but escaped again. Many of the traps were, as I had feared, too weak to hold them, or else the wolves had pulled the stake loose to which the traps were fastened and dragged it away. And the thaw had obliterated all tracks, so I could not follow them. I lost several that way, and had good reason to curse my luck. But oh, how they had investigated! They had been at every trap. The fact that the usually sly and wily wolves, who shun traps like the devil, had been so careless meant that these had wandered far south from their homes on the remote tundra where they had had little experience with traps. Their great numbers also helped; all animals tend to become careless when they are numerous, and are then easy to catch.

Despite the thaw, and the frost that followed, putting the traps out of order, this trip was good. The last day was the best—in fact the best I ever had during my years of trapping. That day I got thirteen wolves, two mink, two red foxes, one cross fox and one marten.

In the first trap was a fox. Good! This morning starts all right! I might be lucky and catch some more today, I thought, as I continued. And on the next lake there was a cross fox in a trap on a point. It jumped, clawed, bit the trap and yelped when it saw us, and tried frantically to escape. I hurried the dogs on, and, with a thumping heart, I watched it as we scooted over the drifts. There is always a thrilling moment when one approaches a trap with game in it. Will it be able to tear itself loose before one gets there?

This time I got there in time. I tapped the fox on the nose to stun him, and wrung his neck. Just then I heard the dogs whine behind me, and out of the corner of my eye I saw the sleigh start. I made a flying leap for it and managed to catch the tail rope just when the dogs, barking with eagerness, made off across the lake. Sprinting a few feet and holding on to the rope, I pulled myself up on the back end of the sleigh. Then I saw ahead of me what had attracted the dogs. There were two wolves caught in traps I had set by a caribou carcass. When we were close I yelled at the team to stop, but as usual I had to upset the sleigh and sit on it to make it plough snow.

When we stopped I sat and fired at the wolves with my .22. It took many shots before they were dead. Not only did they jump around, but the dogs also spoiled my aim by jerking the sleigh and sometimes moving into the line of fire, making me nervous and afraid of hitting them instead. And when I had killed them both I spotted a third one by the next island. Hardly glancing at the others, I drove away towards that one, my heart pounding like a trip-hammer from excitement. This time I did not even bother yelling at the dogs. I just turned over the sleigh and started shooting at the wolf, which frantically tried to tear himself loose.

When he, too, was still, I rolled a cigarette with shaking hands and smoked it to the end before I moved. Then I walked over and started skinning him.

Then I returned to the other two, skinned them, threw the cross fox in the toboggan and went on. After this it was something of an anticlimax to catch one more red fox, a couple of mink and a marten, before I came to Ena Lake.

It was evening when we reached the lake. The sun was just setting and threw a rosy glow over the snow. It was still warm, and I sat down on the sleigh. Now it was only three or four miles home, and I was happy and contented as I squinted against the sunlight over the lake. I had had a successful trip, in spite of so many wolves escaping and so many traps not functioning. And this last day had been a very good ending to it.

The dogs trotted briskly on. They also knew that we would be home soon. We had only two more points to pass and then the cabin would come into sight. The dogs broke into a gallop; I urged them on.

We rounded the point. A swarm of ravens rose, screeching raucously, from the ice. I swore softly. They had been at my wolf bait again. I strained my eyes and saw that there was not much left of the caribou. They had eaten it all. But what were those greyish snowdrifts out there? I sat up straight. They were wolves —wolves almost covered by snow! I counted them with growing excitement as we came nearer. They were now easy to see, as they contrasted sharply with the snow. Six, seven, eight. . . . No it was impossible. Yes, there were that many! When we got there I jumped off the sleigh and ran back and forth, and turned them over and counted them again. I could hardly believe my eyes, but there were ten lying there, with legs stiffly outstretched, within a circle of two hundred feet. But the ravens had torn two so badly that I doubted if they would be any good.

They were all frozen stiff, so that I could not skin them, but I gathered them in a pile on the shore and covered them with spruce boughs and snow and drove on home. Sometimes one is lucky. Sometimes, but only sometimes, everything seems to go just right, even better than expected.

But that is not often. Usually everything goes plumb to hell. Then it seems that everybody and everything is in a conspiracy to make one's life a trial. There were, of course, days, often many of them in a row, when one did not catch anything, when the wind was bitterly cold, the trails all blown in by fresh snow, and the lakes covered with slush, so that one had to break trail on snowshoes every inch of the way or stop and scrape ice off the sleigh every few hundred feet. Or the dogs would tire, so that one had to let them stop for a rest so often that it was late at night when one arrived in camp exhausted and hungry. Those days were common, days that one expected and took as a matter of course. They were a part of one's life.

But then there were times when one ran into streaks of really infernal luck, when all possible and imaginable things contrived to make one's life bitter. I will relate one of those, just to give the reader the right perspective on the life of a trapper.

When I woke up in the morning it was cold and overcast, and a whining wind was blowing down the lake. When I wanted to hitch up the dogs one had got loose during the night and stolen a caribou steak that I had saved. As a result of his guilty conscience he did not dare come to me, but hid so I had quite a job to catch him, and lost a lot of time before I got started.

Out on the line it started fine. The first trap I came to had been smashed, and the beast—a coyote judging from the tracks—had escaped. I replaced the trap, and struggled on against the cold wind which blew stinging snowflakes into my eyes. A bit farther, a trap was gone. A fox that had been caught had dragged the toggle with him. The tracks on the lake had been obliterated by the wind, and it took me a long time to find where they entered the bush. Now followed a regular ring around the roses. The fox track circled around and around and in and out among the spruce and willows, and it was only after much work that I managed to untangle it and follow it straight up a slope. There I found a fresh bed; it was still soft. Reynard had apparently rested here until he saw me coming, and then fled. Up the hill I went, and there I ran into another tangled skein of circles and bends. Then I caught sight of Reynard. He had tarried too long in making his puzzle. I ran as fast as I could after him as he started straight up the slope of an esker again. I just about caught him when he reached the top, but then he scurried down the other slope, toggle and all, so fast that I was left practically standing. It took another twenty minutes before I caught him—a measly red.

When I returned to the lake, wet and tired, the team was gone. The dogs had started back for camp. I walked a mile before I found them. The sleigh had become hooked on a stump and turned over.

As the day wore on I found several of my traps dug out of the snow and the bait gone. A coyote had been playing around. And a caribou I had shot and hidden on the shore had been found by ravens, which had eaten part of it and dirtied the rest.

In the next rapid the water had overflowed and covered some mink sets with several feet of water, and it had changed the landscape, so that I could not even find them. I lost them with the game that possibly was caught in them.

To top off the day I broke through the ice in a place where I had travelled all winter without mishap, and had to stop and build a fire to dry myself and then spend the rest of the afternoon there. It was late when I got home that night, tired and frozen.

Days like that were not common, but they did come along occasionally, and oftener than lucky days.

Among other causes for irritation I had my feud with a coyote. He was a big specimen, much slyer than any wolf or fox, and had a malicious nature besides. Between my trips over one of my lines he visited it, ate the bait, dug up the traps and turned them over to make them spring, or just left them contemptuously uncovered on a pile of snow. Sometimes he was so insolent that he defecated right beside them before he left. Sometimes he just pulled a trap aside by the chain. And this theme he varied *ad infinitum*. It made me see red to see my—as I thought— skilfully made sets treated in this cavalier fashion.

I tried all imaginable tricks to catch him. I set new traps beside the old ones, and followed his tracks and set traps or snares in them, or set traps in my own trail where it crossed a portage. But I had no luck. He always walked around them in a neat circle.

Finally I caught him, though. That time he had extended his marauding beyond his usual beat and had come to a trap he did not know. He got caught in a set where I had had a fox once, and its scent was so strong that he did not discover all the traps, and stepped in one. Perhaps also his contempt for my fumbling efforts to catch him had become so great that it made him careless. There he was, at any rate, firmly planted in a No. 2 trap. He yelped and barked and bit the trap and scratched around when he saw me come. And he almost escaped me that time, too. Just when I was swinging a stick to stun him with a blow on the nose he made a frantic jump. The stick hit the trap instead, and the trap broke. He was so surprised that he hesitated just a split second too long before making his escape. My second blow caught him right on the black tip of his sharp, wily nose, just when he made a long leap. He keeled over and I wrung his neck.

He was a fine specimen, and that he was my sworn enemy soon became apparent, as all depredations on my trapline ceased. He had, however, done much damage. I had lost many pelts because of him and I got only eight dollars for his hide.

Upon my arrival home from my second trip I found a note on the table. It said laconically: 'We have caught eighteen wolves, fourteen foxes, three lynx and eight minks. Gone north. Back in a week. Good hunting! George.'

The race was getting close.

I had one more encounter with wolves that winter. I was out on one of my short lines, when the dogs chased a caribou herd in full gallop. As I had enough meat and did not want more, I let the dogs run and yelled at them occasionally to make them increase their speed. The caribou fled like the wind through a strait between an island and the main shore, and we followed, the dogs yelling and I whooping. Then a grey shape hurled itself out of the bush on the island and streaked for the shore right through the galloping caribou herd. Behind it in single file came a pack of others. With their bellies close to the snow and their tails straight out, they seemed to go even faster than the caribou. I counted eight of them; the last one passed only a couple of hundred feet in front of me.

But I could not shoot. All I could do was to hang on to the bouncing sleigh and keep it upright as we careened over the drifts. I could not even think of picking up my rifle which was pushed under the ropes on the load. In a few moments the wolves had disappeared into the bush, and we had gone by on the heels of the herd.

The wolves had obviously lain in ambush for the caribou, when our wild appearance, which stampeded the caribou, spoiled their hunt and made them so nervous that they abandoned the island for the safety of the main shore.

They were still there when I returned an hour or so later. Now they sat in the shelter of the bush and hurled their howling curses at me at the top of their voices as we passed. But this time I did not catch a glimpse of them, although I scanned the shore, with my rifle ready in my hands.

My expectation of a good season was being fulfilled. The only thing I could complain about was the quality of my foxes. Only reds blundered into my traps. I caught a dozen of them to each cross or silver. My irritation was all the greater when my neighbours told me that their catch consisted of about forty per cent of cross and silver foxes. It is often that way. I knew two trappers who caught about one hundred foxes each one winter on the shore of Lake Athabaska, but one got only reds while the other got only the more valuable kind.

The quality of my wolves compensated for this, though. Mine were all arctic white, while August and George had caught several blacks and steel-greys that were worth much less.

After the first two trips I did not catch many more wolves. The big packs had roamed by and only a few remained. But I got many other fine pelts, and the bundle in my cache grew in size.

That winter I saw for the first time the damage that wolves do. Everywhere there were remains of caribou. On most lakes, no matter how small, lay a carcass or two, the ribs sticking out of the snow. And more numerous still were those that wolves had killed and only partly eaten before leaving.

On a sandplain I found half a dozen caribou, dead but otherwise hardly touched. They were all in a space the size of one acre. Only a couple had been partly eaten.

Some expert has stated that a wolf kills fifty caribou in a year. That estimate is surely wrong. Perhaps a wolf eats fifty, as one a week is not too much for a full-grown wolf. But, judging from signs, it kills at least twice that many from pure bloodlust. The assertion that a wolf kills only when hungry is a dangerous untruth.

It has also been stated in the wolf's defence—by equally dependable experts—that they improve the strain by weeding out old and sickly individuals, because these are easy to catch. That argument is preposterous. Every trapper knows that the wolves always pick healthy and fat caribou for their kill. Why should they not take the best when they can choose? On a short run wolves are faster than the healthiest caribou. They lie in ambush until the caribou come close, and attack with a tremendous burst of speed that leaves the slow-starting caribou practically standing still. If one examines wolf kills one sees that they are always near a shore or in the bush, never away out on a lake.

The bounty paid on wolf pelts should be increased manyfold, and if the authorities knew the true facts they would be. If a representative of the government had visited, for instance, the district in which I trapped that winter he would have seen enough.

It has also been said that trappers in the north are a real danger to the survival of caribou. That argument is also stupid. A trapper needs on the average fifty caribou a year for himself and his dogs if he has no fish; and he does not kill from bloodlust, but of necessity. That is exactly the same number that 'experts' claim a wolf kills. At the same time a trapper kills many wolves every year. The conclusions are obvious.

There is today much stress put on so-called scientific observations of wild life, and allegedly trained observers are sent into the bush. But these observers are often no bushmen and therefore are incapable of making a thorough investigation. Conclusions are hastily reached from too few observations, and are the more dangerous because they are supposedly unbiased. More attention should be paid to the opinions of successful professional hunters and trappers. They have a wide knowledge of wild life, plenty of experience and keen powers of observation. After all, their livelihood depends on these qualities. True, they are not talkative with strangers; but a truer picture of the wilds and, for instance, of this question of caribou and wolves would emerge if their opinions were gathered.

It is significant that, although every nook and cranny of the north has been visited and hunted in by professional trappers, great parts are still practically unknown to the world in general. And I know of one or two loquacious 'experts' on the Arctic who have achieved international fame and whose opinions are listened to by governments, but whose reputation for veracity is very poor among those who live in and really know the north. Can the authorities afford to be misled by experts of that kind—

at a time when the north is growing in military importance, and costly mistakes must be avoided?

But back to the wolves. Ed Clauson, a Norwegian who trapped in the area east of the Great Slave Lake, killed during three consecutive years six hundred wolves in all; two hundred and forty of these during the last winter. He probably has the record, and incidentally saved the lives of a sizeable herd of caribou.

A much greater danger to game than the inhabitants are some so-called sportsmen who invade the north in increasing numbers and kill only for the fun or to get a trophy. Often many animals are wasted before a set of antlers, worthy of a place above the living-room mantle, is obtained. And the meat incidentally is left, at least most of it. Unscrupulous fly-by-night mining companies have also been known to slaughter caribou to feed their crews, in places where the cost of bringing in beef is high.

The caribou killed by wolves did not go to waste, however; foxes, minks, weasels and ravens, especially the ravens, saw to that. They were a regular plague that winter. They also followed the caribou and cleaned up on what the wolves left, and if I left a caribou somewhere without hiding it carefully under snow and branches the ravens found it and feasted on it.

If they had been content with caribou it would not have mattered greatly, but if a fox or wolf died by a bait and a raven spotted it the pelt would be torn to pieces in a short time, making it worthless. It's a queer fact, though, that ravens did not touch a fox that had died in a trap.

George had an adventure with a wolf which I must tell. He had the habit of killing those that were in traps with an axe or a stout club. This he did, he maintained, to save ammunition. When I warned him, he just laughed and pointed out that the beasts were firmly caught.

One day he, as usual, walked up to a wolf he had caught. In his left hand he held his axe and in the right two dog-chains doubled. His idea was to shove the axe at the wolf, and make it snap at it, and then knock it senseless with the dog-chains. He thrust the axe towards the wolf, which lunged at him. George thought that it came uncomfortably close and backed up a step. The wolf followed. And now George noticed to his surprise that the trap had come loose. He jumped backwards quickly, trying to hit the wolf on the nose, just as it made a lunge. But the beast just kept on coming and snapped for his throat, missing by a hair. It got hold of his parka instead and tore a big hole in it. Just as it was about to spring again, George's dogs, who by now saw that their master was in trouble, piled in and pulled it down in the snow.

Now a ferocious fight started. The wolf was practically snowed under by a pack of snarling and biting dogs. They were taking hold wherever they could and bit and tugged with all their might. Meanwhile George skipped around them, waiting for an opening in the tangle of wolf, dogs and harnesses. Finally the wolf's head emerged for a moment, and George let him have it as hard as he could with the heel of his axe. The wolf dropped with a broken skull, and lay still while the dogs continued to chew the carcass triumphantly. 'I bet you they thought they had finished him themselves, they were that proud,' said George. 'I sure got to watch them next time I get one in a trap; they are liable to try it again. And if that wolf had been fresh, instead of tired from many days of fighting the trap, I'd have had it, too,' he added.

Then he showed me the skin, and it looked as if the beast had died from smallpox, so full was it of red marks from the dog's teeth. But I think George, after that, gave up the idea of saving ammunition by killing wolves with a club.

And so the trapping continued, and Christmas was approaching. Soon the time came to start in to the fort again. I did not take all my furs with me, because cached in the snowdrifts there were still sixteen frozen wolves that I had still to skin. But there would be plenty of time for that in January and February, when the cold weather set in and I would be at home a lot.

# CHAPTER XVIII

## *Christmas and carousing—Life with wolves—*
## *Redskins in the vicinity*

A FEW days before Christmas I started for the fort. Because I had to traverse unknown terrain and had a lot of trail to break before I came to Lake Athabaska I left early. George and August went in quite another direction, south-west to Camsell Portage.

But I was lucky. After one day's trail-breaking from the end of my trapline I came upon a fresh sleigh track that took me all the way to the fort. Some Indians had gone before me.

The merchants greeted me like a long-lost brother, and one of them would not give in before I promised to stay with him while I was there. And all my utterances were received, according to their nature, either with laughs or sympathetic tchk-tchks, enthusiastic smiles or compassion. One inquired about my health, how I lived, if there were lots of caribou in my district and—had I caught much fur? That was the most important question. I lodged with Black Ali, a levantine businessman.

By Christmas Eve many other trappers had arrived, and we decided to celebrate it together. The party started with much good food; and then a bottle, the first of a long procession, came on the table. As the evening wore on the discussion became livelier and the gestures wilder. Then our furs were inspected. We laid them out in piles on the floor and admired them. Everybody had some unusually beautiful pelts that he wanted to show off. When we tired of looking at them, we laid them in piles in a corner of the room and watched with amusement Ali's avaricious eyes that every so often caressed the furs. One could almost see him wonder how cheap he would be able to get them. He became, if possible, friendlier than ever and proffered his bottle. Later, when his own spirits had risen, he produced a couple more, and the party got into full swing. We talked, bragged and sang.

Finally somebody shouted: 'Now, let's get a dance going!' Yes, let's, that was a splendid idea, we all thought, and went out to round up partners. But it was queer. None of the ladies were willing to come. They were either too tired or had too much to do or had a headache. We became a little downhearted. But we had decided to dance, and we would. Let the women go hang! We will dance with each other. Ali's old portable phonograph was wound up, and so the dance began.

I had Karl for my lady, but somehow we started squabbling about who was to lead. And, in some way, the squabble became a fight. Before we knew it we were batting each other about and rolling around on the floor accompanied by old-time music and Ali's anguished shrieks, as we tumbled into the furs, so that pelts and fox-tails whirled in the air. It looked—as one of the spectators put it the next day—like a hurricane in a barnyard. Finally the others managed to separate us. Struggling and shouting insults at each other, we were led away.

Next morning I had a nice black eye, but Karl's face was not so beautiful to look at either, with a gash and a swollen nose. When we met we first glared angrily at each other, but both thought the other looked so funny that we started laughing. And then we viewed the damage to our furs.

Many were the jokes and innocent questions that were put to us as we were matching foxes and tails and sewing them together again. And so we sat there in amity and stitched while our grinning friends looked on. The only one who did not smile was Ali. He did not see anything funny in the whole business. He just shook his head and lamented people's foolishness.

On my way back from the fort I stayed overnight with a local chief. He was very hospitable and proud of having a white man for a guest. In my honour the first meal was eaten at the table; in that house there were both a table and some chairs, and even a rocking-chair, that the chief had made himself. We even had forks to eat with. But for the second meal the housewife tired of this sort of snobbery and set the food for herself and the family on the floor, leaving me in splendid isolation enthroned at the table.

It was New Year's Eve, and that was an occasion as important as Christmas for the Chipewyans. In the evening many members of the tribe gathered at Jeremiah's, the chief's house. Teams arrived from all over the neighbourhood, and the yard teemed with people and dogs.

First they had a service. The Chief came and apologetically explained that they were going to pray, but that I could stay inside, anyway—it was all right. I did not belong to the true faith, but it was so cold out that one could not banish even a heathen there. So I stayed and watched the proceedings.

The Indians are really religious, and the ceremony was moving. Jeremiah read a little sermon in Chipewyan, and led the song. It surprised me to hear them; many of them had really beautiful voices. The hymns had words in Chipewyan. After that there were many Ave Marias and Pater Nosters. Although I did not understand a word, I recognized them immediately, the inflection and tone is the same in any language.

It was twelve o'clock midnight. They had received the New Year with prayer. Then Jeremiah walked outside with his rifle, and fired four shots, one each north, south, east and west. Then we listened. Far to the west there were four weak reports in reply, and also the south. 'Everybody shoot—for luck,' explained Jeremiah.

When I left in the morning I received some disapproving glances. 'No good work, no good travel this day. Bring bad luck much,' ventured Crooked Back finally, when I was ready. It was plainly a great crime in their eyes to do anything. I have noticed that, even if the Chipewyans do not follow the other Commandments very scrupulously, they are very careful not to break the one about honouring the Sabbath. Perhaps because it is the easiest one to obey. At any rate they have a really legitimate reason for being idle; those, that is, that still need a justification. The majority are such hardened drones that their consciences need no sedatives.

In the fort I had bought a new lead-dog. After the trip home I was very satisfied with him. My other dogs were transformed.

From a mediocre team they changed into a really splendid one. A good leader ahead was all the pups needed. Now Chum sped straight from point to point, obeyed in a wink and never procrastinated. That spring I made some real record-breaking trips. Once I drove the six miles to my neighbours' in thirty-three minutes, and in March I made a forty-mile trip in a little over four hours—and that with a load and a toboggan over bush trails, not with a racing outfit of light sleighs and specially trained dogs on a hard road.

Right after the New Year it was very quiet; the real winter had set in. The thermometer hovered around forty and fifty below, and neither man nor beast was abroad. For me it was a period of hard work, though. All those frozen wolves that I had buried in the snowdrifts had to be thawed out and skinned. I hauled them home and hung them from the rafters of my cabin. And there they hung for a week, before they had softened enough for me to skin them.

But oh, my gosh, how they did stink! The cabin was only ten feet square, and sometimes there were five wolves suspended at once from the ceiling. And I had to stay at home all the time to keep a good fire going. It was a real trial to live there then. The place smelled like a morgue, and it was so crowded that I almost had to crawl around on my hands and knees in there. The wolf smell permeated everything, and wolf hairs clung to everything. I had them in the water-pail, on my clothes, in my hair and, no matter how careful I was, even in the food. I drank, ate and breathed wolf hairs. Since there was room only for five at the time and I had sixteen, I lived with them for three weeks before they were skinned.

When I at long last had skinned the last one and carried the carcass outside I was very happy. Then I had a real house-cleaning. I washed, scrubbed, ventilated and bathed. I carried all my clothes out to be aired. But still the wolf odour clung. Many weeks afterwards, when I returned to the cabin after a day in the fresh air, I could still smell it plainly.

One day Joe stopped by. He had been out on his trapping grounds to the north of me since September and not seen a single soul all winter. He was going to stay only for lunch and then continue to the fort. But he did not get away that day. We talked till one o'clock that night, and it was two o'clock the next day before he left. Joe had so many interesting things to tell, and to have somebody to talk to was a luxury he had missed for so long that he now enjoyed it to the full.

'What's the date?' he asked.

'The twenty-fourth,' I replied, and Joe considered for a while. 'It's January, isn't it?'

'Yes, and 1934, too,' I said.

Joe grinned in appreciation. 'Well, I guess I was out about ten days this time, but it could have been a lot more.'

At the end of January I drove over my traplines again for the first time since Christmas. I did not expect many pelts in my traps, but wanted to see that the traps were in working order and that they would be ready when animal life again stirred as the weather warmed and fox and mink started thinking of love. Then it was time to visit the traps oftener.

However, one of my lines had become so poor that I picked up all my traps and started making a new line along a big creek. Along it there were many good lakes and I found quite a few signs of fur.

I had gone up the creek perhaps fifteen miles and was snow-shoeing along the ice, breaking trail for the team, when the snow suddenly gave way underfoot and I found myself swimming in the creek, snowshoes and all. The strong current had eaten away the ice so that only a crust, just strong enough to support the snow, remained.

I tried to swim upstream, but could not make any headway and turned hurriedly, keeping my feet, to which the snowshoes were still tied, horizontal, so that they would not be pulled down and under the ice. Trying to keep my head up, I swam down-stream, breaking the ice with my fists. As I worked, the hole was filling up with snow and made it difficult to move in any direction except down, and I did not want to go that way. By working methodically and pushing the crowding snow aside, I reached ice that was too thick to break. After clearing some snow from it I managed to roll up. Very gingerly, not daring to rise, I then rolled and crawled towards shore until I could grab hold of a willow and drag myself up on land. I never found out how deep the water was; I was too busy getting out.

Then I led the dogs, who had been watching my peculiar performance with their heads tilted sideways, up in the bush and started chopping wood. There was luckily a stand of dry tamarack handy.

It was a race with the cold. My clothes were freezing fast in the thirty-below weather. They were crackling like paper as I worked, and I felt the cold creep through, and could not even keep warm by chopping as fast as possible. I knew that soon I would hardly be able to move. Before that I had to have a fire going. When my clothes were so stiff that I hardly could bend my elbows and knees I lit the fire.

Soon the flames were leaping up merrily, and I could start peeling off my clothes. They were then so stiff that they really could have stood up by themselves. A tamarack fire is not the best in the world. It sputters and crackles continuously, and throws sparks around it. I could neither sit nor lie without being burned by flying embers, and I had to watch my clothes incessantly to keep the sparks from burning holes in them. And so I sat stark naked all night bundled up in my sleeping robe, snapping sparks from my clothes and myself, and cutting wood for short intervals at a time. It was morning before I could resume my trip, now carefully avoiding all suspicious-looking spots on the ice.

But the new trapline was worth the trouble. When spring came I caught more fur on it than on all the others together.

On a lake I one day unexpectedly encountered some strange sleigh tracks that joined mine. And beside the trail, stuck in the snow, was a whittled stick written full of Chipewyan characters, Well, the red brothers had arrived.

During the first part of the winter the Chipewyans usually live by some lake where the fishing is good. But when the caribou have quit moving around and settled down for the winter, the Indians move out to some district where the moccasin telegraph reports that they are plentiful. There little groups of two or three families live in tents all winter. When the Caribou eaters, as this branch of the Chipewyans is sometimes called, come to a place where there are lots of caribou, they live like kings. They eat tongue, make dry meat, render marrow fat and visit their neighbours. A thirty-mile trip in fifty-below weather is nothing for them.

It was probably a group like that which had invaded my territory, I thought, as I followed the trail. That guess was correct. From the top of a ridge I saw two silvery-white clouds, whiter than the sunlit pink snow, hover over a lake ahead. It was the breath of two dog teams, that froze into white steam in the bitter cold and could be seen for miles, farther than the dog teams themselves. The latter were too far off to be distinguished. From the western shore three huge clouds of smoke drifted slowly, in the hardly perceptible breeze, out over the lake.

I drove down the portage and towards the camp, and came there just after the teams I had seen.

"Ello! B'jour Chelutshee!' shouted two voices, and two grinning smoke-brown visages turned towards me, and then their owners came over with outstretched paws. Chelutshee means 'the dwarf' or something similar; that was the name they had given me because of my large frame.

These two were Ari Chilahsee and Pete Crooked Back, both of the Fond du Lac tribe. Crooked Back was not called so because of any deformity, but because he was so poor that he always had to go with a bent spine and beg assistance from his more fortunate brothers. Ari Chilahsee, ragged Harry, had received his name because he was one of the best-dressed and most energetic men in the band. The Chipewyans do not lack a sense of humour. The third member of the party, John Wolverine, whose tee-pee was pitched alongside the others, had received his name because of a weakness for lifting fur out of other people's traps. He was away on a hunting trip just then.

We stepped into Ari's tent. As the leader of the party, he claimed the honour of treating the white guest to tea, dry meat and bannock. Ari's tent was new and clean, like his bashfully grinning squaw and shy, silent children, and he smoked real tobacco. None of that awful mixture of willow bark and cranberry leaves for him.

As I had supposed, Ari had moved out after caribou a few days before and been given two of the band's good-for-nothings to take along and take care of. They had heard there were lots of caribou in the area. How they knew that was a mystery; I had not seen an Indian track all winter, and white men do not broadcast the fact that there are any on their grounds. Unless they just love their red brothers. Here they were, however, and intended to remain. 'Good place, caribou lots,' Ari summed up the situation and told me that other families lived to the east. Pleasant news.

Crooked Back was very proud because, on the journey out, his wife had borne him a son. This had happened in forty-below weather, in a ragged tent, heated by a tin stove with the kind assistance of his friends' women. Because it was a boy, Crooked Back had graciously permitted her a day's rest before she again took her place walking before the dog team—this time with the baby on her back, though! Tough stock! It must be said in Crooked Back's favour, however, that he always changed off with her and let her ride at times, and did not, like some, just stand on the back of the sleigh and drive.

His and Wolverine's tents contrasted with Ari's as much as the owners themselves. They were black from smoke and age, and so full of spark holes that, looking from the inside, they were like planetariums. Their outfits were of the same calibre; even the dogs had something of their masters' abject and unsure appearance about them.

Ari lorded it over them, but practically supported them, too. This is the custom. One has to care for all members of the band, no matter how useless they be. This way everybody lives; some not as well as others perhaps, but nobody starves.

While we sat in Ari's tent, the Cow, Wolverine's wife, who had the reputation of being the flightiest bag in the band—which is saying a lot—entered. She grinned broadly, shook hands, put her pipe back between her amber-coloured teeth, and started nursing her child. Reaching inside of her blouse, she produced a breast of ample proportions, which the baby grasped avidly.

The scene was one of contentment, but I stared, fascinated. This well of life was unique. The nipple that the child sucked, and the area closest to it, was a light pink; but spreading outward in concentric circles there was a territory of increasing darkness. I contemplated the sight with interest, wondering which one of these shades of brown represented the true hue of the Cow's skin. She looked up and smiled, probably misunderstanding my interest. She took the pipe out of her mouth, and said invitingly: 'John go away, two days', smiled again, and stuck her pipe back. Whether these words were meant as an invitation I never found out. The proposal was not very alluring, anyway. But the Cow still smiled when I left.

After this the Indians often came visiting, especially Crooked Back, who always begged. He taxed me every time, although I tried my best to resist. But he never gave up until I gave him at least some tea or tobacco. It would probably have hurt his pride to go away empty-handed. And he did not have much of that left, so I gave in.

He also visited August and George. But there he met his match. Crooked Back had one regrettable habit. When one offered him a smoke, he filled his pipe, lit it, and took a few puffs. Then he would put it in his pocket, and, when it had gone out, surreptitiously empty it. After a little while he would fill it again out of the can and repeat the procedure. In this manner he succeeded in transferring a considerable amount of tobacco into his pocket in one evening.

But the brothers were equal to him. Next time he came visiting and happened to lay his pipe on the table, August, by some subterfuge, lured him outside. Meanwhile George took the pipe and removed the stem. Then he put a match in the hole, pushed it in firmly until it stuck and broke it off flush, and put the stem back, at the same time wedging a thin sliver of wood in the crack so that the stem stuck as if welded on.

When Crooked Back came back in George put his tobacco can on the table and offered him a smoke. The Indian filled his pipe carefully and tried to light it. But it did not draw. He tried to pull off the stem to clean it. But it did not budge. Then he tried to clean it as it was with a piece of wire, but did not succeed. He reamed and toiled, and blew in it until he was blue-black in the face, but without result. The pipe would not draw, and the stem stuck as though glued on.

At the same time the boys proffered their tobacco cans and urged him to have a smoke and puffed mightily themselves. When Crooked Back finally gave up and with unaccustomed fingers rolled a smoke he was a broken man. When would he again get a chance like this to replenish his tobacco supply?

But he must have discovered the perfidy later, because from then on he treated August and George coldly and seemed to carry a grudge against them.

Crooked Back only begged and was therefore pretty inoffensive. But Wolverine was different. He would not leave my traps alone. Once I caught him almost red-handed. I came to a mink set from which he had removed the prey so skilfully that it looked as if the animal had broken its foot and escaped. But although he had obliterated his tracks carefully, it had happened so recently that the snow had not yet become hard. And in the very thin film of frost that had formed in my trail to the trap there were faint but fresh tracks made by a pair of moccasins smaller than mine.

I drove after Wolverine, and arrived in the encampment shortly after him. Instead of talking to him, I told Ari Chilahsee, who in fluent Chipewyan bawled out the now very humble John. He berated him for stealing from their good friend Chelut-shee, threatened him with God knows what, and finally ordered him to return what he had stolen. John, now looking like a schoolboy caught in mischief, slunk off. Imagine my surprise when he returned not only with the mink but also with a red fox already stretched and the trap in which it had been caught. It was one that he had found on an island, he explained. I knew then; that fox had dragged away the trap and toggle and I had not been able to track it.

What terrible thing Ari threatened him with I do not know, but Wolverine left my traps strictly alone from then on. The

Indians stayed in the district until spring, but they were less bother than I had feared.

One day, when the sun was shining and a fresh wind blew, I hung my furs out in the air. I admired the pelts as they swayed with the breeze. Some of the wolves were really fine. One was all white, with long silky hair, and others had only a grey stripe along the back, while even the darkest ones were only light grey.

Just then I heard a plane, and a while later it landed on the ice in front and out jumped Ali. He had just come visiting to see how I was getting along and, incidentally, had brought my mail, he said. But when he caught sight of the fur that fluttered in the wind he hardly wanted to leave me. He wanted to buy all my fur on the spot. But I pulled in my horns. A trader does not visit a trapper out in the bush by plane unless the market is rising and he expects to make a good bargain. Ali treated me to drinks out of a bottle he had brought along and argued and raised the price. He was so persistent that I had to sell a few pelts to get rid of him. After all, he *had* brought my mail and given me some drinks. But he still eyed the furs greedily when he left, not completely satisfied.

Once more that winter the wolves visited my district. They came in great numbers again in March, and for a few days the neighbourhood teemed with them. But now they had been in more populated parts and had gone to school. They were now at the same time both bolder and warier than before. They avoided traps carefully. They followed my trail until they came to a set. Then they made a little detour around it and went on.

Once when I had been away from the cabin for a few days, I found that a pack of about twenty wolves had been rummaging all around it. They had tramped regular trails all around the cabin and eaten a caribou that they had somehow pulled down from my meat cache. And a net that I had left to dry on the stage and that probably still smelled of fish they had torn to little pieces. A caribou hide that I had nailed to some trees had been chewed to shreds. They had examined the dog-houses thoroughly, and had eaten every bone and every scrap of meat. The only thing they had not touched was a doped caribou I had put on the ice a mile from my camp. This, although they had passed within a few hundred feet of it. They were 'civilized' now. When the snow melted in the spring I found pieces of fish-net away out on the ice.

Although I hunted them every way I knew, I caught only two all spring. I made ordinary bait sets, set traps near caribou guts, put traps where the wolves had cocked their legs against a stump or boulder, and also in my own trail between two lakes. But it was no use. When they howled around the cabin or tent at nights they sounded derisive. They certainly had reason to be.

By the end of March they were all gone. They had probably returned to their homes far to the north on the barren grounds. Now followed a time when I caught only an occasional mink or lynx, and prepared for the spring hunt. Now also was the time to go in to the fort for fresh supplies. I followed the trail the Indians had broken after Christmas and which they had kept open since then.

On my way to Fond du Lac I met Louis. He said with emotion: 'Albert, crazy, plumb crazy! He try to shoot me, and take my Rosa!'

Louis was all worked up. I tried to find out what had happened, but got a jumbled explanation which told me very little. All I gathered was that Louis, after some trouble when visiting Albert, had gone to Fond du Lac, where he probably had told and retold his story, which naturally had grown with each repetition. Now he was going to get the police to put Albert in the nut factory. He warned me earnestly against going near Albert, and looked scared when I said that I thought I would visit him. Maybe Louis thought me crazy, too.

Albert lived by the shore of a lake. As we approached the dogs increased their speed. They knew the place and liked visiting, too. While I was still some way off I saw a big cloud of smoke rise from the stove-pipe. Albert had spotted us and put more wood in the stove and the pot on. And when I arrived he stood on the shore, with a wide smile of welcome on his honest face, and asked me in. 'I recognized you way off; the dogs always look so small beside you. Step in! It's a long time since I had any visitors.'

While we ate I asked him how long it was since anybody had

been there. Albert said it was funny, but nobody had called for more than a week, although several dog-teams had passed by, away out on the lake. I laughed, and when Albert looked surprised I asked if he knew what he had done.

'Louis goes around,' I told him, 'and says that you are nuts, and that you tried to shoot him and take Rosa. What have you really done to them? He was all worked up when I saw him.'

Now Albert understood why nobody had called. He laughed till the tears ran down his cheeks, slapped his knee in glee and told me.

Louis and Rosa had come visiting. Albert had treated them to tea, with some stronger stuff added. After a few drinks Louis had become boastful and then quarrelsome. He had started bragging about how good a rifle shot he was and how he was the best hunter in the area. Albert then challenged him to some target shooting, and when he won Louis became angry and started to fight. Rosa interfered and was pushed over in a snowdrift by the now angry Albert. Weeping and shrieking, she ran into the cabin and locked the door. When he could not get in any other way, Albert climbed in through the window. He then chased her out, threw hers and Louis's parkas and mitts after, and told them both to scram. They then left, Rosa still screaming and Louis threatening him with dire revenge. Nobody had been there since.

'Now you better come in to Fond du Lac with me and show them that you aren't crazy. The Indians all think so already, since they haven't dared come to see you, and soon everybody else'll believe it, too,' I said. Albert agreed reluctantly.

When he approached the fort the sun was high and warm, and a flock of children were playing out of doors. We were maybe a hundred yards away, when Albert shouted at his dogs. It was as if a bomb had exploded among the children. For a moment they all stood motionless, then in a few seconds the yard was empty. There was not a soul in sight when we drove up; even the grown-ups had disappeared.

Albert thought it was very funny. He was used to having all the children in the place crowding around him a few minutes after his arrival, but now they had scattered like chaff in the wind at the mere sound of his voice.

First we went to Hudson's Bay, where we were warmly received. But an Indian who was in there edged gingerly to the door and sneaked out while we were talking to the clerk. After a while some timid faces appeared in the window, and finally some of the braver men came in. But they all watched Albert apprehensively, and seemed ready to jump at the first sign of danger.

However, their fear gradually subsided; after a couple more visits they became calm. They found out that Albert still was as sane as everybody else. Some of them even started making joking remarks about Louis and Rosa.

And when a little later Albert walked over to the Hudson's Bay store he again had a long train of expectant children behind him. He was again that nice man, who always bought them candy.

I stayed in the fort only a day, long enough to gather my supplies, and returned to my trapline.

The days became longer and warmer. The sun shone brightly on the crystallized snow over which the sleigh slid so easily. The dogs, who were now full grown, pulled the toboggan like the wind, so that I travelled distances in a few hours that had taken me a whole day before Christmas. And I rode on the load, too. The weather was made for living out of doors; one was sorry when evening came, and loath to go in. Then the stars shone clear and the drapes and jagged roses of the aurora flamed like huge roman candles in the sky.

Then, with a rush, came spring. The snow melted in a week, all the valleys became brooks, the ice quickly became bare and black and treacherous in the little lakes. When bare spots appeared on the slopes the first mosquitoes came out, the first frogs croaked, the first buds swelled on the bushes. The sun burned—spring had come.

# CHAPTER XIX

## *Spring hunt—Good and ill-luck—Bruin comes visiting—Reducing diet—Farewell*

DURING March and April I had explored the neighbourhood for beaver-houses, and found several little lakes close together that all had lodges in them, with fresh feed in front. The area had apparently been overlooked by earlier hunters, and the beavers had increased unmolested. The houses were all near the east bay of the Ena Lake, where a large creek fell out and where I could expect open water early. I thought it would be a good idea to move there while I hunted beaver; only a short distance to walk, and at the same time I could set my net in the creek.

So one morning I loaded my outfit and my newly built hunting canoe on the sleigh and drove to the camping spot I had chosen. I pitched my tent on the shore. It was wonderful to hear the sound of running water again and to see the bravest birches already taking on a tint of green, although ice still covered the lake.

That evening I visited my first beaver family. They had been out foraging for fresh food already and had cleared the ice from a large space around the house. Along the narrow band of open water near the shore they had felled several birches. Fresh chips of wood littered the ice and the shore. I slipped quietly down to the house to wait.

It was a quiet spring evening. While I waited I heard spruce grouse drum in the bush and the frogs croak in a muskeg slough behind me. Then I noticed a slight movement among the ships on the water. As if it had floated up, the first beaver appeared. I fired, and the beaver turned over and lay there as if it never had been living at all. Shortly after, another came swimming rapidly along the shore. It dived and came up again right in front of me.

I aimed behind its ear and shot. This one was a little tougher, and splashed for a while, but soon it also lay still beside its mate.

I shot two more that night before it was too dark to see the sights. I was happy as I stumbled homewards in the dark with my heavy load. The dogs were also glad when they got fresh beaver steak for supper. My spring hunt had started well.

That week I was lucky. I came home every night with at least one beaver. All the lodges were so close to my tent that I could skin and stretch my catch in the daytime and visit a new house every night. I got sixteen beavers that week, nine of them large. Although I have never been a master marksman, it seemed that week as if I just could not miss. But my best shot was a pure fluke.

I had visited one of the houses farthest away and was on my way home with a heavy packsack. My course took me around a bay of a lake and I walked along the shore, intent on getting home without caring how much noise I made, stepping on branches and pushing through the undergrowth.

Suddenly I heard a loud splash. Bang went the tail of a large beaver on the water. The sound echoed through the still night. I stopped, astonished. I had examined this lake earlier and had not seen any sign of beaver there. But there were some, anyway, because out there, fifty yards away, on the smooth mirror of the surface that reflected the evening sky, the outline of a beaver showed plainly, with wide silvery rings around it. Almost as a reflex action I raised my rifle and fired, although I hardly saw the sights. I scored a bull's-eye. The beaver kicked once and turned over.

However, I had to get it ashore. The lake was dead calm and a very weak current moved the animal parallel to the shore. I tied several poles together, but I could not reach it with these. Then I tied a stone to a string and threw it out, but the string was too short. There was no dry wood around to make a raft. The beaver floated slowly with the current, and I tried to reach it again from every point it passed. After hours of wasted effort, I decided to wait for the morning breeze, and so I camped. I lit a fire and boiled tea. I could not sleep on such a cold spring night without blankets, and I did not dare leave the lake for fear that some bear, of which I had seen plenty of signs around, would find it if it floated ashore while I was away. So I sat through the night by the fire and waited. Frequently I heard splashes out in the darkness of the lake. The beavers were curious, but also uneasy. But I could not see them with my fire-dazzled eyes, and it was too dark to shoot with any hope of success, anyway. When it became light enough to see they were gone.

With sunrise came a light breeze, which silvered the water and made the young leaves flutter. Now my beaver started moving towards the opposite shore. I broke camp and walked around the lake, where I sat down to wait. Then the wind changed and the beaver floated right down the middle of the lake. By now I was tired, hungry and frozen, but if swearing had warmed me I would have had a fever. Slowly, infinitely slowly, the beaver moved on. 'Oh hell!' I thought. 'I suppose I have to sit here all day, too.'

It was already afternoon when the beaver at last reached the end of the lake, but the closer it came the more slowly it moved. Finally it lay almost still thirty yards from shore. I tried my rock and line again. Just as I threw it, something splashed only a few feet away. The beaver's mate had been sitting there, a wonderful target, and I had neither seen nor heard it.

I was suddenly furious. Gone completely berserk, I jumped in the lake and waded out until I stood up to my waist in the bitterly cold water. I threw the line again, and after a couple of tries it caught, and I pulled in the carcass. It was a huge brute, the biggest yet. Although I was sleepy and hungry, I was happy, just the same, as I walked towards camp, with the water squishing around my toes with every step. That night I did not go out. When I had skinned my beavers I went straight to bed.

But that was the turning-point of my luck. In a whole week I did not get a single pelt. If I sat by a house the beavers were all down by the dam and never came near, and those few shots I got in were either clean misses or else wounded the beavers so lightly that they escaped. I decided to go home after one more day.

The last evening I went to a lake where I knew a great big beaver lived. I had seen him several times, but he was always out of range. He was a wise old cuss. It was his habit to swim underwater far out from the house, so that he was far out of range when he came to the surface. After patrolling the middle of the lake for a while, he would swim to a point on the opposite shore and start eating. I had not been able to go there before; the wind had always been wrong, and he would have caught my scent.

But that day the wind was right. Now, I thought, I could catch the old beaver. When I approached the shore I walked as lightly as possible, parting the bushes carefully and taking care not to step on any dry branches that would snap, and I picked every spot where I set down my foot. It was still early. The beaver would still be in the house, but I was cautious, just the same. I had to find a good hiding-place from which I could see the point clearly. I decided on a spot and sneaked slowly towards it.

Suddenly there was a deep growl, and with a loud splash a huge black bear leaped into the water right in front of me and swam for dear life across the lake straight for the beaver-house. There he clambered ashore and made off through the bushes like a stampeding tank, breaking bushes and branches in his haste. I jumped high in the air, and probably growled, too. While Bruin was still in the water I shot him in the end to speed him on his way, and sent several more shots after him as he galloped up the slope.

Bruin had had the same idea as I, and had sat down in his blind with the obvious intention of grabbing the beaver by the neck when it came ashore. My arrival had been an unpleasant surprise, and he had thought it best to call it a day. But that did not gladden me much. His splashing and blundering had certainly warned the wily old beaver. Now he would not show himself before late at night, when it was too dark to shoot. So it was no use to stay. I went back to my tent.

There I loaded all my stuff in the canoe and paddled to the cabin. The beavers in the lakes I had visited were all too wary now. Still I decided to have one more try. There was one more beaver-house I knew a couple of miles from the cabin; one I had saved for the last.

It was afternoon when I arrived at the lake and saw the beavers, who until then had not been disturbed, swim and play out in the middle. They dived for water-lily roots, and called to each other with their funny *toot-toot*! It sounded just like a little steam-boat whistle. I watched them dive and chase one another, their wet backs shining brown. Sometimes one would take a root and swim to a little platform by the water's edge, crawl up and start to eat. One of their favourite spots was a flat rock a few yards from the other shore. There most of them went sooner or later.

I made a wide circle around the lake and walked in the shelter of some trees towards the flat rock. I waited until the beavers, who still were playing out in the middle, were all under water at the same time, and sprinted quickly to a little knoll fifty feet from the shore. I reached it undetected and sat down behind a spruce. From here I had a good view.

Soon one of the beavers swam to the smooth rock, crawled up and sat up on its flat tail like a squirrel, turning the root between its paws, taking a bite here and there. It afforded a perfect target, sitting there sideways to me with its wet fur shining in the sun. I raised my rifle a bit reluctantly. I hated to spoil the perfect idyll, but I needed the pelt. Then I fired. The bullet whistled clean over the beaver. I saw it hit the water beyond. The beaver slid into the water, there were a couple of mighty splashes, and the lake was empty. I just stared. How could I miss at a short distance like that? Then I discovered the reason. The backsight of my rifle was bent. It had caught on something in the bush and been bent out of shape. I stood up, both angry and relieved at the same time.

But this was the end. I had had enough. I had hunted for ten days without getting a pelt. My good luck in the beginning had changed into the most infamous kind of misfortune. I had had enough of beaver-hunting. It was time to quit.

As I paddled homewards I thought the thing over. I had to admit to myself that my enthusiasm for hunting had cooled, and that might be the real reason for everything going wrong. I just did not enjoy this wholesale killing.

When I paddled around the last point I saw a yellow canoe on the shore by my cabin. August and George were there.

They stood on the shore when I landed, and almost the first thing they said was: 'Are you ready to go to town soon?'

'Damn right I am!' I replied. I started telling them about all my tribulations. While I ranted, the smiles on the boys' faces became wider, and when I finished my tirade they just grinned.

'Boy, am I comforted,' said George. 'We've also had a devil of a time these last few days, and I can't say we've been any menace to the beavers in these parts.' And so I had to listen to the story of their troubles, looking as sympathetic as possible.

Then we held a council of war. When it ended it had been decided that August and I were to leave right away. George intended to stay behind. He would take care of all our dogs for the first part of the summer, then August was coming in to relieve him by plane. I told them that I was not sure that I would come back, but that they could have my dogs if I did not.

So we left. I packed my belongings and we went to the boys' cabin. There August and I loaded all our furs and clothes, and supplies for a few days, into a little fourteen-foot hunting canoe that was easy to portage. We said goodbye to George and pushed off.

It was already full summer. Spring had lasted only a couple of weeks. As soon as the ice had melted all the trees were suddenly in full leaf.

The canoe was easy to take across the portages. But unfortunately it did not carry much of a load. With two big men and furs and packsacks, we had only three inches of free board. We could not cross any big lakes if it was windy, but then we had only one of any size on our way in. We estimated that the trip would take three days.

In good spirits we paddled down the rivers and lakes and ran across the portages. My first holiday outside for years loomed only a few days off. My hunt this year was so good that I could afford that. And now, when the decision was made, I could hardly think of anything else. I would sell my furs there and have a good time.

But we had not allowed for a storm, which started on the second day. We managed to cross some small lakes during the lull that came just before sunset, but on the north shore of a big lake it was definitely: Stop! The waves that rolled over the three-mile stretch of open lake were such that we could not think of attempting a crossing. We were stuck here until the storm blew itself out.

When the storm showed no signs of abating, we passed the time wandering around in the bush and hammering at rocks. The formation here was considered favourable for gold. We found a large quartz vein with mineralization, and spent the day pounding and digging, finally wandering back to the tent loaded with samples.

It was evening when we arrived at our tent. August, who was walking ahead, suddenly yelled, 'Damn it all!' and started running towards the tent.

A big black bear was investigating our grub-box. The box was upset, and all its contents scattered on the ground. Bruin raised his head and growled and showed his teeth at us. I pushed a shell in the rifle and fired. Bruin roared, but turned and made off at a gallop. At the same time we heard some shrill yelps, and two small cubs scurried away after it for dear life, but changed their minds, when we took after them, and climbed quickly up a poplar instead. I sent another shot in the direction in which the she-bear had disappeared, but she was away and stayed away.

August ran over to the poplar. 'Keep a look out, I'll try to make her come back,' he yelled.

He shook the poplar furiously. The cubs yelled to high heaven, but hung on like leaches. August laughed and shook harder, and I stood with my rifle cocked and scanned the bush where the old she-bear had disappeared. But she did not return. She had left the cubs to shift for themselves.

'Fie and for shame! What a mother!' said August. 'But I'll show her something.' He started chopping down the poplar. Soon it swayed and, while the cubs yelped yet more, crashed to the ground. August rushed towards them, but they had landed unhurt, and stood all ready for him on their hind feet, with bared teeth and snarling. They tried to growl and look as dangerous as they could. Jet black and not much bigger than cats, but just as furious as a cornered rat, they were ready to slap any attacker with their claws. They made such a funny sight that we laughed. August simulated some attacks and ran a few times around them. The cubs turned quick as weasels, hissed and growled and almost fell over in their hurry.

Finally August quit teasing them, and we retreated a little way. The cubs took their opportunity to escape immediately. They turned, and in a jiffy they were hidden by an alder thicket. Still laughing, we went to the tent.

But there was certainly nothing to laugh at. The sugar bag was in shreds, its contents poured on the ground, trampled and mixed with dirt. Here the cubs had really enjoyed themselves. The butter tin was licked clean, all other cans squashed and chewed until they resembled sieves. Dishes, pots and pans were tossed around and dented. All the other food was destroyed in the same way. And flour was spread over the whole place. The bag had been dragged around and torn to bits. There was hardly anything left that could be used. A little tea, some flour that remained in a corner of the bag and which we carefully saved, salt, baking powder and some spices—that was all. The she-bear had probably just finished the sabotage, and was giving the grub-box a last look, when we arrived.

But the tent was luckily intact, except for a few tears. There they had not yet had the courage to go. And that was really lucky; that saved our clothes, and, above all, our furs.

'Damn it! That's the way it is, when one has no dogs along,' said August. I nodded. It was true, as a trapper seldom experiences such mishaps, just because bears fear his dogs. But prospectors and other campers are often victims of roaming bears.

We were now practically without provisions. Except for pancakes and stick bread—strips of dough wound around a stick and baked by an open fire—tea was all we had in the way of food.

And the storm blew unabated. We were only ten miles from the fort, but that did not help us much. It was still blowing the next day, and we hunted for food along the lake shore and the surrounding bush. But there was no game now, when we needed some. Our foraging netted us only a jack-fish, a fingerling, that made only one bite apiece. There were not even any ducks.

'Oh yes, this is a regular banquet,' said August, as, two nights after the mishap, we divided a pancake baked from our last flour. 'Won't you have some jam? Here, take some, there is lots more.' He offered me the cup with some last year's cranberries, which we had picked on the north slopes of a hill. But we did have tea, which we drank strong and hot.

The next day was dreary. The wind still blew, and the white-caps still raced over the lake. Three miles away was the south shore from which we could walk to the fort in two hours. But that thought did not satisfy our complaining stomachs. It was getting dark, and we made ourselves ready for another night with empty stomachs.

August stared fixedly at me:

'Have you seen Chaplin's *Gold Rush*, Erik?' he asked.

I looked at him and grinned. 'Sure, I remember it. Do I look like a chicken? They ate their shoes first though,' I suggested.

'Yes, and licked the nails, too,' said August and walked out for a look at the lake.

Then I heard a shout: 'Hi, Erik! Come here!'

I rushed out. There August was slamming away with a big stick at something on the ground. A porcupine! God bless all porcupines! In spite of quills and so on we skinned it in record time, and before I had taken out all the innards August had brought the water in the pot to the boil.

'Look how fat it is,' he sighed, as he grabbed a big piece and sank his teeth into it. We ate the whole thing in one sitting, although it weighed at least eight pounds. It tasted better than tenderloin.

'Oh, oh! This is bad for my girlish figure,' squealed August, sinking back happily and folding his hands over his bulging middle.

We were certainly full, and ready for bed.

I woke up at three o'clock. It was peculiarly quiet. I lay there for a moment before it dawned on me what that meant. Then I rushed out to the lake. Yes, there was no sighing of the wind in the trees. The storm had abated considerably.

I shook August out of bed, and in a flurry we tore down the tent, loaded the canoe and headed out on the lake at full speed. If we only got across while it was calm it could blow again as much as it wanted afterwards.

But when we had passed a couple of islands that so far had sheltered us we realized that it had not calmed as much as we thought. The rollers were still plenty high, and the crossing was risky.

But we had started, and it was calmer now than before, and it might blow again at dawn. So we decided to risk it. We paddled on, partly against the wind. When a big roller hit us we turned the canoe straight against the wind and slowed down. It was slow and tiring work, the canoe rocked and pitched in the hissing combers. We had to be very alert not to ship water. To make it worse, the wind increased again. It had changed during the short lull in which we had started, and it now blew straight against us. Soon we were in the middle of cross-waves of increasing size. Now we had use for all our skill with the paddle in snaking over and dodging the combers that plunged towards us from right and left alternately. We turned quickly now in one direction, now in another; now we dug in for all we were worth, now we had to rest and just steer against the biggest white caps. And in spite of all our care, we shipped some water when some really big wave hit us. Our freeboard became lower and the water in the canoe made it tippier than ever. Besides, we were tiring. But we toiled doggedly on, cursing bitterly when some big comber forced us to stop and lose several precious feet which we had just gained.

It became easier. At first we did not even notice it, but after a bit the really big seas became scarcer, and we started getting closer to shore. Soon the waves became so much smaller that we got a chance to stop and bail out some water. We were definitely beating the storm now. The shore came closer and closer, and finally we paddled past the last point into a sheltered bay.

When we stepped ashore to rest our benumbed knees and aching arms, I was wet through, and not just from spray but from sweat. Neither of us said anything for some time. We just lay stretched out in the moss and panted.

Then August reared up on an elbow and said: 'Damn it, I forgot my tea-kettle! We'll have to go back for it!'

I said something very nasty, and August laughed heartily.

We examined our equipment and found that our furs were pretty dry. We had placed them uppermost in the canoe next to the tarpaulin. Only our bed-rolls and clothes were wet, and they could be dried later. After this we continued our trip in sheltered waters to the last portage. When we had completed the portage and pushed out from shore to paddle the last stretch into the fort, it was almost calm. The wind had died down almost completely.

One hour later we paddled into the fort. It was only six o'clock when we landed, and everybody was still asleep, but half an hour later we sat before enormous portions of ham and eggs and steaming cups of coffee. Hunger and hardships were forgotten. Our summer vacation had begun!

A few days later the first plane for the season landed; the plane that was taking me outside. I had not seen a city, a show or a white girl for several years; it was time to live like a civilized human again for a while.

As I sat beside Bill in the plane, with my fur sacks behind me, I thought of all these things. I took a deep breath. Soon I would enjoy them all again.

Bill turned his head and smiled. 'How does it feel to go out, Erik?' he asked. I told him. He laughed and said: 'Oh yes, I've heard that before. But you just wait a few weeks, and you'll be ready to go north again. There's nothing like it for a guy who has once lived here.'

As we flew on I looked down. Below us lay the green summer land with its endless uninhabited woods, its muskegs dotted with stunted spruce, its steep eskers and bare hills and park-like sand-plains, among which gleamed unnamed rivers, winding creeks and thousands upon thousands of nameless lakes, their bright-blue eyes looking towards the sun. We passed over the countless islands of Cree Lake, among which ice-floes lingered, and the steep cliffs below which, if they faced north, snow still remained in the shadow.

This was a great land, a good land, about which little was known to the average man, and much of that knowledge false. It was also a land which had been good to me, and that had been my home. I thought of Bill's words. Would I return? Perhaps. He whom the north has tormented and fondled is hers. She is a demanding mistress, who never lets her lover stray far from her arms.

Bill suddenly wakes me out of my musings. He points, and puts the plane into a dive. Down there in a muddy little lake stands a moose up to his shoulders in the water. He lifts his head as we approach, and takes a few steps towards safety, but when we have passed, he stops and stands still, a statue of dark bronze in a wild landscape. A last symbol of the northland and a farewell greeting. As we climb again, and I turn my eyes ahead, I see the smoke-stacks of the city above the horizon.

THE END